32384

Fracke
Buena V

Date Due

MR 30 '64			
	PRINTED	IN U. S. A.	

THE Great Rascal

JAY MONAGHAN

The amazing Ned Buntline, adventurer extraordinary and creator of the dime novel, lived a life far more fantastic than that of any of his imaginary heroes. If he hadn't actually existed and thus become the subject of this lively biography, it is doubtful if any novelist would have had the temerity to create so incredible a hero. In fact the story of Ned Buntline reads like all the dime novels rolled into one super-duper.

Edward Zane Carroll Judson (the famous pseudonym of Buntline is a nautical term for a rope at the bottom of a square sail) was born in 1823, ran away to sea as a boy and, by the time he was fifteen, was a midshipman in the navy. Resigning four years later, he led a life of incredible adventures in the Seminole Wars, and later in the Northwest fur trade. When he was twenty-three, he was tried for murder in Nashville, was lynched by a mob, and was cut down in time to be brought back to life. He could sport more scars, including a bullet hole in his chest, than any man he met — and he had a whole supply of yarns to go with each wound.

Generally in trouble, whether financially, romantically or with the law, stocky, red-bearded Ned Buntline had at least as many enemies as friends. Unscrupulous, often accused of blackmail, defendant in several trials, he once jumped bail in St. Louis, and was heavily implicated in the 1849 riot in Astor Place in New York. A reformer who frequently got drunk after delivering a lecture on Temperance, Ned was also one of the founders of the Know Nothing Party.

In the 1840's he established *Ned Buntline's*

Own. In this sensational weekly he published not only his novels but also stories exposing gambling, prostitution and drinking in New York City — championing the cause of the Know-Nothing movement. During the Civil War he served in the Union Army as a sergeant (later broken to private) and afterwards undeservedly assumed the rank of Colonel, a title which stuck until his death.

It was on a Western trip that he met handsome William Cody, dubbed him Buffalo Bill and wrote a series of dime novels based on Cody's life as a hunter and scout. He also launched Cody on a theatrical career in a play he wrote in four hours — *The Scouts of the Plains* — with himself playing a leading part. But despite the renown, infamous or otherwise, of his exploits, Ned Buntline is perhaps best remembered for his dime novels. Typical of his four hundred-odd stories are: *The Mysteries and Miseries of New York, Navigator Ned; or, He Would Be Captain, Stella Delorme; or, The Comanche's Dream, The Black Avenger of the Spanish Main; or, The Fiend of Blood,* and *Buffalo Bill.*

Jay Monaghan, *State Historian of Illinois in charge of the Illinois State Historical Library, and author of* THE GREAT RASCAL, *is the author of the two-volume* Bibliography of Lincolniana *and* The Overland Trail.

BOOKS BY JAY MONAGHAN

Bibliography of Lincolniana, 1839–1939

Diplomat in Carpet Slippers: *Lincoln Deals with Foreign Affairs*

Last of the Bad Men: *The Legend of Tom Horn*

The Overland Trail

This Is Illinois

The Great Rascal: *The Life and Adventures of Ned Buntline*

THE GREAT RASCAL

The Life and Adventures of

NED BUNTLINE

From a photograph by Sarony

Ned Buntline

The Great Rascal

The Life and Adventures of *NED BUNTLINE*

by

JAY MONAGHAN

Fracker Library
Buena Vista College

With Illustrations

Little, Brown and Company · Boston

COPYRIGHT 1951, BY JAMES MONAGHAN

ALL RIGHTS RESERVED. NO PART OF THIS BOOK IN EXCESS OF FIVE HUNDRED WORDS MAY BE REPRODUCED IN ANY FORM WITHOUT PERMISSION IN WRITING FROM THE PUBLISHER

LIBRARY OF CONGRESS CATALOG CARD NO. 52-5003

Published January 1952
Reprinted February 1952

Published simultaneously
in Canada by McClelland and Stewart Limited

PRINTED IN THE UNITED STATES OF AMERICA

TO MILDRED

Contents

Illustrations

THE GREAT RASCAL

The Life and Adventures of

NED BUNTLINE

I

The Discovery of Buffalo Bill

IN THE LATE SUMMER of 1869 a short man with a seamed and weatherbeaten face limped down the steep steps of a Union Pacific coach at North Platte, Nebraska. He had heard about an Indian skirmish at Summit Springs on July 11, and he wanted to interview the veterans. At the same time he hoped to impress them with his own prowess, and lecture about the evils of alcohol. On his breast glittered row on row of semimilitary decorations[1] – emblems of many secret organizations. Ned Buntline (a pen name for E. Z. C. Judson) was nationally known. His stories of life at sea, of adventures in the Seminole, Mexican, and Civil wars, sold by hundreds of thousands. Moreover, his popular little pocket books had proved to be exactly what the soldiers wanted. A clever publisher had printed the picture of a ten-cent piece on the cover of popular romances of this type, thus preventing sutlers from overcharging enlisted men for them.

A crowd of loafing soldiers and civilians, as well as a few blanketed Indians, stood outside the railroad station watching the train. Hacks, carriages, army wagons, and an ambulance or two waited to take passengers to the hotel or down to Fort McPherson, eighteen miles away. Ned was obviously perplexed. Should he ride to the fort in the hack with a motley assortment of plug-hatted salesmen, gamblers, and calico-clad soldiers' wives – the kind of people who haunted the outskirts of every army post? He would enjoy talking with them about his importance. On the other hand, a man of his means should hire a carriage and drive to the fort in a style that befitted his prominence. Ned Buntline was reputed to be the best-paid writer in America, boasting an annual income of $20,000, and he liked to lavish it with open hands.

The fight at Summit Springs, which Ned had read about in the papers, seemed an apt basis for his next dime novel, or for one of the sensational serials he frequently wrote for *Street and Smith's New York Weekly*. A band of Sioux and Cheyenne renegades under Chief Tall Bull had been pursued by General Eugene A. Carr with the 5th Cavalry, aided by Major Frank North's battalion of Pawnee scouts – irregulars enlisted to kill their tribal enemies.[2] On the trail of the hostiles the soldiers discovered the unmistakable shoe print of a woman prisoner. Ned could ask no better beginning for a story, and the subsequent events were more thrilling than the beginning.

On the day of the skirmish, Tall Bull's renegades at Summit Springs were dallying during the hot July afternoon in the shade of their tepees. They did not suspect lurking enemies until they heard a roar of hoofs and looked up to see the Pawnee scouts, stripped naked and riding bareback, sweeping down upon them – manes, tails, braids, and whips flying. Tall Bull's braves ran for their picketed ponies, jumped aboard, two and three tandem, and raced away with the red scouts behind them in hot pursuit. Blue-clad cavalrymen galloped into the deserted village and prowled through the tepees while the Pawnee scouts, including Frank North and his brother, Captain Lute North, ran down and killed the fugitive men, women, and children out on the plains. Two, instead of one, captive white women were found in the encampment. One was dead, her head crushed with a tomahawk. The other, still alive, proved to be a German immigrant, a Mrs. Weichel, who could talk no English. Neither was exactly the type of heroine for Ned's popular books but that detail was unimportant. The high light of the entire skirmish was the manner in which Frank North tricked Tall Bull to his death. This incident, as it had been told to Ned, rivaled his own best stories. He was eager to meet the hero out here on his native heath and write about him in his next novel.

Frank North, according to the stories Ned heard, had been riding across the plains beyond the Indian village with his brother. From a "wash" where Tall Bull lay hidden a shot rang out. Frank fell off his horse as though hit. Lying on the ground he told his brother to gallop away with both horses. The hidden Indian would hear the pounding hoofs, Frank said, and peep out to see if he had killed the rider. That was the chance that Major Frank wanted. He knelt, aimed his rifle at the edge of the wash, and waited. A rifle appeared over the bank. Frank North drew a bead on it. Then an Indian's head came up, and North pulled the trigger. The head disappeared, and the rifle lay unfired on the bank. Frank North reloaded and waved triumphantly for his brother to return. Soon a woman with a little child appeared and made signs of surrender. She came forward begging for mercy. Her husband, Tall Bull, she said, lay dead with the last of his warriors in the gulch.[3]

Ned Buntline had gone first to Fort Sedgwick near Julesburg, Colorado, hunting for Frank North. Soldiers there told him that the great man would be found down the Union Pacific at Fort McPherson, near North Platte. So Ned traveled farther east. He found Major North at Fort McPherson, true enough, but the major did not measure up to Buntline's literary standards. Instead of greeting the author cordially, North scarcely concealed his contempt for writers. He did not care to become a paperback hero. "If you want a man to fill that bill," he told Buntline, "he's over there under the wagon."[4] Ned stumbled across the area, among prostrate men who were trying to sleep in the fly-infested heat. Lute North, watching, thought the heavy-set little stranger tipsy, but old and mysterious wounds made him walk that way. Unsteadily he poked beneath the wagon. A young giant, with sleepy eyes and straw in his long hair, looked up at the gnome whose stories would soon make him the fabulous Buffalo Bill.

William Frederick Cody was well known in his narrow frontier circle. Now twenty-three years old and handsome as Apollo, he had served without action in the Civil War and had driven a scraper team for a contractor laying rails across the plains. Above all he liked to hunt, having supplied buffalo meat for the section crews. Recently he had served as scout for General Eugene A. Carr, Frank North's commanding officer. The general and Buffalo Bill had missed the scrap at Summit Springs but they had galloped into the Indian village shortly afterwards. Cody knew the details of the fight and all the participants. What was more, Ned Buntline found him both engaging and talkative. Cody invited the novelist to ride his horse, Powder Face. He noticed that the crippled man sat a saddle with a skill not learned by writing books. Cody suggested that they go scouting for Indians. "I was to deliver a temperance lecture tonight," Buntline replied, bristling his red mustache, "but no lecture for me when there is a prospect of a fight."

Ned proved to be a bold and tireless rider. He seemed thoroughly familiar with cavalry equipment, recounted experiences in the Civil War and told how his troop swam the Blackwater River in Virginia under fire, showed his wounds – one bad one in his chest – and talked about storming the Halls of Montezuma when he and the famous Civil War generals were all young men together. He also confided that his real name was Colonel E. Z. C. Judson. His skill with firearms won the respect of young Bill Cody and the other frontiersmen. He kept his sense of direction on the plains, said it came easily to a man who had lived years at sea. His eyes noticed tracks along the way, a habit he had acquired trailing Indians in the Seminole War, Buntline said. The soldiers believed him – some of them at least. Moreover, he proved his prowess by swimming his horse recklessly across the Platte ahead of all the troopers.[5]

Ned Buntline spent several days – weeks perhaps – on the Platte but he encountered no hostile Indians. His vacation over, Ned returned to New York with his head full of stories. In December 1869, Street and Smith advertised a new serial by Ned Buntline in their *New York Weekly*, to be entitled "Buffalo Bill: The King of Border Men – The Wildest and Truest Story I Ever Wrote." The sobriquet "Buffalo Bill" did not originate with Buntline. For a dozen years the name had been popular on the frontier.[6] Ned appropriated it for Cody just as he had copied titles and literary style from other writers all his life, but Ned Buntline, with the *New York Weekly*, introduced Buffalo Bill to the world.

The time was ripe for cheap literature about the West, and Buntline's story appeared just as hundreds of thousands of immigrants arrived to claim homesteads on the plains. Investors were also talking about the millions to be made in the cattle business out West if the Indians could be removed. One railroad had reached the Pacific and three others were planned. A great rush for new settlements loomed, and also an unprecedented demand for steel rails – a bonanza for industry. Everyone, rich or poor, was talking and thinking of new opportunities.

Cody himself must have gasped when he read Buntline's account of him as the greatest scout in the West and also a temperance advocate, for Cody liked his drink as well as the next Western youth. In fact, he admitted enlisting in the Civil War when he had drunk so much he did not know what he was doing.[7] He must have been doubly surprised to learn that he had killed Tall Bull, but, before long, Cody himself would permit his press agents to make him the sole hero of Summit Springs, a gallant figure riding into the village at the head of the charge instead of four hours afterward. Tall Bull, according to these later accounts, was found in the act of raising his tomahawk to strike down Mrs. Weichel, and Buffalo Bill, rather miraculously, held his reins in one hand, shot Tall Bull with a pistol held in the other, and raised his magnificent sombrero in a heroic flourish to Mrs. Weichel – presumably with his third hand.

Bill Cody was very hard up when Ned's first stories about him appeared in the *New York Weekly*. He was out of a job and his wife expected a baby. Fame, but no money, came to him weekly as installments described his horse, Powder Face, his associate "Wild Bill Hitchcock" and the "M'Kandlas gang." Evidently Ned was writing about things he had heard, not read, for Wild Bill spelled his name "Hickok" and had shot it out with the McCanles – not M'Kandlas – gang in 1861 at Rock Creek Station, Nebraska. Cody's real wife Louisa and fictitious sisters, Lillie and Lottie, all shared in Buffalo Bill's hairbreadth escapes. While Ned wrote about them for an ever-widening circle of readers, he divided his own time between Kate Judson in Westchester County and Lovanche Judson in New York. For the latter he kept a house at 13 East Seventh Street.[8] One day a letter from Stamford, New York, awoke the busy writer from dreams about his three loves – the two women who claimed to be his wives, and the charming Knight of the Plains. Ned read that his uncle, Samuel Judson, had died on August 18, 1870.[9] Buntline traveled by boat and stage to the western Catskill village. (The first railroad reached Stamford that year.) He found Samuel's estate to be moderate, but the dead man had shrewdly willed $1500 to establish a village library, provided that the community matched his bequest.[10] One heir, in addition to Ned, survived. This man, N. Pratt Judson, owned a small garden spot in Stamford, and made his living by occasional blacksmithing.

Ned returned to his wives in lower New York State in the fall of 1870, but it was plain that he had left his heart in the highlands, his ancestral home. He planned to return in the spring to raise the endowment for the library.[11] During the winter Ned spent many months traveling, writing for Street and Smith, and corresponding with Buffalo Bill. In November Cody's son was born. The scout wanted to name him for Judson, but Frank North dissuaded him. The dime novelist had always appeared like a paste diamond to North. He saw scars of Ned's past that were invisible to the younger man and he suggested that Kit Carson seemed more appropriate. Cody acquiesced,[12] but he still cherished memories of himself in Ned Buntline's stories.

In May 1871, Lovanche Judson noticed that Ned's payments for her living became irregular and much smaller than usual. To make ends meet she displayed a sign soliciting dressmaking. Then she learned that Ned had spent $300 for a watch, chain, and other jewelry which she had not received.[13] Lovanche became suspicious and in June swore out a complaint for desertion. But before the officers found Judson he bounced beaming into her house, took down the seamstress sign, paid some of her bills, stayed a day or two, and then disappeared, to be heard of next up at Stamford, where he pitched a tent at the edge of a grove and settled down in surroundings that were reputedly comfortable for a pioneer Indian fighter. Small boys came across the fields and stood openmouthed around the tent. In moccasins and fringed trousers, with trusty gun on shoulder, Ned Buntline strode down to the village. There was no doubt about the deadliness of his marksmanship. Stamford accorded him amused tolerance that grew to respect when a downstate newspaper reported his income at $15,000 a year from Street and Smith alone.[14]

Ned organized the Judson Library Foundation to meet the requirements of his uncle's bequest, and on July 4, 1871, a marble obelisk was dedicated to the memory of Stamford's benefactor.[15] Between stories for Street and Smith and for Beadle and Adams, leading dime novel publishers, Ned offered to deliver lectures for the Foundation. In addition to a talk on temperance he prepared a new one entitled "Woman as Angel and Fiend."[16] Often he tied down the flaps of his tent and drove away to lecture in small towns within twenty miles of Stamford. Usually he charged ten cents admission, pledging it to the Judson Library fund. Was he really rich or only a charlatan?

During the summer of 1871, Ned became enamored of and proposed marriage to Anna Fuller, daughter of a Stamford farmer who owned a butcher shop in town. Rumors of Ned's reputation had followed him, and the Presbyterian minister, L. E. Richards, inquired about Ned's past and found it questionable. Ned admitted that he had been married, but claimed to have been divorced. As a matter of record, he does seem to have separated from Kate Judson and to have bought off Lovanche – that is to say, on September 2 he paid her $100 to "renounce all present and future claims." Lovanche admitted taking the money, but she also remembered that Ned came back to see her once or twice during the following month, bringing flowers and a canary bird.[17] Lovanche confessed later that she succumbed to her perennial weakness for Ned and became thoroughly convinced that she had won him permanently. Her mother was not so sure, and suspected that Anna Fuller possessed the inside track in Ned's affections. In her daughter's behalf, she wrote the Reverend L. E. Richards at Stamford asking if Ned Buntline was engaged. She received the reply that Ned and Anna were not only engaged, but had been married on October 3, 1871.[18]

News of the marriage was printed in the newspapers. Kate Judson, the mother of Ned's four children, decided that she had had enough. Her divorce was granted on November 27.[19] Lovanche, always more assertive, did not intend to let Ned get away with such a prank. She threatened to upset his playhouse and ruin everything. Ned learned about the correspondence between Lovanche's mother and the Reverend Mr. Richards. He hurried to New York. After a scene, Lovanche agreed to accept $50 a month from him and signed a stipulation "to not disturb, trouble, or annoy him, or any one connected with him, in any way, place or manner, so long as he faithfully and promptly fulfilled this agreement." Then Ned returned to Stamford and his bride.

In the New York papers he read that Buffalo Bill's fame was growing apace. James Gordon Bennett, son of an old enemy of Ned's, had gone West with a party of wealthy friends, all guests of General Phil Sheridan. The young man belonged to a fast set of wealthy New York bachelors. He had recently inherited the *New York Herald* from his father and was constantly watching for popular features to add to the paper. In all probability he knew nothing about Ned Buntline's altercation with his distinguished father some twenty odd years before.

For Bennett's Western trip Sheridan prepared a sumptuous camp outfit. Sixteen wagons were detailed to haul tents and supplies, two to carry ice for the wine. The young men got off the cars at North Platte, Nebraska, and drove across the broad shallow stream, then through the cottonwoods to Fort McPherson below the bluffs at the south. The hero of the *New York Weekly*, Buffalo Bill himself, rode over to their camp on a snow-white horse, a gallant stepper. With a white buckskin suit he wore a crimson shirt, and a white sombrero crowned his flowing locks. James Gordon Bennett noticed that the hero was every bit as handsome as Buntline had pictured him, and his guests were delighted when General Sheridan assigned him to them as guide. Moreover, they found him as affable as he was good-looking, and they pronounced him a "mild, agreeable, well-mannered man, quiet and retiring in disposition." He taught them the old-fashioned Western custom of taking a snort of bourbon before breakfast, a delightful habit "more refreshing than brushing the teeth." [20]

After the New Yorkers left, Bill Cody was out of a job again; and he was now spoiled for manual labor. He realized that opportunity beckoned back East, where money seemed plentiful. Perhaps his old friend Buntline could recommend him as a coachman for some rich man or, better still, get him a job driving a fire engine — anything connected with horses. Then, in the fall of 1871, Buffalo Bill had another stroke of good luck. The Grand Duke Alexis was touring America. Government officials showed every consideration to the blond Russian youth of nineteen. Russia had been the best friend of the United States during the recent Civil War. The purchase of Alaska had cemented the friendship. Now the Grand Duke traveled from ovation to ovation. He signified that he would like to hunt buffalo on the plains. Again General Sheridan was ordered to provide the entertainment. Again he employed Buffalo Bill and outfitted a wagon train from North Platte. Spotted Tail, a famous Sioux, and his village accompanied the expedition to give it color.[21]

Only a few bison were killed, but the Grand Duke expressed his pleasure over the camping trip, especially the exhilaration of a mad ride in a stagecoach behind six fractious horses with Cody holding the lines. Back on the railroad, the royal party traveled down to Denver, a rapidly growing plains town which already prided itself on having outgrown pioneer rudeness. Ned Buntline read of the trip in the New York papers and set to work promoting a great debut for Buffalo Bill at the end of the excursion.

In the meantime, a formal ball was tendered the Grand Duke in Denver, and before the festive evening ended a telegram set all the merrymakers agog. Out on the plains, in Kit Carson County, Colorado, a herd of buffalo had been sighted. Little Phil Sheridan ordered cavalry horses loaded on the Grand Duke's train. He selected a detail to escort the royal Russian. One of the musicians at the ball, Chalkley Beeson, knew the plains where the game was reported to be, and went with the party. At daylight the train stopped in the hunting country. The horses were unloaded and saddled, and the huntsmen rode away. General Sheridan stayed behind. On foot with Chalkley Beeson, he walked to the top of an elevation to watch the distant figures coursing across the flats. The bombardment sounded like a battle. Black spots on the plains showed where bison had fallen. Little bands of surviving animals galloped hither and yon into coulees. A wounded calf came straight toward the men as they stood on the swell above the special train. Dragging its hindquarters, the crippled animal seemed to have lost all fear of man. General Sheridan turned to Chalkley Beeson: "Catch that little fellow," he said. "I'll put him out of his misery." The fiddler ran toward the calf and caught its tail. Sheridan, a short man, panted up and shot it with his pistol.

Years later the fiddler became the leader of a well-known cowboy band. He liked to tell how he once sat in a group of raconteurs when Sheridan "sounded off" about his buffalo hunt with Grand Duke Alexis. Beeson remembered commenting: "I too was on that hunt."

Sheridan had turned his balding head toward the musician. "I don't remember you," he said.

"You should," the band leader replied. "I'm the man who held the buffalo by the tail while you killed it." [22]

The Grand Duke's eight-day hunt ended. He presented Buffalo Bill with a Russian fur coat, jeweled cuff links and studs. Young Cody watched the royal train steam away to social receptions and ovations while he sank back into pioneer squalor. Before spring, however, General Sheridan notified Cody that James Gordon Bennett had sent $500 for the scout to spend on a trip East. Ned Buntline may have been behind the invitation.[23] At any rate, his serial in the *New York Weekly*, "Buffalo Bill: The King of Border Men," had been rewritten as a play by Fred Meader [24] and promised a successful run, with the character called "Buffalo Bill" drawing loud applause.

Bill Cody pocketed Bennett's money and started East. Newspapers announced that he was coming to visit the two journalists, Ned Buntline and James Gordon Bennett.[25] At Chicago Cody stopped between trains to be measured for suitable clothes. When he stepped off his car at Niagara reporters described him as wearing the Alexis jewels. At Stamford, Ned and Anna Judson packed their carpetbags and hurried to New York to meet the incoming celebrity. On the train Ned wrote detailed stories about the trip for publication in his home paper. He called his young and latest wife "precious Hazel Eye" and seemed to have no fear of encountering Lovanche.

Ned and Anna registered at the Brevoort. The New York to which they had come boomed with the postwar prosperity that preceded the panic of '73. Millionaires were building mansions along Fifth Avenue. Poor people, less poor than ever before in their lives, crowded prize fights, dogfights, cockfights, and rat-killing contests in the slums – all new to Anna but too close to Ned's past. Barnum had expanded his museum. Circuses, dime peep shows, cheap theaters were packed with smelly people, many of them foreign. Ned called on old friends and arranged for a series of lectures to urge membership in a society that interested him – the Patriotic Order of Sons of America. Ned was an expert at conducting organizational rallies. The redheaded rabble rouser had learned the technique before the Civil War, in activities which were best forgotten.

Ned's campaign had hardly started when Cody arrived in town and registered at the Union Club. With a bevy of newsmen, the scout strolled over to the Brevoort for a call. Stubby Ned bumbled into the reception parlor and formally presented him with a long-range rifle, made to order for a British nobleman who had not lived to use it. The reporters scribbled in their notebooks during the presentation, and the next day people read that Buffalo Bill had told Ned Buntline that he would have to load such a long-range gun with rock salt, otherwise the meat would spoil before he got to it.[26]

Buffalo Bill became the city's lion. James Gordon Bennett carried stories about him in the *Herald*. August Belmont invited the Wild Westerner to dine. At the Academy of Music, Buffalo Bill became a feature of the Liederkranz Ball. The festivity started with a pageant. A cortege of Russian bears hauled in a huge snowball, from which emerged a striking likeness of the Grand Duke Alexis. The *Herald* announced that Buffalo Bill, the Scout of the Plains, was also present, having "come from the land of the buffalo and red skin to see for himself the difference between an Indian powwow and a genuine masquerade." [27] But Cody's great night came a week later at the Bowery Theatre. Ned invited him to attend the dramatization of his life and see himself portrayed on the stage. The bashful plainsman sat in Ned's box, where the audience recognized him at once, cheering "with an ovation such as actors at the more aristocratic theatres never received." [28]

"Speech! Speech!" Cody felt himself half lifted to the stage. He looked at the pool of pink faces, thousands and thousands of eyes. He stammered incoherently and was glad to get back in the box – but the glare of the footlights made him feel good, too.

The drama was simple, easily understood, full of action, blood and thunder. Bill Cody saw his counterpart, in an imitation buckskin shirt, run onto the stage amid war whoops from Indians in the wings. The make-believe scout crawled into a hollow log just before the bloodthirsty warriors rushed into the scene. Then in an act of great suspense the Indians decided to encamp. They built a fire by the log and talked in monosyllables about the horrible things they planned to do to the white man once they caught him. Soon the eager audience noticed that the hollow log was on fire. The trapped scout must burn to death or come out and be tortured by his captors. Watching breathlessly, pit and gallery saw the blond wig of the scout emerge from the end of the log. With elaborate stealth, the actor scout poured the contents of his powder horn onto the fire. The redskins were blown to smithereens, and the actor bowed heroically before a hurricane of applause. Successful acting seemed as easy as that, and Bill Cody was impressed.

Acts two and three proved equally dramatic. The performance ended with a hand-to-hand duel between hero and villain – "Buffalo Bill" and "M'Kandlas" – followed by a brief love scene.

Ned was busy with his lectures during most of Cody's six-week vacation. He and "Hazel Eye" rattled away on local railway trains to organize chapters of the Patriotic Order of Sons of America in the suburbs.[29] He composed a "Hymn of Devotion," and introduced Red, White, and Blue degrees, which had proved their appeal in his earlier secret organizations. But Ned was never too busy to keep himself in the limelight with Buffalo Bill. One day the two traveled down to West Chester, Pennsylvania, a town beyond Philadelphia. Cody's uncle, Colonel Henry R. Guss, operated the Green Tree Hotel there. Ned and Bill, the tall and short, with swinging canes, called formally at the hostelry, met "the family," pronounced Cody's cousin Elizabeth a "most beautiful girl,"[30] and returned to Gotham. Cody's $500 was almost all gone now and he decided to spend his last fifty on a grand banquet at Delmonico's. After the meal he learned that his money scarcely covered the price of one plate. Ned Buntline generously paid the bill and saw his handsome Western friend settled on the cars bound for Nebraska.

At North Platte, Cody got off the train, borrowed a horse, and galloped over to Fort McPherson flaunting Ned's rifle, a high hat, white tie and tails. Late in May 1872, he was awarded the Congressional Medal of Honor for heroism in a brush with some hostile Indians. Ned, in the meantime, followed Buffalo Bill's departure with a show of his own – a temperance talk in the Bowery Theatre, scene of his recent triumph with the Western scout. At the theater door a table held pens, ink, and a pledge to be signed. The press reported the meeting as one of the largest ever to pack the Bowery.[31] Next Ned hurried off to the national encampment of the Patriotic Order of Sons of America at Allentown, Pennsylvania, where he was elected vice-president, master of forms and ceremonies, and custodian of the Red, White and Blue degrees – honors that had been denied the grim-faced little man who had first conceived these degrees back in the days when they were part of a political upheaval that rocked the nation.

After returning to New York, Ned had an accident, but as usual he was prepared for the emergency. According to his story, printed in the newspapers, he and Anna attended the theater with another couple. After the show they all boarded a streetcar — all but Ned. Thugs grabbed him, but our hero pulled out his trusty pistol and they ran away.[32] Ned, with intrepid mien, joined the party in the car before they knew anything had happened, and he reported the event to the press instead of to the police.

In triumph the aging colonel with his "precious Hazel Eye" returned to Stamford, announcing grandly that they had come to rusticate for the summer. But on Memorial Day Ned visited Philadelphia to attend a grand rally of the Patriotic Order of Sons of America.[33] When he returned he drew up plans for a gentleman's country residence, an estate to be named Eagle's Nest after the hunting lodge of that name which he had owned in the Adirondacks. Ned selected a site on his father-in-law's farm a mile out of town, and work was begun [34] with no apparent consideration for cost. Ned designed a special gun room or armory to display his rare weapons and fancy fishing rods, a library, glass conservatory, and everything imagination could conjure. Outside, he said, a gameproof fence would surround the property. Then Ned set to work in earnest to get sufficient funds for the Judson Library Foundation project. In addition to proceeds from his own lectures, he planned to raise money with a series of talks by several eminent people — Josh Billings, "Brick" Pomeroy, the Reverend T. de Witt Talmage, "Grace Greenwood," and Professor Le Roy Cooley of the State Normal School at Albany. Season tickets were offered for $2.50, and the *Stamford Mirror* reported the opening performance a howling success. "That the lecture was appreciated can be best estimated by the quality of hooks and eyes, as well as buttons picked up on the floor next morning." [35] However, no other lectures followed. Perhaps the election excitement of 1872 was taking up everyone's attention.

In November, Grant won a second term, and Delaware County, New York, Ned's bailiwick, elected every local Republican candidate. A news note from the West announced, too, that Buffalo Bill had been elected to the legislature in his home state.[36]

After the election Ned tried to revive the lecture course. On November 26 he announced that he had engaged a Rocky Mountain trapper, Cale Durg, to give a free recital at Seminary Hall in Stamford. Children and their elders came and saw Ned himself in fringed buckskin with an ostrich feather in his hat. The success of the performance gave the colonel an idea. He wrote Cody to come to Chicago with some other Westerners and a group of real Indians. They could all make a fortune with a Wild West Show.

Out in Nebraska, Cody read the letter and remembered the thrill of the footlights and the things Ned Buntline had shown him. "Mamma," he told his wife, "I know I'd be a fizzle at legislatin'. I don't know just how bad I'd be at actin'. I guess maybe I'd better find out." [37]

II

Wild West Show

NED BUNTLINE beat Buffalo Bill to Chicago by hours or by days. The records are conflicting. Some years afterwards Ned said that he arrived in the Windy City on the same day Buffalo Bill did, but that, as will be seen, made a good story.[1] Chicago was rising from the charred rubble of her great conflagration of the previous year, and Ned, strangely enough, came to town as a fire insurance agent as well as a theatrical promoter.[2] He certainly had written Buffalo Bill to meet him in Chicago, so selling insurance was probably only a side line. Years ago he had made expenses by selling Cuban scrip and temperance tracts when he organized the Know-Nothings.

Chicago's crudely constructed amphitheater, with unfinished board sides and canvas top, seemed ideal for the rough show Ned had in mind for his scouts of the plains – if not for a covering policy. Ned had learned a lot about running a road show before he met Anna Fuller and settled down at Stamford. He discussed his new plans with the manager, Jim Nixon, saying that two real scouts and twenty Indians were on their way to the city. Nixon thought that Chicagoans would pay to see these Wild Western men and he made a deal with Buntline. Then, to Ned's chagrin, Bill Cody arrived with an ex-scout from Jeb Stuart's Confederate Cavalry,[3] "Texas Jack" Omohundro, and no redskins. Jim Nixon was furious. People, he said, would demand to see real Indians. Ned displayed the scouts' fringed shirts and beaded leggings. He said that twenty professional actors might be hired to take the Indians' parts. The play would be better with them. Nixon grunted disconsolately, "Let's see your script."

Ned said that he had not written it. "Not written it," Nixon snorted, "and this is Thursday with the opening scheduled for Monday." The theater manager was indignant. Ned loved to tell the sequel. It was typical of the way he pictured himself. Nixon, according to Ned, canceled the contract. "What rent will you ask for your theater for next week?" Ned queried.

"Six hundred dollars," Nixon told him.

Ned counted out the greenbacks, then hurried his scouts to a hotel and ordered pen and paper. Within four hours, Ned boasted forever after, he wrote *The Scouts of the Plains*. It was, of course, Meader's play, *Buffalo Bill, King of Border Men*, almost act for act, but with a new character added – Cale Durg. Ned set the bellhops to copying his script for each actor to memorize, while he hobbled off to employ suitable men who might look like Indians if dressed in tan frocks and cambric pantalets. To take the sole feminine part, Dove Eye, he hired Mlle. Morlacchi,[4] described later by the *Chicago Tribune* drama critic as "a beautiful Indian maiden with an Italian accent and a weakness for scouts."

His troupe hired, Ned hurried back to the hotel to drill the scouts in their parts. He himself was to act Cale Durg, the character he had impersonated at Stamford. Ned found the real scouts dismayed at the prospect of memorizing so much. "Bill," Texas Jack asked his companion in misery, "how long will it take you to commit your part?"

Cody grinned. "About seven years, if I have good luck."[5]

The opening curtain for *The Scouts of the Plains* rose on December 16, 1872, with all seats filled. The box office had taken in $2800 – enough to pay the week's rent and leave a handsome profit. Before the footlights Buffalo Bill, Texas Jack, and Ned Buntline stood resplendent in fringed buckskin. None of them said a word. The opening line belonged to Cody, but stage fright

Buntline as Cale Durg

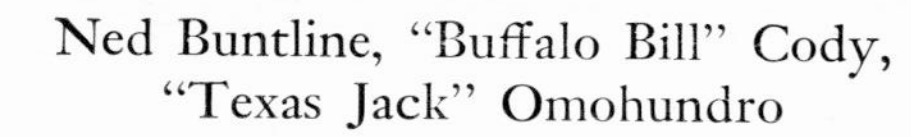

Ned Buntline, "Buffalo Bill" Cody,
"Texas Jack" Omohundro

numbed his mind. Ned tossed him a cue: "Why, you've been off buffalo-hunting with Milligan, haven't you?"[6] Cody knew that Milligan, whom he had guided recently, was in the audience. Consciousness returned partially to the handsome scout. He repeated a few simple facts about the hunt. The audience knew this to be extemporaneous and no play acting. Men and boys by hundreds felt that they were out on the plains listening to a real scout at the campfire. They rocked the house with wild applause.

Ned fed the stage-struck scout encouraging questions until the end of the act. Then he signaled the manager to turn loose the red men. "Supers" in cambric pantalets bounded upon the stage. Buntline shouted, "The Indians are upon us!" Texas Jack and Buffalo Bill understood this cue. Tongue-tied as they were, they flew at the painted and befeathered actors and "killed" them to the last man. The curtain came down accompanied by a thunderous ovation.

In the second act Buntline's anemic plot began to unfold. The scouts did not know their lines, but they were active. The *Chicago Tribune* summed up the play as a triple warfare between the scouts, the Indians, and a party of renegade whites, one of whom, named Cale Durg, "managed to keep drunk for several days without a drop of anything." The Indians divided their time between homicide and "bombastic speeches about the dew, the clouds, and the baseness of white men." The *Times* critic remembered: "They have a strong desire to capture somebody and, consequently, jump about and yell," until Cale Durg, the trapper, rushes "unarmed, in the most inexcusable and uncalled-for manner, into the midst of twenty or more of his mortal enemies." Immediately the Indians lashed the captive to a tree and kindled a torture fire.

At this point in the drama Ned prolonged the suspense before the torture fire by lecturing on temperance. His lengthy monologue resembled the speeches he had been giving for twenty years. The *Tribune* reporter summarized it in a terse sentence.

"Buntline," he wrote, "delivered some opinions on the use of liquor which he said was injurious and had done a great deal of harm." The sermon over, the redskins returned to the torture at hand, to be interrupted by Buffalo Bill and Texas Jack, who ran in from the wings with smoking pistols. Amid shots and shrieks, the savages and the curtain dropped. The next act was similar except that the rescue was made with lassos instead of pistols. In the last act Cale Durg died in agony while the scouts rushed in for a belated revenge with bowie knives.

To weave heroines into such a drama would have taxed the ingenuity of any playwright but Buntline. He repeated the love scene from *King of Border Men*, this time with the real Buffalo Bill furnishing both profile and arms. The *Times* concluded:

> On the whole, it is not probable that Chicago will ever look upon the like again. Such a combination of incongruous drama, execrable acting, renowned performers, mixed audience, intolerable stench, scalping, blood and thunder, is not likely to be vouchsafed to a city for a second time, — even Chicago.[7]

A matinee was advertised for Wednesday, December 18. Ned added an innovation. Since his trouping days in the midlands he had always appealed to women. Now instead of offering them free seats he advertised that every "lady" at the matinee would be presented with a "photograph portrait" of Ned Buntline, Buffalo Bill, and Texas Jack.[8]

The successful engagement closed and the troupe moved to St. Louis, where some politicians remembered that Ned Buntline had led a riot in the city twenty years ago and had jumped bail. People were also reminded of Ned's tumultuous past by a news note that announced the sudden death of Edwin Forrest in his dressing room in Philadelphia.[9] Forrest had been instrumental in helping Ned to a much publicized year in jail.

The first St. Louis performance opened at the Grand Opera House on Monday, December 23, 1872. The night was bitter cold and snowy but Buntline's show drew the biggest theater crowd in town. Mrs. Cody had come East to join her husband. She sat in the third row and Buffalo Bill saw his Louisa at once. He leaned over the gas footlights and called, "Oh Mamma, I'm a bad actor." The audience roared applause as they had in Chicago. They were seeing real scouts – not play actors – and they loved it. Ned added to the studied amateurism by telling reporters again that he had written the script in four hours. An artless newsman passed the word on to his readers, with the additional remark that he wondered why it had taken so long.[10] A writer on the *Missouri Democrat*, which had deplored the Buntline riot twenty years before, announced: "Buffalo Bill is a beautiful blonde, and wears the Alexis diamond on a shirt, whose fastenings are in the rear." All the reviews were jocular, and none recommended arresting Ned for jumping his bond.

On Christmas Eve Ned announced to the *St. Louis Globe* that the scouts had subscribed to the *Temperance Monthly*. Then two days later came the shock. The actors were lounging in the lobby of the Southern Hotel at two o'clock in the afternoon. Ned, up in his room, was writing advance publicity for the troupe's opening performance in Cincinnati. A messenger knocked on his door and delivered a telegram. Ned said he had no change in his pocket. Would the boy wait while he went down to the hotel desk to draw some money? The lobby was full of men who seemed to be waiting for someone. A stranger slapped Ned on the back with authority: "Mr. Buntline, I want you."

Ned turned and looked up into the face of Deputy County Marshal Reinstaedtler. "I'm an officer," the tall young man said. "Consider yourself my prisoner."

"What for?" Ned asked in a serious tone and with a sad side-glance toward Buffalo Bill and Texas Jack. The scouts laughed, and one of the city-bred actors pulled out a revolver. He had been with the troupe less than two weeks and did not understand the true nature of Western men.

"If we were out on the plains," said Jack, "we might have

something to say; but here in the city it is no use. We must take what comes." The Chicago actor pocketed his gun sheepishly. Deputy Reinstaedtler explained to Ned the charge against him: assault with intent to kill and rioting twenty years ago.

"Will you allow me to go to my room, to pay for a telegram I have just received?"

"Certainly," replied the officer, "and I will go with you."

Ned requested the officer to make no scene, keep the arrest a secret. He said that he wanted no sensation to harm the play. With the officer he walked up to his room and the crowd melted away. Many of them were newspapermen who hurried to court for the hearing. Up in his room Ned paid the messenger. Alone with the officer, Judson said, "I'm sorry this thing did not come up earlier. All my witnesses are dead. I am innocent of the charge, but I will obey the law without a murmur. I had nothing to do with the riot. I was living in the city at the time, publishing a paper. Word came to me that a riot was going on at Soulard Market, and that a dear friend of mine had been beaten and nearly killed. I went down and took him home, and that is about all there is to it."

Ned and the deputy walked downstairs and out into the street. In Circuit Judge Primm's court they found the press waiting. A friend of Ned's, Captain George D. Martin, volunteered to represent the prisoner as "friend." The judge looked down at the wizened little showman. "Is this Ned Buntline," he asked, "whose yellow-covered literature I have heard of? I expected to see a big, piratical looking fellow, as tall as that door, with bowie-knives and pistols in his belt."

"You are not the first person who has been disappointed at my appearance," Ned replied. Then he let go one of the chivalrous statements that often won him friends among the women. "Once, when I was in Cincinnati," he said, "Amelia B. Welby, who, you know, was a little golden-haired thing, more like an angel than a woman, called to see me. She stood amazed when I presented myself, and said she had imagined I was a great whiskered monster with tarred breeches and a tarpaulin hat. At that time I had a smooth face, like a girl's, and was younger and better looking than at present. But about this arrest; I assure you I know nothing about the charge. I have been in the city several times since the occurrence. Back in 1855 I was with Sumner at Ash Hollow, and was wounded there, and came to the city and laid for three months at the Planter's House. Here is the scar." Ned opened his shirt bosom proudly and disclosed a bullet wound received in Nashville more than twenty-seven years before. "An Indian arrow made that. At the breaking out of the rebellion I took the first company to Washington – the mounted rifles. There were sixty of us, and only fifteen were left – all the rest were killed. I have never avoided the city, and supposed the charge had died out." [11] The judge informed Buntline that he was still liable for trial on the rioting indictments in spite of the passage of twenty years. A thousand dollars would be required for bail to release him from custody.

Ned did not have sufficient money, but his friend Captain Martin hurried away to raise it, and before the evening performance he returned with Carlos S. Greeley, treasurer of the Kansas Pacific Railway and president of the Provident Savings Institution. Greeley signed Ned's bonds, and when the curtain rose at the Opera House Cale Durg limped grimly into the first act.

Newspapers in Chicago hinted that the arrest was all a publicity stunt – an improbable conjecture, for Ned jumped bail again and the court ordered Carlos S. Greeley to pay the thousand-dollar forfeit.[12] The records show, too, that the troupe's cash box was attached before the show left town. Ned wrote grandly to friends in Stamford that he chased the officer away at rifle's point,[13] but the play's name changed suddenly to *Scouts of the Prairie*. Without doubt the reorganization of ownership, not a rifle, cheated the law. This was the old game by which Ned had saved his yacht in 1849.

Under the new name the troupers opened in Cincinnati at Pike's Opera House.[14] To the consternation of serious drama critics, this show drew "the only satisfactory receipts of the week."

People in New York who had been following the progress of *Scouts of the Prairie* read a perplexing article in the *Herald.* What did this item mean?

> CINCINNATI. W. J. Halpin, actor, died at noon today from the effects of injuries received last Thursday night when playing his part as Big Wolf with Ned Buntline's Company.[15]

Manhattan wondered if this could be only an invention of the enterprising Buntline, or if it was grim truth about an extraordinarily realistic show. Grim truth seemed right, for the troupe went into seclusion for a month, then in February opened in Albany. In March the *Scouts* reached Boston, fountainhead of pre-Civil-War abolitionism. Ned advertised himself as a prodigious warrior. He said that he had fought seven years against the Seminoles, in the Mexican War, and that in the Civil War he had not quit with the surrender of Robert E. Lee on April 9, 1865 (Ned was discharged August 23, 1864), but had fought on with Sherman until Johnston surrendered on April 26 – thus falsifying his service in the first war considerably, in the second war considerably more, and in the Civil War by exactly eight months and three days. The ghastly imprint of the bullet he had received in his chest at Nashville was now attributed to an Indian knife instead of to an arrow, as Ned had told Judge Primm. In Boston Ned commenced a huge publicity campaign for his New York debut. The performance, he said, was to be given on horseback with a hundred extra people and twenty more Indians. Boston, Ned continued, was known to be "the most critical city in the Union"[16] and the *Scouts* had played before 1400 Bostonians and always received enthusiastic applause. Gorgeous new scenery had been prepared, and the troupers expressed no fears about Manhattan.

Ned's repeated assertions of confidence sound suspicious. Competition in New York was keen and expenses were high. Mrs. Judson had joined the troupe in the northern states, but she returned to Stamford[17] when the show moved to Broadway to compete with the nation's best talent—Lawrence Barrett in *Julius Caesar*, Joseph Jefferson in *Rip Van Winkle*, and E. A. Sothern in *Lord Dundreary*, a play so popular that it was revived by the actor's son, E. H. Sothern, a generation later. Such competition looked bad, but there were good omens, too. New York had become the dime novel capital of America, winning the laurels from Boston after the Civil War. Publishers like Beadle and Adams, Street and Smith, and a half-dozen others, had made the name of Ned Buntline famous. Poor people read his books and wanted to go West. Wall Street bankers discussed Western investments. Daily the newspapers carried accounts of the progress of Indian wars involving the Apaches and the Modocs. Eccentric long-haired scouts and Western authors were social lions. Bret Harte had just come from California to write in New York's congenial atmosphere, and be arrested for skipping a tailor's bill.[18] Mark Twain was looming into prominence. His *Roughing It*, a vivid yet romanticized picture of the West, was published in 1872. Joaquin Miller, poet of the Sierras, with more hair on his face and head than Buffalo Bill ever had, was attracting crowds to recitals delivered in fringed leggings.[19] A Leatherstocking show similar to Buntline's was playing at the Theatre Comique the same week Ned planned to open. This was direct competition hard to offset. Moreover, Ned's dream of enacting his show on horseback had to be given up. To add to the *Scouts'* bad luck, James Gordon Bennett's mother died on the night of the opening performance.[20] If Buntline expected the *Herald* to shield him from criticism on account of his services in discovering Buffalo Bill, he was disappointed. The morning after the play's debut he read:

> The long promised production of "The Scouts of the Prairie" at Niblo's was accomplished last night without accident. The drama, of

which we understand Ned Buntline is the author, is about everything in general and nothing in particular. Every act ends with a fight between the scouts and the Indians—the first act being still further embellished by a characteristic war dance. The Indians, as well as the scouts, are the genuine article. The real hero of the piece is Cale Durg, the part represented by Ned Buntline, the American Bulwer. Mr. Judson (otherwise Buntline) represents the part as badly as is possible for any human being to represent it. The Hon. William F. Cody, otherwise "Buffalo Bill," occasionally called by the refined people of the eastern cities, "Bison William," is a good-looking fellow, tall and straight as an arrow, but ridiculous as an actor. Texas Jack is not quite so good-looking, not so tall, not so straight, and not so ridiculous. Ned Buntline is simply maundering imbecility. Ludicrous beyond the power of description is Ned Buntline's temperance address in the forest. To describe the play and its reception is alike impossible. The applause savored of derision, and the derision of applause. Everything was so wonderfully bad it was almost good. The whole performance was so far aside of human experience, so wonderful in its daring feebleness that no ordinary intellect is capable of comprehending it.[21]

The critic of the *World* saw something his colleague had missed. With unerring judgment he singled out the one star in the performance:

As a drama it is very poor slop. But as an exhibition of three remarkable men it is not without interest. The Hon. W. F. Cody enters into the spectacle with a curious grace and a certain characteristic charm that pleases the beholders. He is a remarkably handsome fellow on the stage, and the lithe springy step, the round uncultured voice and the utter absence of anything like stage art, won for him the good-will of an audience which was disposed to laugh at all that was intended to be pathetic and serious.[22]

This "utter absence of anything like stage art" proved immensely popular with audiences surfeited with the conventional dramatic bombast of Booth, Beerbohm Tree, and the elder Sothern. Box-office receipts disclosed the show's real popularity.

In May the *Scouts* moved to Philadelphia, where Ned, at a

reception in the Continental Hotel, was presented with a cane made from wood allegedly cut at Valley Forge. At Harrisburg the troupe disbanded for the summer.[23] Ned wrote his home-town paper that the show had cleaned up $200,000, but he probably added one cipher to the total. Buffalo Bill's share came to $6000 [24] — the largest sum hitherto possessed by the young man — and he promptly invested some of it with his uncle in West Chester.[25]

Ned returned to Stamford determined to play the *Scouts* next season out of doors with horses. During the summer he lectured at lodge meetings, and on the Fourth of July he treated the town to a fireworks display in the meadow sloping down to the road from his mansion, Eagle's Nest.[26] In the streets of Stamford and chatting with guests on the front porch of the Delaware Inn, Ned said that the Western show would take to the road in late August. He had been offered a six months' engagement at the Adelphi in London, he explained, but was holding out for Drury Lane, as he should net $15,000 a night there.

This daydream was broken by a statement from William Cody that he and Texas Jack proposed to continue the show without Ned. They had employed Wild Bill Hickok, a genuine gunman, to take Ned's place. Buntline did not flinch. Nonchalantly he rearranged the laurels on his brow and announced that he had a genuine show of his own and, what was more, he had real Comanche Indians, fresh from the plains. These Indians, Ned said, had been employed by P. T. Barnum for a rival Western performance, but Ned had purchased the contract for $16,000 and intended to bring them to Stamford for his friends to see. True to his word, Colonel Judson brought real redskins and two white scouts. He introduced them as Arizona Frank and Dashing Charlie, the Texas Whirlwind, heroes of his last year's story for Street and Smith. Ned hoped that the yellowback novel would sell his new men and new show the way earlier Buffalo Bill stories had sold *Scouts of the Plains.*

Ned trained his actors at Eagle's Nest. On the day scheduled for his performance he led the troupe through town in Indian file to the hall he had hired. His red men stamped out the corn dance rhythms on the stage, shot targets with bows and arrows, beat drums, and sang. One of the chiefs delivered an oration in his native tongue. Dashing Charlie played on a banjo. Arizona Frank sang while performing a jig step – and the show was over.[27]

From Stamford Ned's troupe went on the road. At Paterson, New Jersey, the Indians delighted the audience with a grudge fight on the stage.[28] This, of course, was part of Ned's advertising, for he reported in the afternoon that trouble was brewing over the favors of a young squaw. With advance publicity, a great mob turned out to see the termination of a genuine Indian combat that night. The *Paterson Daily Guardian* reported:

> Long before the doors were open, the sidewalk was obstructed by a thick crowd of half grown men and boys, who scrambled towards the entrance, and extended as far as the middle of the street, looking for all the world like a swarm of exaggerated bees climbing over each other at the entrance of a monstrous hive.[29]

Ned, an old hand in rural show business, knew where to find his audience, how to play medium-sized towns and stay away from the biggest cities, but in spite of the show's popularity he did not make money. In October word came back to Stamford that showman Buntline had got into a quarrel in Louisville, had been overpowered and kicked around. The editor of the *Stamford Mirror*, S. B. Champion, was evidently disgusted with Stamford's new and already notorious citizen. He had welcomed Colonel Judson to the village in 1871 as "our new fellow townsman," and as late as June 1873,[30] he had printed a letter from Ned protesting against proposed blue laws to prohibit the operation of railroad trains on Sundays. But by August 1873, when Ned tented with his Comanches down by the railroad station, the editor had evidently lost his patience, for he referred to

Ned's "old tricks" and "blood and thunder show." Barefoot boys loitered around the tents, but respectable citizens did not. It is possible that the editor may have learned about Lovanche, too, for Ned's payments stopped at the time of the Louisville gun scrape,[31] and Lovanche was not one to take adversity meekly. However, there are no records to indicate that she created any scenes in 1873 like those that shocked the village a few years later.

Ned returned to Stamford soon after the Louisville fracas, and Editor Champion did not deign to mention his arrival. For the Eagle's Nest stables Ned purchased a pair of Hambletonians which he considered the fastest on the road. His strong arms made driving easy. Snow came early in the Catskills, and Ned's sleigh, with Anna in furs, sped along the roads. The couple seemed very happy, but Lovanche threatened trouble. To keep scandal out of the village, Ned took Anna down to New York late in December, hoping for a final settlement with Lovanche. A sum was agreed upon, and in February 1874, the court gave her an uncontested divorce with $15 per month alimony.

At the time of the divorce Ned was back at Eagle's Nest writing diligently for both *Street and Smith's New York Weekly* and Beadle and Adams's *Half Dime Library* – nickel novels that cut into the trade as dime publications had into the shilling shockers of an earlier day. News of Ned's final divorce and his continued literary success partially restored him in the eyes of the few villagers who knew his past. In June he was invited to deliver an oration at the cornerstone-laying ceremony for a new schoolhouse, and on the Fourth of July he presented a great pyrotechnic display. Then he boarded the cars for a busy summer throughout New York and Pennsylvania, organizing camps of the Patriotic Order of Sons of America. Ned himself became a member of a Grand Army of the Republic post in Philadelphia. (Perhaps he preferred to join where his record was unknown.) He was constantly called on to speak before patriotic societies, and weak chapters could usually depend on him for financial aid. Glorying in civic responsibilities, Ned claimed to have founded the Order of the Sons of Temperance and continued his lectures on abstinence for the Order of Good Templars.[32] In Stamford he prided himself on his importance as a member of the school board and the Judson Library Foundation. He and Anna entered grandly into the social life of the community when he was not called elsewhere for lecturing appointments.

In this atmosphere of civic and cultural accountability, Ned followed the careers of his erstwhile Wild West partners. In the newspapers he read that Texas Jack lasted but one season longer with Cody. Then he married Mlle. Morlacchi and retired from the stage. Wild Bill Hickok, most famous scout of them all, did not last so long with Buffalo Bill's show. He proved to be a popular attraction, but theater discipline irked him. When he was passed the jug in a whiskey-drinking act, he spat the liquid on the stage saying, "Any damn fool would know that was cold tea." Hickok also refused to remember such lines as, "Fear not, fair maid; by heavens, you are safe at last with Wild Bill, who is ever ready to risk life and die if need be in the defense of weak and helpless womanhood." [33] Before the season ended he left word with Cody's stage manager: "Tell that long-haired son-of-a-gun I have no more use for him and his damned show business." [34]

Hickok, like Ned, had dreamed of adorning a Wild West Show with horses and buffalo. He had tried them once at Niagara Falls in 1870 [35] without success. When he left Cody he experimented with a show of his own, as Ned had, and again failed. Before long he was obliged to play in honky-tonks at Kansas City, St. Joseph, and Cheyenne, going downhill constantly. Yes, Ned was fortunately free from the old life. Times were never better for his cheap literature. He was happily married, he lived in a mansion furnished with treasured relics, and he had regained the respect of the community. His early life had been hard, often dangerous. He never referred to the time when he had almost been lynched and was saved only by a breaking rope. He did not talk about his revolution and a New York riot which cost him a year in jail. The St. Louis riot case had kicked back when he was trouping with Buffalo Bill. More notoriety might revive other ugly phantoms out of his past. Even his service at sea was not clear from shadows of homicide. As a country gentleman, Ned had time to think about these things. Remorse came to him with prosperity and he lied desperately to cover his past. Then, sorry for himself, he made excuses and told about the unhappiness of his boyhood. A review of the first fifty years of his life explains much. It also tells the story of the rise of cheap literature in America. Perhaps the Buntline books devoured by hundreds of thousands of boys between 1850 and 1886 may have had something to do with the American point of view before the turn of the century. Certainly their popularity must have had more influence on so-called "good literature" than is usually conceded.

Look Aloft! Look Aloft!

THE PLACE AND THE DATE of Ned Buntline's birth are controversial. Biographers state that he was born in Harpersfield, New York, and also in Stamford. Strangely enough, both are correct. The village of Stamford extends across the head of the Delaware into the town, or township, of Harpersfield, and Ned was born in that area of Stamford – not to be confused with the hamlet of Harpersfield some four miles away. The problem of the time of Ned's birth is more difficult to solve. One date was given when he joined the navy, another when he enlisted in the army. His application for pension gives a third date and his tombstone a fourth. The latter, March 20, 1823,[1] has been accepted in this book. Ned liked to recall in later life that a terrible storm racked the heavens on that eventful night. Always full of poetic self-appreciation, he wrote:

> Born when thunder loudly booming
> Shook the roof above my head –
> When red lightning lit the glooming
> Which o'er land and sea was spread.[2]

Of course Ned could remember nothing about that important event. The first memories to whisper in his toddling mind were stormy, however, and the clouds of unhappiness never cleared entirely from his life. His family moved away from Stamford when Ned was still in dresses. The new location promised great rewards but proved a great disappointment. Ned's father, Levi Carroll Judson, was a writer, an orator of Revolutionary War sentiments, and a man who never made little plans. He returned home from one of his periodic absences with the grave announcement that he had accepted the principalship of Beech Woods Academy, at Bethany, Pennsylvania – honor enough alone, but that was not all. Great riches awaited citizens at Bethany. The town had become the focal point in a life-and-death struggle between New York and Philadelphia for the Pennsylvania coal fields. The Delaware River offered a natural water grade for transporting coal to the Quaker City. But Mayor Philip Hone of New York saw an opportunity to dig a canal from the Delaware to the Hudson and thus float the black diamonds to Manhattan. The battle of the titans was meat and drink for a man with Levi Judson's confidence and grandiose imagination. Moreover, the principalship of the academy would support his family until the speculations materialized. Full of enthusiasm, Levi packed up his little household: wife, daughter Irene, and his cyclonic son Edward Zane Carroll Judson – name enough to force its owner into the pseudonym "Ned Buntline."

Ned remembered only a few unfocused impressions, fragmentary pictures in his mind, of the early days when he grew from dresses to little breeches. The Bethany to which his family had come was a bit of old New England on a hilltop above the hazy valley of the Lackawaxen. This country had been a part of Connecticut in colonial days and Pennsylvanians still called the descendants of these people "foreigners." Probably Levi Judson soon left Beech Woods Academy for larger undertakings. Certainly Ned's small-boyhood world centered around a farmhouse on Dyberry Creek eight miles away. The sun peeped above a stony pasture every morning and set at night behind a long forest-tufted ridge. Dyberry Creek meandered through a meadow across the road from the homestead. Occasional expeditions with his mother to the springhouse [3] offered excitement, cold milk, and recollections of boulders with green wavy slime. These things would remain in Ned's mind always. Then there was the memory of a Fourth of July on the Bethany village green – the shrill piping of a fife, men erecting a great pole with a liberty cap on top, Papa Judson on a platform haranguing against redcoats, taxation without representation, and the tyranny "that tried the souls of the patriots of '76."[4]

Ned remembered another picture in the gallery of his mind, a picture tinctured with fright – with murder. He had trudged down the road between stone fences to a neighbor's house. The children there yelled at him, called him "Mason," threw stones, and made him run home with terror tingling in his flying hair. Ned remembered pictures, too, of being dragged unwillingly to bed while his father sat by candlelight, writing furiously with a quill pen. He remembered other times when his mother watched the road from the kitchen window, looking anxiously in the direction of the "corners" – a Pennsylvania name for the cross-roads where people met to trade.

As Ned grew older these pictures became part of a story about the murder of William Morgan, who was killed, people said, because he told the secrets of Masonry. Ned's father had dared the wrath of his neighbors on Dyberry Creek by writing articles defending the order. Poor settlers who could not afford membership in the fraternity complained that Masonic secrets were not democratic – un-American, vicious even – as this murder showed only too well. They pointed to the Judsons as public nuisances, Whigs out of all sympathy with hard-working Democrats. Levi fought back with his pen, and impressed on his son that the Judsons were superior people, and Ned himself the sixth generation of a Connecticut family, now here in hostile Pennsylvania.

Little Ned understood dimly that an Anti-Masonic Party had been formed in Wayne County and that its members were his enemies. He had no friends of his own age, and shunned "the haunts of men" – a phrase he loved. Small physically, but hard as a nut, he liked to climb the ridge behind the house, trudge through waist-high fern brakes, clamber over lichen-covered rocks, and disappear into the oak forest – a small redheaded boy flickering through sunshine and shadow, scents, sounds, and silence.

Ned learned to tie trout flies and to jerk speckled beauties from tinkling ice-cold streams. He liked to make believe that he had a gun and the proudest day in his whole life, so he said later, came in his eighth year when his father gave him a real one. Next morning the lad swaggered into the kitchen with dried blood on his hands. He had killed a doe in the field below the house.[5]

His father paid no attention. Plans for a patriotic rally over at Beech Woods Academy and a new paragraph for his book defending Freemasonry engrossed his mind. Ned slunk away crestfallen, but good health and outdoor activity always restored his cheerfulness. Levi Carroll Judson believed that he had good reason to be more concerned about the future of his country than about the doe which his son had killed in the meadow. American politics trembled, as always, on the verge of a great crisis.

The Anti-Masonic Party threatened to grow to national proportions. Neither Whig nor Democratic, it opposed secret societies, Catholics – their reputed secret organization – and foreigners, who were mostly Catholics. It stood also for a high tariff to keep out foreign goods. In 1831 the Anti-Masons polled big majorities. The next year the major parties adopted many Anti-Masonic planks and practices, including the democratic convention system for nominating candidates. This killed the Anti-Masonic Party, but gave birth to a permanent political convention system in America. In 1832 Andrew Jackson returned to the White House with an overwhelming victory; Masonry was vindicated, but the Whigs lost. Levi Carroll Judson bemoaned the triumph of Old Hickory and at the same time put the finishing touches on his manuscript defending the ritual of the aristocratic Democratic Masons.

To little Ned Judson politics did not make sense. He wanted nothing to do with such contradictory affairs. The boy was growing into a backwoodsman with no apparent interest in his own education or in his father's effort to write convincingly against the Anti-Masons. Only one book, a cheap novel entitled *The Three Spaniards*[6] which his mother had found somewhere and brought home, interested him. Papa Judson worried about his son's backwardness.

In addition to defending the Masons with his pen, Levi wrote for the local paper about agricultural experiments on his farm. He had become a director of the Young Men's Bible Society of Wayne County, and was secretary of a turnpike (toll road) company that he had helped to organize.[7] These civic responsibilities had to be abandoned in 1834, when Levi found it impossible to make the land payments he had planned. Moreover, the New Yorkers had won the fight for the coal fields. Their canal was a success, and a town named Honesdale – for New York's former mayor – promised to be the metropolis of the future instead of Bethany. Broken financially and with no hope of recovery, Levi Carroll Judson announced to his creditors, in the *Wayne County Herald and Bethany Enquirer*, that he was bankrupt[8] – another calamity which added to Ned's assurance that he had been born "when thunder loudly booming shook the roof above my head."

Levi Carroll Judson realized that his iridescent dream of wealth had vanished. He was too proud and too ambitious to remain in Wayne County. A man of judgment should "tot up his parts" and decide where they would be most valued. He could return to Stamford, where his brother Samuel lived on the farm which had been in the family since 1797,[9] but Levi would have to admit defeat there. Another idea appealed to him. Philadelphia had been the city of his choice in the contest for the coal fields. He admired the Quaker City's culture. Her schools of higher learning were famous – just the thing for Ned's education. Levi, himself, might "read" law and establish a practice there. Philadelphia was one of the great publishing centers of America – ideal for Levi's literary ambition. The city's presses turned out books, newspapers, and such well-known magazines as the *Saturday Evening Post*, *Godey's Lady's Book*, *Burton's Gentleman's Magazine*, and *Graham's Magazine*.[10]

Levi Judson announced to his family that they were going to Philadelphia. The women – mother and daughter – acquiesced. Redheaded Ned objected. He did not want to live in a city. His father sternly ordered them all to prepare for the journey. Household belongings were loaded into a wagon and the family set off. Ned pouted, rebellious and stubborn as only an adolescent boy can be.

Philadelphia was the most imposing city any of the Judsons had ever seen. In all America no finer metropolis could be found. The town was noted for its homes, its wealth, and its ease, the neat squares of brick houses shaded by trees, with sidewalks scrubbed to the curbing. On almost every street Negro servants with bucket, brush, and leather hose sprayed the house fronts, scrubbed the marble steps, window sills, and lintels.[11] Philadelphia smelled fresh and clean, like Wayne County's trout streams. The city was proud of its running water, its good hotels with stationary washbowls in all rooms. New York's best hostelries still supplied guests with only a basin and pitcher.

Ned said later that the Judsons moved into a large house on Girard Square, Chestnut Street,[12] where his father began studying Blackstone with the resolution of a Revolutionary patriot, while he, Ned, read the same books sullenly. Levi went out from time to time with letters of introduction to people who might publish the books he hoped to write, or help him meet future colleagues and clients in the law. Ned moped at home. He determined to slip away by himself and explore the city at the first opportunity.

Little by little Ned learned to know the streets. Once he followed a crowd into Chestnut Street Theatre and sat entranced by the acting of Ellen Tree.[13] In the days that followed he attended other plays. Ushers at the Southwark pointed out the box where George Washington had sat. Drama and dramatic presentation would influence Ned all his life and be apparent in all his writing. Sir Walter Scott might spend thousands of words describing a background before introducing his characters. Ned Buntline always began like a play, with people striding across the first page of his story. In his books the reader sat before characters on a stage – obtuse characters perhaps, but always dramatic ones. Music also appealed to the boy, and in later years the roar of a storm at sea would remind him of a Wagner opera. But Ned never cared to sit and listen long. Boundless energy tugged at him constantly. He hungered for romance and adventure. He wanted to emulate the heroes of the Revolution and he craved the excitement he had read about in *The Three Spaniards.* Levi Carroll Judson might feel reverence for Philadelphia's literary atmosphere, for the popular author and playwright Robert Montgomery Bird, and for Charles Brockden Brown, father of American fiction, who had lived in this city – but not Ned. He must have redheaded action.

One day Ned wandered farther than usual from home and came to the Front Street docks. He forgot about Blackstone and the wrongs of an unjust world as he watched rows of sailing ships straining at their hawsers. The wharves were unlike any other part of Philadelphia. Here all was noise and bustle: drivers shouting to their teams, whips cracking like pistol shots, frantic horses lunging in harness, striking sparks from the cobblestones, then moving away with rocking drays of goods. Ned watched the scene entranced. In shop windows he saw delicate sextants, impressive chronometers, elaborate pocket watches with little colored ships pitching across engraved waves on the dials. In front of other stores oilskins with red flannel collars turned slowly in the breeze. Ned heard the compelling screech of a fife in a grogshop. He peered into the dark interior and saw the tattooed arms of seafaring men in checkered shirts, earrings, varnished hats, pumps on their feet. Red sashes held up their canvas drawers – a sailors' name for trousers with bell bottoms that rolled easily to the knees when decks were swabbed. Here were *The Three Spaniards* in the flesh!

All along Front Street fast clipper ships – race horses of the sea – stood in their dock stalls. Ned looked up at their bowsprits. The ships' figureheads – frozen females – stared blankly over his head at the brick buildings across the cobbled street. Ned learned from these wooden ladies whether the ship had been long in port. Heavily loaded vessels floated deep in the water. Day after day when Ned came to the docks these ladies appeared higher and higher above his head as the vessels were unloaded. Great mounds of boxes, casks, and bales littered the wharf beside them. Owners in tall beaver hats checked the goods with supercargoes. Ned learned to recognize West Indian tubs of molasses, straw-bound crockery, and chests of tea from China. Under long sheds, ridges of bagged wheat, flour, bales of stockings and belting waited for outbound passage. One day a packet arrived from Liverpool, the passengers bragging that they had made the trip in thirty-six days.

Ned ventured on board a fruit clipper. He peered into the hold, with its oranges and the hot spiced smell of the tropics – air from the Indies here in Philadelphia. Ned looked up at the ship's rigging. Sea gulls circled and screamed in the sky. Ned looked down the quay at the forest of masts. Wind in the rigging whispered a tune of far countries in a language which Blackstone would not have understood. Ned never concentrated on legal lessons again. Day after day he squirmed in his chair. At last he could stand it no longer. The tiger in him rose above the sand. A plague on Blackstone! The angry boy threw the volume into the burning grate. His father struck him, an openhanded slap across the face, knocking him to the floor. Ned got up, mouth bleeding, eyes flashing hatred. For a moment he glared at his father, then turned and ran from the house, down toward the Delaware – an angry, freckle-faced boy, trotting desperately past stores, markets, stables, mansions where liveried coachmen held fine horses and carriages before their masters' doors. At Front Street he turned north up the quay to Arch.

A West Indies fruiter had just cast off. She drifted slowly out from the pier, loaded deep in the water. Ned ran alongside and bounded on board. The startled captain looked at the boy's long auburn curls, the straps at the bottom of his pantaloons. Such clothes belonged to landsmen – a rigging for horseback riders whose trousers worked up their legs – not to men who followed the sea. But the captain needed a cabin boy, and so let Ned stay on board.

Ned never forgot that first day on a sailing ship. Men were perched aloft on all the masts and spars. Reefed canvas hung like snowdrifts on the yardarms. A steam pilot-boat turned the vessel into the channel. The mate barked an order through his trumpet. Two topsails fluttered from their yards and filled with air. The ship moved slowly away, water rippling against the bow as she gained speed. Ned looked up into the rigging. He had learned in Wayne County the strength of his own arms, the joy of climbing to the tops of tall trees. Squirrel-like, he bounded from the ship's deck and scrambled up the ratlines. At the main-truck the yard captain winked at him. Out on the yardarms sailors lay at ease where the furled sails bagged like hammocks below the spars. These seamen lying in the bunt, as it was called, grinned at the boy. Ned climbed higher up the mast – up, up to the skysail pole. He looked down on the South Street steam ferry going to Camden. He saw League Island and the Navy Yard. Soon Philadelphia passed by the stern and shrank in the distance. Ned felt at home in the sky. His strong arms gave him confidence;

he had no fear of falling, no thought of what might happen as the ship gained momentum.

The Delaware widened to an estuary. The mate called another order, a mainsail broke out, and the clipper jumped ahead as though alive. Ned gloried in the speed. Chester and Wilmington slipped past the starboard bow. Ned looked with sentimental eagerness at the plains of Brandywine, made sacred in "the times that tried men's souls." He watched New Castle glide to the rear. The vessel entered Delaware Bay and picked up a southwest breeze. The masts heeled to leeward and the ship leaped forward, cutting the water with a rush. Ned liked it – no foreboding yet. The wind pulled his long red curls. He resolved to braid them as sailors did. Let deck officers who seldom came aloft wear long locks on their shoulders! Soon the Cape May lighthouse appeared on the lee beam. Then Ned felt the heavy swell of the sea, the long steady roll that sailors know so well [14] – a new thrill to Ned, with still no thought of danger in his lofty perch.

Ned looked below. Under him there was nothing but hissing water – whitecaps of tossing spray. The clipper's sloping deck was far to windward. How could he ever get down in this gale? Terror gripped Ned's heart. His brain reeled. Sea and sky swam giddily before bewildered eyes. His nerves weakened. He was on the verge of dropping into the seething sea when an old salt on the truck yelled, "Look aloft! Look aloft! Damn your blue eyes, look aloft!" [15]

Ned recalled these words years later when he struggled against adverse winds in the literary tempest that was to come with the practice of democracy in America.

IV

The Spanish Main

FOR EIGHT DAYS the *Mary C* flew before the breeze. No new sail was set, no rope hauled. Watch followed watch monotonously. The seamen with no duties aloft were put to work picking frayed rope into oakum on the deck. They all groused good-naturedly and Ned reveled in their company. One said that the *Mary C* was the meanest craft he "had ever saw." Last trip he signed on a good ship. The captain had let the crew do as they pleased when the winds were fair and steady. They didn't pick "no oakum." Instead, men whittled sea shells, made model ships in bottles and other things they could sell at the first port of call. A second man said that he had sailed on a brig out of Hong Kong "onct" and the skipper let all hands fiddle and dance when winds allowed. A third sailor said that he had served on a three-master out of Rio de Janeiro with a woman cook in the galley, and wenches to make a man's bed in the fo'castle. Ned knew that the last story must be a lie, but all the men nodded solemnly.

The ship passed from the soft cool air of the temperate zone into the balmy breath of the trade winds. On the ninth day the captain came on deck as usual at daybreak. He scanned the horizon with his glass, then went below. A few minutes later he reappeared, swathed from head to foot in oilskins and huge sea boots. Ned looked at him and at the clear blue sky. The captain raised his trumpet and rumbled an order. Men scampered aloft.

Ned watched them. He had learned to love the captain, hoped continually to attract his admiration in return, and he watched for the smallest approving glance.

High in the rigging, men furled sail after sail. As they toiled in the sky a black cloud appeared from the north and grew rapidly in size. Seamen looked at it and muttered, "Hurricane!" The men worked furiously to beat the storm. All sails were stowed. Then the gunter masts came down. Preventer stays were passed up to the stumpy lower masts for bracing fore and aft. New ropes were tossed over the cookhouse and the longboat, then lashed fast. Ned felt a solemn awe as the ship was stripped for action against the elements.

All was ready. The dark cloud reached half across the heavens, but still the sea was calm. At last the sun disappeared. In the unnatural gloaming, Ned remembered later, the silent ocean seemed to draw in its breath for the tempest. He heard a distant shriek over the slow heaving waters. On the horizon, racing toward the the ship, he saw whitecaps of foam – "dancing demons of the storm," he described them. The ocean began to boil with milky spray. Nearer, nearer, then, as Ned said later, the solemn silence crashed with a deafening Wagnerian burst of sound from the tempest-band. The ship pitched on her side. Stumpy masts and cordage disappeared in a heaving swell. The staggering helmsman regained his balance on the wet deck, spun the wheel, and the masts sprang upright, showering spray.

Square before the wind now and without a shred of canvas, the ship raced with the waves. Foaming crests broke over the poop, poured a cataract into the ship's waist. Then the stern rose over the mountain of water and reared back as the wave rushed ahead, burying the stern in the next swell and rising again with a new waterfall over the poop.

Ned, drenched to the skin, clung to the catharpins on the mainmast. He licked the salt water on his lips and thrilled at the spectacle. Here was material for a book better than anything his father could ever write. He watched a breaker slap the stern and spatter spray against the mast above his head. If he survived he would write fiction and shame the Old Man for his unreasonable exactions.

The storm raged for an hour. Suddenly the shrill voice of the lookout rang above the wind. Ned heard the captain answer through his trumpet, "What saw you?"

"Land ahead! A long black rock, sir, with a hole in the center and white seas showing on the other side."

"Luff up half a point," the captain shouted to the helmsman. "That's the Hole-in-the-Wall. . . . East end of Abaco. We'll be in Havana in sixty hours." [1]

Another hour passed. The wind raced away and the sea lost its anger. The clipper skimmed by the island into the green waters of the Bahama Banks. Men climbed up the wet rigging to bend new sails. The lowering sun lighted many magic islands with splendor. Ned leaned on the wet bulwarks, watching until the sun sank into the ocean. After dark, spray from the bow glowed with luminous yellow light. The captain paused beside him for a moment, looking at the phosphorescent sea. Sentimental always, Ned recalled later that he, with his first friend at his side, had glimpsed tropic headlands as through a cloth of gold.

At dawn, two days after the storm, the seamen sighted the mountains of Cuba. Before noon Havana hove in sight. The ship entered the harbor between Morro Castle's bright brass cannon and the bristling Punta's guns – Havana's jaws of fortifications. Inside, the old town appeared to be a disorder of huts and palaces, parks, and churches.

The captain had a lady love in the Spanish city. He thought he could find a girl for Ned, too. "Rig yourself in your shoregoing togs, and stand by to take a cruise ashore with me," he said encouragingly. Ned hurried below.

It was dark when the boy and man set off. Distant music came from a plaza – military music, not Wagnerian like a storm at sea.

People in holiday costumes trooped toward the cathedral, and Ned and the captain joined the throng. They passed the Governor's Palace, where moonlight illuminated a sparkling fountain. Ned saw his first palm tree. The man and boy entered the vast cathedral and knelt for a moment, then wandered through the nave looking at ancient paintings and the altar – "a pile of perfect gorgeousness," Ned described it.

At a door not far from the Plaza the captain stopped and knocked. A little sliding shutter opened and two eyes peered out. The Americans heard a cry of welcome and then the heavy door swung open. Ned looked down the passageway and his jaw dropped. The inside of a Spanish house, he remembered later, differed from the outside as much as a silk shawl differed from a horse blanket. The hostess, a Spanish *doña* named Mrs. Boyd, was the widow of an American sea captain. Her daughter's hazel eyes attracted Ned. Youthful Carolina sparkled with mirth and mischief. Brown hair hung to her waist; every limb was rounded to perfection. Ned fell in love at once.

The captain and Ned stayed at Mrs. Boyd's home during the entire time required to reload their ship. The days passed all too quickly, and Ned always remembered Havana as a part of Paradise. Even grumbling seamen could find little to complain about in such surroundings. A cargo of fruit was loaded for the northward voyage. Such perishable goods must be moved at once, but another hurricane threatened. The captain, ready to sail, studied his barometer and the sky. Should the trip be risked? Ned watched his idol hesitate, then make up his mind, order the ship to clear for the sea. Sailors climbed to their places aloft. The mooring cables were cast off and the ship drifted away from the pier. On the yardarms, sail after sail dropped from its fastenings, filled with air, and the vessel began to move. The magic city slipped past the bulwarks. Morro Castle and the Punta were left behind. Ned watched the receding coast wistfully.

Ned Judson returned to Philadelphia more self-satisfied than ever. On Front Street he met his father face to face. The boy wrote down his version of the interview later. He said that his father greeted him with:

"So, Sir! You have returned? I suppose you are sick of the sea, and are willing to ask my forgiveness; and, if I permit you to come home, to do as *I wish*, not as *you* will—eh?"

Ned looked at his father. "No, Sir," he answered, proud and priggish. "No, Sir, I ask no home from you." Ned loved adolescent melodrama. He reported himself as concluding: "Remember, no locks, bonds or bars can bind my spirit. It is free; free as the glad albatross that skims far and wide over the ocean, and sleeps when it listeth on the bosom of the wave that feeds it."

The father turned away, disgustedly no doubt—"sternly," Ned called it—and the lad signed on for a cruise to Rio de Janeiro. For five or more years Ned Judson followed the sea. As a sailor he visited New York, Boston, Charleston, New Orleans, and many Caribbean ports. On merchant ships he found and devoured the works of Cooper, Scott, and Irving. Here was literature that held him—sweeter fare than Blackstone and Chitty in his father's library. For hours at a time he read in the lee of the longboat, reveling in Miles's history of the crusades and the *Chronicles* of Jean Froissart.[2]

Ned stored into his memory ideas that furnished sea tales for the rest of his lifetime. Often his stories contained good-natured complaints about life in general. His heroes were always victims of a thousand wrongs. Primeval nature fascinated him. He marveled at the tropical waters. Perched on the bowsprit with white foam curling under the prow, Ned looked deep into blue waters. Once he noticed that the ship sailed silently over a submarine forest of coral, sea fans, and sponges.[3] Tropical fish, gay as birds of brilliant plumage, darted through the marine jungle. Above him in the Caribbean sky the jibs, foresail, fore-topsails, topgallant sail, foreroyal, skysail and moonraker piled one on the other, white and billowy as a summer cloud. Ned, boylike, felt himself Prince Ahmed on a magic carpet in the *Arabian Nights*, riding above the treetops of fairyland.

Another sight delighted Ned. Hour after hour he watched dolphins. A dozen or more of them would rush across the water, circle the vessel, and gobble bits of garbage. Many times the sailors climbed down onto the ship's martingale to spear a dolphin as it romped around the bow. The unfortunate monster would be hauled to the deck, gasping in death agony. On its hard slimy body, color waves—blue, green, gold, copper, and silver—spread and vanished. Back in Wayne County, Pennsylvania, Ned Judson had seen similar colors play across a bar of hot iron as the blacksmith tempered it. Dolphins were so playful, so full of the joy of living, it seemed like murder to kill them. Yet the cook was ready enough to slice dolphin fillets for his pan. They did provide a welcome change from fo'castle salt pork.

On the Spanish Main Ned heard stories of pirates. Once or twice his ship was followed by sinister looking vessels with raking masts, like slavers, but with more hands on deck than were needed to man commercial ships. The captain eyed such craft suspiciously, tried to outsail them and at dark changed his tack, hoping to be free from pursuit in the morning. Occasionally Ned saw a distant vessel mistake his ship for a pirate and race away. Sometimes the Americans followed for sport, and once pursued a frightened merchantman for over two days. She finally gave up, surrendered, and discovered the joke.[4]

News came to the merchant seamen that Indian trouble was brewing in Florida, the long flat peninsula usually shunned by sailing vessels. Treacherous winds and currents made the Florida Keys a notorious graveyard for ocean vessels, and great ribs of broken ships marked the Florida coast for miles. Professional wreckers made a living by salvaging shipwrecks but these gentry were considered little above pirates. Seamen accused them of posting false lights to lure ships to destruction. Corrupt captains were suspected of wrecking vessels on commission.

Ned felt patriotic pride in knowing that the United States had acquired Florida from Spain in 1819. He was not so proud when he learned that after almost twenty years the Indians still kept white men from the territory. In 1832 and again in 1833 the government had induced the Seminoles to sign treaties for their own removal west of the Mississippi. Some villages migrated dutifully each time, but many remained. In 1835 President Jackson lost his temper. "By the Etarnal," the Indians must abide by their treaties and go. Old Hickory ordered the military to see that the red men went, so recalcitrant chiefs were invited to a council with army officers. They came proudly in moccasins and feathers and sat down on the ground. The white men talked; the Indians talked. Many agreed to go, as they had before, but few complied. Ned heard that one chieftain, Osceola, had refused point-blank. Dramatically he had drawn his knife and plunged it in the treaty paper. Soldiers seized him for his insolence. Then Osceola became contrite. He too agreed, if released, to gather up his village and migrate. So the whites turned him loose, but he did not come in with his people. Instead, a terrible massacre followed. Major Francis Langhorne Dade, marching a column of soldiers from Tampa Bay to Fort King, was ambushed, and of 110 men only 4 escaped.[5] Everyone blamed Osceola, while other Indian depredations flared up around all Florida army posts. In the White House President Jackson smote the carpet with his cane. He ordered troops far in the North to go down and crush the Seminoles once and for all, ship the last one out of the swamps.

The United States Navy was ordered to patrol the dangerous Florida coast and to transport soldiers to military posts and land them on palm-fringed strands. Everywhere Ned heard stories of the approaching war. All the adventurous spirits of the Mississippi Valley seemed to be congregating in Florida. John J. Audubon, artist, and George Catlin,[6] Indian painter, both famous for their work on the upper Mississippi, came down to see and paint the Seminoles.

Then news of another nature was gossiped along the wharves. Crews were wanted for an antarctic exploring expedition to be led by Lieutenant Charles Wilkes. Ned decided to enlist and write the world's greatest adventure story. He was mustered into the service at the Philadelphia Navy Yard on August 7, 1837, the same year that his father first appeared in the city's directory as a practicing attorney. Whether or not Ned visited his family on this last trip to Philadelphia cannot be determined. He said merely that he enlisted at the age of fourteen "after three cruises and four sweethearts."[7] He was assigned to Wilkes's flagship, the *Macedonian*.[8] Then that frigate was withdrawn from the exploring expedition.

Ned found himself stranded in the Brooklyn Navy Yard without a chance of seeing the antarctic and writing his book, but there was a possibility that the West Indian squadron might get into the Seminole fracas or, better still, chase pirates in the Caribbean. Then, too, there was a blockade on the Mexican coast that promised excitement. The French Navy was preventing all ships from entering the Latin-American republic until certain debts were paid.

There was a peculiar angle to the Mexican business. South of the Rio Grande the Catholics and the Masons were both organized in political parties. The former controlled the government, but the latter bided their time for a revolution. Loyalty to the Masons was congenital with Ned, yet here he was tied hand and foot to inactive naval duty. He was still grumbling in October 1837, when word came to the Brooklyn Navy Yard that Osceola had been captured and sent to St. Augustine in chains. But the Seminole War was not ended. Most of the tribesmen remained on the warpath under other leaders.

In January 1838, Ned learned that the United States Army had encountered a large force of Seminoles in a great battle on

Christmas Day, 1837, at Lake Okeechobee. American regulars, in uniforms suitable for Napoleon's army, advanced in solid ranks against an invisible foe. Indian observers, wrapped in gray moss on water oak limbs above the soldiers, signaled to hidden warriors. The solid ranks of soldiers came to a wall of waving saw grass. Well-marked trails entered it, and the men did not suspect an ambush.

Behind the green wall invisible Indians waited with their chieftains, Alligator, Sam Jones, and Coacoochee the Wild Cat. A prophet, or medicine man, had prepared magic relics and cast spells over the naked warriors before they went forward to their hidden positions. The soldiers outnumbered them three to one, but after the first volley the regulars realized their own disadvantage. For three hours the Indians fired as rank after rank came forward. Then the red men retired, leaving ten dead warriors on the battlefield. General Zachary Taylor inspected his army and counted 138 casualties.[9] Military men called it a victory according to the Napoleonic rules of war taught at West Point, for the Americans had won the field.

Ned Judson and other good-natured American grumblers did not call it a victory. They had not studied West Point textbooks and did not understand the fine points of military achievement. They did know that the Indians were still on the warpath in Florida, and that the war promised to last long enough for them to get in it.

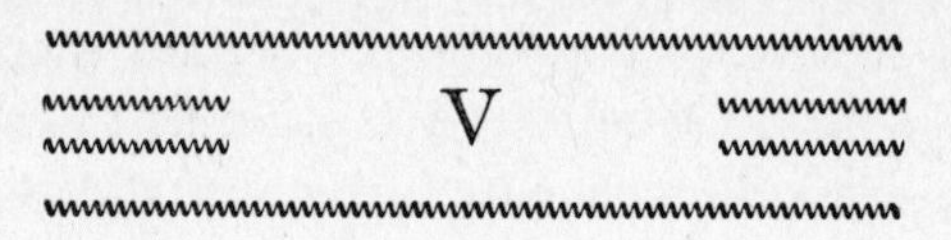

The Seminole War

NED JUDSON was really angry. He pouted good-naturedly, grumbled about his bad luck and laughed at it, but he had certainly never expected to serve these exciting months in the dull old Brooklyn Navy Yard. He could get no material here for the book he hoped to write – the great literature that would shame and confound his stern parent.

Then, to make things worse, Ned discovered officers in the navy with more irascible dispositions than his father's, more exacting and rigid in discipline. Life in the navy was far from pleasant. A man ceased to be a man, Ned complained.

He had never seen so many humans packed into such close quarters. Many of the seamen were not Americans. Some were Negro slaves hired from their masters by the navy. The law prohibited this but it was done.[1] Nearly half of the petty officers over Ned were foreigners. Most insulting of all were the midshipmen – youngsters like Ned, terrible little boys who ran errands for the officers. They strutted the deck, slapped the hilts of their dirks, and sputtered oaths at seamen older, wiser, and larger than themselves.[2]

Ned soon got into trouble with the United States Navy. In his own account, which cannot be verified, he admitted talking back to an officer. For punishment he claimed to have been sent to Staten Island with other culprits for a boatload of sand. Being small, Ned acted as coxswain. On the long way down to the sand pit, both tide and current helped the men. The air was cold, with "mush ice" in the East River – great weather for seamen eager to serve in Florida! All the men rowed smartly to keep warm and they arrived in record time. The trip seemed short and easy. They did not reckon how long it might take to load the boat and return against the tide. Late in the day they started back. The open boat made slow headway, row as they might. Night settled over the East River. One by one, lights appeared in the houses on shore. The sailors had no light themselves, and they realized the imminent danger of being run down. In addition to traffic up and down the river, a steam ferry crossed to Brooklyn every five minutes.[3]

In the inky blackness the men saw a Fulton Street ferry bearing down on them. To attract attention they yelled and waved their arms in the dark. It was no use. The steamboat rushed at them head-on. The oarsmen evaded the ferry's bow, but their boat was hit a glancing jolt, throwing the men overboard. The big vessel careened away, oblivious of the accident. In the blackness the sailors splashed in the icy water. Judson, pert as could be, helped every man to get hold of the foundering rowboat. Then, under his orders, the sand was dumped and the boat floated high enough to keep the men's heads above water. A sloop, the *Helen Morley*, rescued the sailors and landed them near the south ferry wharf. The drenched tars wanted to scatter, every man for himself, to warm up in neighboring grogshops, but Coxswain Ned still held the tiller. With this weapon he marshaled the seventeen half-mutinous men and marched them all to the Navy Yard. Then he fainted and for ten days lay in the sick bay.[4]

The exploit, begun as a punishment, ended with a reward. The lad gained wide renown in his small naval circle, and his immediate superiors are said to have recognized officer material. A recommendation that Ned be commissioned was sent to the President. On February 10, 1838,[5] Martin Van Buren signed his midshipman's papers. In March of that year Ned was fifteen years old. Precocious? No! Midshipman Farragut had commanded a prize ship in the Pacific at the age of twelve and put down a mutiny in the crew. Ned was ordered to report to Captain Paulding on the eighteen-gun man-of-war *Levant*[6] for transportation to the Caribbean. Active duty with the West Indian squadron at last, and he was an officer to boot!

According to tradition, Ned's second trouble in the United States Navy began at once. On the trip south he is reputed to have challenged thirteen of his new messmates to duels because they did not approve his family's social standing.[7] To stop the carnage Captain Paulding ordered target practice on deck. Ned's magic marksmanship convinced his fellows that a challenge from him was tantamount to suicide. At Pensacola he was transferred to duty on the United States Sloop of War *Boston*, patrolling the coast of Mexico, where the French were attempting a blockade – not, as he had hoped, to the Florida Keys and the Seminole War. At Tampico the man-of-war called for water. Two French ships, a corvette commanded by the Prince de Joinville and a brig, lay at anchor outside the bar and barely beyond cannon range from the Mexican fort. The Americans anchored nearby. One afternoon Midshipman Judson climbed to the maintop with his sketchbook and pencil. The yard crew lolled on the truck, some napped in the bunt. Ned stowed himself comfortably on a spare studding sail and commenced to scribble. The yard captain called Ned's attention to movement on the decks of the French ships. Out on the horizon a sail had appeared. Evidently the Frenchmen suspected that she might be a blockade runner. They were taking no chances. One of them made sail and set off to meet the stranger.

Ned ordered a man to go below for his glass. The cocky little midshipman enjoyed showing his authority. He waited impatiently until the sailor came aloft with his telescope. Then Ned squinted one eye at the distant horizon and reported to the crew.

The stranger flew a Texas flag. She was evidently a Lone Star warship, come to join the other nationals anchored along the bar. France was particularly anxious to be on friendly terms with Texas. A treaty was said to be pending between them. The French brig approached the Texan, then "wore" around her, and the two vessels raced back playfully side by side.

At the anchorage the French brig clewed up her sails, hove to, and fired a national salute. The Texan did not stop, as everyone expected, or even reply to the salute. Instead she scudded ahead under the Frenchman's bow. Ned looked at her in wonder. He noticed red-coated marines leaning against the masts and bulwarks. A shining brass swivel showed plainly on her deck, and along her sides was a row of masked portholes, "symptoms of a sharp set of teeth." She was plainly a Lone Star cruiser, yet she did not heave to with the other nationals but skimmed across the bar. Then a strange thing happened. The red-coated marines dived ignominiously into the sea, and the Texas flag was replaced by American and Mexican flags. Already the clipper was under the guns of the Mexican fort. She was a blockade runner that had got safely into port.

The next day Ned went into the Mexican town. He learned that the clipper *Nella* was commanded by an old friend, Will Allen. The red-coated marines had been made of straw. The brass cannon was a log painted yellow.

Outside the bar the Frenchmen swore to get the blockade runner whenever she came out—even if they had to sink her. Ned knew his friend Allen to be resourceful, but he wondered how he would ever get away. His own ship's refueling was not complete when the barometer began to act up—a storm surely. Would Allen use it to escape? Here is Ned's account of what happened:

One of the most certain omens of an approaching gale on that coast is a singularly clear atmosphere. Distant hills, seen at no other time, show their blue peaks plainly; thus forewarning the mariner to be ready to cut and run. We, as well as our French neighbors, commenced preparing for it by sending down our light spars, housing top-gallant masts, close-reefing topsails and coursers, and refurling them snugly to the yards, intending if possible to "lay it out" at anchor.

Night came on, and as the sun gradually descended behind a gathering bank of black clouds in the west, the wind increased, beginning to pipe the sailor's warning in its loudest key. The ground-swell rose very high, causing us to labor heavily, and to pitch bows-under into it. The distant thunder began to echo the hoarse moaning gale, and lightning played fitfully through the flying clouds. "This is the very night for such a dare-devil as Will Allen," said I, as I hurried on deck, enveloped in the folds of my storm-jacket, with my sou'-wester lashed on my head. The thought had barely passed through my mind, when the look-out on the night-heads sung out "Sail ho!"

"Where away is she?" said I, straining my eye-sight in the gloom.

"Right ahead, Sir. I believe it's that clipper that tricked the Johnny's the other day, trying to come out over the bar."

"Great God, she'll be lost!" said I, as I caught a glimpse of her, struggling through the heavy range of breakers that ran mountain high entirely across the bar, one moment hidden in their tumultuous boilings, the next seeming to leap high above their snowy crests. Oh! it was beautiful; grandly, sublimely, terrifically beautiful! As the lightning flash illuminated the scene, the eye in one hurried glance would cover the high, rolling breakers, tinged with the prismatic hues of the rainbow, that seemed to leap madly up from the quicksand bar; the gallant and beautiful vessel rushing swiftly through the flashing waters, her spars bowing to the full strength of the storm-king's breath; her sails white as the cloud-spot whence the lightning bursts forth; her crew hurriedly flying from one post to another, as their varied duties required, in the dread time of danger.

Again the lightning-cloud closes, and the imagination is left to picture the scene from the wild uproar of warring elements. Once more the jagged rays of lurid light flash forth; the vessel has passed the bar in safety; here she comes, right down in our midst! The gale had increased to a height that rendered our anchorage unsafe, and all together, French and American, were obliged to slip and scud.

The ire of the Frenchmen was aroused. It was galling to their pride to see a little Yankee clipper pass into a blockaded port, in fair weather, under their very port-holes, but doubly galling to see the audacious craft again laugh at them, and defy their power in the teeth of a hurricane. As the Nella came on, the French ships beat to quarters, determined, as one of their officers afterward told me, to sink her. We were now all in a huddle, driving out to sea before the gale. As the treacherous lightning betrayed the position of the gallant Allen, the French opened a rapid fire upon him, but they were too nervous to do any harm; their shot flew wide, the quick flash of light hardly enabling them to take an aim, which the succeeding darkness would set entirely at fault. On, on we sped before the whistling blast, amid the roar of the hurricane, the loud-booming cannon, the lightning's glare, and the red flashing of the guns; but the Nella had the heels of us. Soon even the far-reaching storm-light failed to discover her situation; she had ran [*sic*] the blockade, in and out, in perfect safety.[8]

From the coast of Mexico Ned went to Florida – the Seminole War at last – where Lieutenant John T. McLaughlin commanded a Florida squadron known as the Mosquito Fleet. Ned was assigned to the revenue cutter *Otsego*, under Lieutenant Edward T. Shubrick. The first sight of Florida from the ocean differed from the West Indies. Ned was accustomed to phantom mountains floating pale as gossamer on the Caribbean. Florida appeared from the ship's deck like a thin white and green ribbon along the horizon – two parallel lines, white sand topped with green myrtle.

In southern Florida, where Judson's cutter anchored, the natives were known as Spanish Indians. They traded with the Cubans and had not felt close kinship with the red men of northern Florida, but that was changing now. Since Osceola had been captured, the Prophet had gained influence. With mysterious herbs and potions, wild songs and incantations, he conjured all the Indians to unite against the whites. The Prophet lived in Big Cypress Swamp, an eerie waste of slimy water studded with hummocks of thick undergrowth that hid his people's villages.[9] No white man knew their location. The Indians, in their canoes, could disappear in gloom beneath hanging moss and live indefinitely on fish, venison, and wild rice.

In July 1839, the sailors in the Mosquito Squadron heard accounts of another massacre. On the Caloosahatchee near the west coast a company of soldiers had been almost exterminated. The commander, Lieutenant Colonel William S. Harney, was one of the few who escaped. He swam out in the dark to a government boat in the river.

Before long Ned learned that the leaders of the massacre were Billy Bowlegs and Chekika, the latter a Spanish Indian. So the disaffection had spread south. The Prophet might yet have his way. Judson and his companions were sure to see action soon.

Sailors in the Mosquito Fleet swore at the army's incompetence. Three inexcusable massacres – Dade's, Lake Okeechobee, and now Harney's men – all because the damned soldiers fought by Napoleonic traditions instead of with common sense! Some of Harney's regiment were stationed at Fort Dallas near where the *Otsego* lay at anchor. These soldiers openly admitted a dislike for their commander. Harney, they said, was one of the handsomest men in the army, a pretty boy with blue eyes, red as a fox and as cruel. Suave with his equals, an infraction of discipline in the men below enraged him to insanity. He had once tried to kill an awkward soldier who splashed with his oar while rowing a boat.[10] Habitually Harney marched in Florida with Indian scouts carrying ropes to intimidate any soldier who might desert.[11] Quite naturally the soldiers blamed the massacre on Harney. His men knew enough to post a guard on the fatal night, they muttered, but they were afraid of their own commander and dared not suggest it. Now the soldiers were all dead and Harney was not even cashiered. Ned Judson acquired a hatred for Harney before he met him.

One day the crew of the *Otsego* was piped aft to hear orders. Land duty – action at last! The commanding officer explained to the men that things had gone from bad to worse during the last three years of fighting. The government was determined to stop the spread of disaffection among the Seminoles, so now the navy must pull the army out of its predicament. Already Gaines and Scott, America's ranking generals – and bitter rivals – had both been removed from command. Next, Florida's Governor Richard K. Call, a friend of Old Hickory's, and Major General Thomas Sidney Jesup, a regular army man, had tried and failed. Now the supreme command was to be given to Zachary Taylor. Under Jesup he had won the "technical victory" at Okeechobee. A real victory now might make him President of the United States. Who could say?

The sailors knew Old Rough and Ready Taylor to be an "Indian man." Things would begin to happen for sure. His backwoods exterior gave common soldiers confidence. West Point concepts did not affect his military thinking. Rough as an old sycamore, he wrote badly and spelled worse, but Seminoles were not to be whipped with pen and paper. He intended to fight them in their own way. No more formations of massed men would march out in military array to be shot down. The lesson of Okeechobee was too fresh in his mind.

Lieutenant Shubrick explained that Taylor intended to scour the country with small bands of soldiers, and capture every Indian man, woman, and child he could find in the swamps. But he did not expect to get them all by this method alone. He had an additional plan. Every Indian village must be burned, every stalk of Indian corn cut down, every melon hacked to pieces. Starve 'em, by God, then they'll come in, surrender, and be glad to move west of the Mississippi. Taylor had even resorted to another drastic measure. He had imported bloodhounds from Cuba – dogs to track runaway slaves. Perhaps they could catch Indians in the Everglades.

Ned Judson listened to Lieutenant Shubrick [12] as he explained the new task. The navy was to co-operate with the army in hundreds of sorties. Florida was to be combed and cross-combed.

Everything Seminole was to be captured or destroyed. The sailors were to be divided into companies and each was to explore a given area. The plan for Ned's detail was to march inland until they intersected the Miami River, then follow it downstream to Fort Dallas on Biscayne Bay. The men were eager to start.

Opposite Key Biscayne, some miles below the mouth of the Miami River, the detail boarded longboats and rowed to shore. The seamen had greased their hair, fixed "love curls" over sunburned ears, and braided their back hair in tight little "swan's neck queues." With bell-bottomed "drawers" and pumps they appeared more ready for a holiday than an Indian campaign, but all were well armed and ardent.

The land west of the lagoon proved to be a pine barren. The seamen had no compass, but they were confident that they could keep their bearings north by northwest to the Miami. For a few miles they marched with the sun at their backs. The woods were deserted – no sign of Indians. Before long the column reached a great prairie, a beautiful plain stretching to the horizon.[13] Mud stains on the grass showed that water sometimes flooded this country, but now the grass was parched and brittle. In the distance, on the skyline, the sailors saw islands of trees, not only pines but the rich hardwood areas known as hummocks. The men marched by column of four into the ocean of grass. Ned looked back. He saw that his company had left a wake of four parallel trails stretching like a whiplash to the fringe of trees behind them.

Rattlesnakes were plentiful. Ned spitted the writhing serpents on his sword and tossed them to one side. From distant clumps of herbage deer got up, looked at the sailors with curious cupped ears, then bounded away. The sailors trudged on. At last the commander halted the column. Horse tracks had been discovered. Ned Judson's Wayne County boyhood came in good stead now. He trotted along the trail, noted that the horses were not grazing.

They were being ridden. Then he found moccasin tracks. Ned waved to the waiting column. Indians!

The men were ordered to examine their arms, see that flints had not been lost and that sufficient powder was in the pans. On the skyline a fringe of pines marked another barren. Look! A column of smoke rose like a magic rope into the hot sky. Indians signaling!

Half an hour later the sailors reached the pines – tall trees with blue sky above the branches, grass underfoot half-leg high. The men deployed and moved forward cautiously. They remembered the way Dade's men had been trapped, how the soldiers were mowed down at Lake Okeechobee. Warily they advanced, eyeing the tree trunks. They saw naked bodies in the distance dodge through the parallel lines of gray bark from one tree to another, always out of range. The Indians did not fire, nor did they give the sailors a chance to do so. Judson was sure that the savages were counting the white men, determining in their own minds whether to attack. He knew that the Indians had mustered over three hundred men for the battle of Okeechobee. A similar force here would annihilate thirty sailors.

For an hour or two the white men challenged the Indians to fight. Then they were ordered to close ranks. The column turned north toward the Miami – or where they hoped to find it. Out in another vast prairie they came to dry sloughs with mud cracked and curled as brittle as dead leaves. In the distance they saw what appeared to be the tops of hardwood trees. This might mean water. They marched across to it. The hummock proved to be dry as a powder house. The sun was setting now, and the men, choking with thirst, bivouacked at the edge of the trees. After dark a wolf howled. Once or twice the men were sure that they heard an Indian war whoop – grim reminder to keep the guards awake.

At daybreak the little column formed and marched off. A hot sun rose over the sultry wilderness. The men traveled north-

northeast, desperately groping for the Miami. By midmorning their suffering became acute. They pulled off their shirts. Some wanted to throw away their guns. The officers watched them constantly. Ned cackled with authority. On the prairie the skulking figures of Indians watched and waited, always out of gunshot range. The red men yonder knew the location of water that would save the whites.

The men had been told that a march of twenty or thirty miles would take them from the landing beach to the Miami. They thought of the tedious miles behind and estimated that they must have walked at least fifty. One and all began to fear that they were lost in the dry ocean of grass. When the sun began to sink in the west on the second night, no water had been found and the desperate men were getting hard to control. They broke ranks, ran to low places and dug with their cutlasses for water. Someone pointed a sword to a single tree in the distance. It looked like a willow and that meant water. The men ran across the brittle grass.

It was a willow! Coats, shirts, varnished hats were discarded in the mad race. Under the tree the green grass felt cool. The men prodded the sod frantically. Their swords came out of the ground wet. All hands pawed down to muddy water. Men wallowed like pigs. Ned took off his neckerchief and spread it over a mudhole to strain the water. Sailors watched him and followed his example. On their stomachs they drank, rested, and drank again. The sun, red as a drop of blood, touched the horizon.

In the distance the men heard a cannon boom — the sunset gun at Fort Dallas. In the cool of the evening the sailors set their course by the stars. Four hours later they stumbled into the army post.

This feat was more heroic than the Fulton Ferry incident in the East River up in New York, but Ned was not cited this time. He grumbled good-naturedly about his new wrong as the little command rowed back to the *Otsego* next morning. He'd write up the scurvy system in a book sometime and expose the whole United States Navy. Of course he could not foresee that this experience would help him later with Indians on the plains. At the time he thought only that if this war was the best Rough and Ready Zach Taylor could do, the old fellow was much overrated.

Give Florida to the Indians

The seminole war seemed far away from Midshipman Judson in the winter of 1839–1840, yet he was in the thick of it patrolling the west coast of Florida from Cape Sable to the Suwannee River. He saw no Indians, but years later, as a feature writer for sporting magazines, he remembered killing the greatest duck bag of his life. An odd war indeed! [1]

Spring burgeoned early down in Florida. Soldiers and sailors whined that a new crop of West Point lieutenants would come with the orange blossoms, "smart young men that did'n know nuthin'." In May, Zachary Taylor was superseded by a new commander, Walker K. Armistead.[2] Old Rough and Ready's "Indian" ways had not been equal to the Seminoles'. A new chief had risen to power in Florida. Coacoochee the Wild Cat had learned, as a minor chieftain in the battle of Okeechobee, to despise white soldiers. Since that time he had distinguished himself by leading numerous raids and by surrendering himself at least twice. Like other Seminoles he liked to visit a military camp and agree to take his village to the Indian territory west of the Mississippi if supplied with bread, powder, lead, and whiskey to enable his people to come in and surrender.

At first, hopeful commanders had furnished the requested supplies. A few weeks later they would learn that the Indians had used the food for a war party against some distant settlement.

This method of financing the Indians' war had become a fixed pattern. The massacre of a traveling troupe of actors on the St. Augustine road made people ask what Indians had been given food recently. Then these murders were forgotten in the face of a more serious butchery in August, down at Indian Key, a short day's sail from the anchored fleet. The sailors knew the ocean keys to be seaswept and bare of vegetation – a strange haunt for Indians. During the summer the seamen had enjoyed going to the keys on moonlight nights to catch turtles for their mess. In hot weather these great green monsters came up on the sand to lay their eggs in holes at the edge of the grass. Sea turtles usually weighed a hundred pounds or more and practically every ship kept two or three on their backs by the galley companionway. Turtles lived thus for days, flippers waving idly, long necks craned in a futile effort to turn right side up, until the cook made them into soup.

The turtle keys seemed an odd place for an Indian raid. Indian Key contained but eleven acres. Close by, on Tea Table Key, the navy maintained a sick bay. Ned knew that a New Yorker named Housman lived on Indian Key and claimed all the island. According to the rumor on shipboard, Chief Chekika, murderer of Harney's men up on the Caloosahatchee, had led the raid.[3] Without doubt all the southern Seminoles had joined their northern kinsmen at last in the war against the whites. Florida, from end to end, must be one long warpath now. Five years of fighting had made a bad situation worse.

Housman had been a prodigal son who made good. His father had set him up in business with a small schooner to ply between Staten Island and the East River. Young Housman sailed away to the West Indies, promptly lost his craft on the Florida Keys, and stayed there. He salvaged the next wreck and soon became one of the most successful wreckers in Florida. Accused, like his colleagues, of posting false lights and bribing captains, he became wealthy, built an elegant mansion on Indian Key for himself, a model village for his men and a fine hotel for shipwrecked mariners. In Charleston he got a wife to grace his island kingdom. Invalids in the North heard about the ocean haven. Already it was fashionable to be ill and spend a few months on Indian Key.[4] Housman brought down a doctor to minister to the health of his people.

When the Seminole War broke out in 1836 Housman had fortified his village, but after three years with no alarms he became convinced that the disaffection was not spreading to the southern Indians. He stopped posting guards. Indians with friendly faces paddled across to trade at his store. The Mosquito Fleet anchored nearby often and added to his fortune. The sick bay on Tea Table Key gave him another source of revenue. All in all, the Seminole War was profitable for Housman. Ned had especially admired the village's neat squares of cottages – more like Philadelphia than the Caribbean area.

Now it was all gone, wiped out. Judson heard how on the morning of August 7, 1840, between two and three o'clock, the village awakened to a war whoop. Sleeping villagers heard their windowpanes shatter under tomahawk blows. Moccasined feet padded through the halls. Men and women in gowns and nightcaps leaped from their beds to be struck down. Housman and his wife jumped out a window and escaped. Their maid was butchered. Dr. Perrine ran out on the porch of his house and told the Indians that he was a physician, he had saved their own little ones. Did they not recognize him? The Indians ran away and entered the next house. The doctor hurried his wife and children into the cellar, which had been walled off as a bathing pool filled by the ocean. A row of posts separated the pool from a turtle pen under the nearby dock. Mrs. Perrine and her youngsters lay low in the water and waited. The doctor covered the trap door to the cellar with a bag of seed. Before long the Indians returned. This time the doctor could not talk them away. He fled and barricaded himself in the cupola. Down in the bathing pool his wife heard the Indians force their way up and murder him.

She lay quietly with her children as the savages ransacked the house, broke her china, tore open her pillows and yelled with fiendish glee at the fluttering feathers. Then they set fire to the house. The dry timbers burned furiously. Beams crashed to the floor. Falling sparks hissed on the water in the pool. The mother held her hand over her daughter's mouth to prevent her screaming. Her son whispered that he would rather be killed by the Indians than boil like a lobster. He forced a way through the posts, waded under the dock, which was now on fire, and emerged outside. His mother and sister followed him. Safe in the water, they saw a boat at the next wharf, loaded with plunder. The Indians were absent getting more loot. The family waded to the boat, crawled over the gunwale, and rowed away. A government ship lay at anchor within a mile. Here the refugees met Housman, his wife, and eight other people who had escaped the massacre.

So much for the tragic incidents. Ned heard other details that made the sailors laugh. Midshipman Francis Key Murray, in command of the sick bay on Tea Table Key, had heard the shooting. He mounted a four-pounder on a barge and with eleven invalids rowed over to blow the red marauders from Indian Key. Instead, the third discharge blew his cannon into the lagoon. The disarmed sick men returned to their quarters hoping that the savages would forget their bombardment and not include the hospital in their plans.

In due time Lieutenant McLaughlin, fleet commander, arrived on the *Flirt* with arms and supplies. The Indians had vanished, and the beleaguered survivors were taken to safety at St. Augustine. Lieutenant McLaughlin rebuilt the Indian Key village into a government depot. Ned landed on the island many times in the next two years of the Seminole War.[5]

In October 1840, Lieutenant William Tecumseh Sherman arrived at St. Augustine, fresh from West Point. Another lieutenant, Braxton Bragg, commanded the post there. Sherman was assigned to Fort Pierce, a quadrangle of palmetto-thatched log buildings on the great eastern lagoon known as Indian River. In November he was detailed to patrol it in a boat from Jupiter Inlet to the lagoon's head almost two hundred miles above.[6] Thus the army which Sherman had come to serve was developing webfeet. Judson, with an equal rank in the navy, anchored at the Mosquito Fleet base off Fort Dallas, where the sailors learned to march on land. Both Sherman and Judson wrote about their Florida experiences. Judson's accounts were less lucid, less restrained, and daubed with more color than Sherman's. For twenty years he would write about newly remembered incidents.

Late in the winter of 1840–1841, Colonel William Jenkins Worth, eager to make a name for himself in the Tampa district under the command of General Armistead, tried a new ruse with the Indians. He especially wanted to catch that young upstart, Coacoochee the Wild Cat. Worth ordered a messenger into the swamps with a banner showing red and white hands clasped above pipes, tobacco, and a bottle of whiskey. The chieftain was impressed by this message. He sent word that he would come in. On March 4, 1841, Worth's sentries reported Indians trooping down the road through the saw grass. In the van strode Coacoochee. Plumes waved on his low-crowned hat, which might have been more appropriate for a Danish prince in the Reformation than for a savage in the Everglades. The chieftain wore a shirt of medieval pattern and on his feet were the unmistakable buskins conventionally worn by tragic actors. Beside this caricature of Hamlet walked a copper-skinned Horatio in simple cotton garb. Behind him strode a hideous savage in the royal purple and ermine of Richard III. Spangles, crimson vests, Falstaff's jerkin, Puck's pointed cap, adorned other wild-eyed Indians of all sizes and degrees. So Coacoochee had murdered the actors on the St. Augustine road! [7]

Solemnly the Indians marched before the colonel, then sat down. Bring on the whiskey! Worth issued the refreshments, got the pipes glowing with white man's tobacco, and urged Coacoochee to bring in his people. Further resistance would be suicide, he said. The chieftain agreed. But his women had not yet made their summer crop. They could not come in without supplies. Worth had heard this excuse before, but the "sick season" was close at hand. He wanted to make a name for himself in the army before he was ordered to withdraw. Supplies were counted out on spread blankets. Red squaws gathered them and trudged away, to be seen no more on the west coast.

Coacoochee reappeared on the Atlantic. He sent three warriors and a Negro interpreter to Fort Pierce to say that he had tired of war and wanted to surrender. Lieutenant Sherman and a squad of mounted soldiers jogged out to get him. The soldiers, with red and black guides, rode four or five miles through the monotonous pine forest. Young Sherman began to suspect treachery. The Negro assured him that Coacoochee was camped only a little way ahead. Before long the riders came to a tangled hummock on the edge of a slough. Sherman saw a group of miserable Indians lolling on the ground. He ordered his soldiers to halt, instructed the sergeant to take sure vengeance in case anything happened to him, then Sherman rode forward alone to meet the Indians. The redheaded lieutenant asked for the chief. A young man about twenty-five years old stepped forward, slapped his breast, and said, "Me Coacoochee." Sherman told him to bring his men to the fort. The Indians tarried, talking among themselves.

Sherman noted that their guns were leaning against a tree. He ordered his soldiers to come up and take the firearms. Coacoochee appeared very angry when the soldiers surrounded his weapons. Sherman spoke to him sharply: "Get ready and come to the fort." Coacoochee deliberated sullenly. First he bathed in the slough. Then he laced his buckskin leggings and moccasins. Next he put on shirt after shirt, then several vests – Sherman noted that one had a bullet hole with a bloodstain over the pocket. Coacoochee pulled out a paper dollar and offered it to the lieutenant. He wanted a silver dollar in exchange. His victim had cheated him by carrying paper money. Finally Coacoochee wrapped a turban around his head and surmounted it with an ostrich feather, sole relic of the plundered troupers. Thus equipped for conference he mounted a pony and rode back to the fort, where he demanded supplies and at least thirty days' time to bring in his people. Once more he was given a chance.

At the appointed time Coacoochee appeared, asked for more supplies and more time. The commander put him in irons and consigned him to the Indian territory out West. But before he reached the distant destination Colonel Worth, whose "Indian sense" had earned him command of the army in May 1841, ordered Coacoochee to be confined on a ship in Tampa Bay. The general hoped to use him as a decoy to draw Indians from the swamps. Coacoochee was still there on the Fourth of July when the navy celebrated Independence Day with booming cannon. Sardonic sailors wondered what the Indian in his chains must think of a Declaration of Independence based on the proposition that all men are entitled to life, liberty, and the pursuit of happiness. Ned Judson and his comrades did not know the answer. They cursed Florida but they liked the Indians.

Up North, other people were tiring of the war. Expenses had been exorbitant – $100,000 per month, not counting soldiers' wages. Election year was coming and voters might stop the extravagance. The administration retrenched, and the army protested, but to no avail. With only a few more months of possible opportunity for military distinction, officers increased their activity. During the summer and fall of 1841 Sherman in the army and Judson in the navy accompanied many little expeditions hunting Seminoles. In November 1841, Sherman scouted across the Everglades. He rode all day long in water to his horse's knees, camped at night on hummocks so thick with brush that a man on foot penetrated it only by cutting his way with a blade. Ned went through the same country with a detachment of the Third Artillery – Sherman's outfit – but neither boy noticed the other if they met.

Judson described one expedition with "leathern stocked and gaiter-footed lubberly soldiers" in some detail.[8] The sailors met the military at the mouth of the Miami River. Sharply at midnight, Ned remembered, drums beat assembly. The men formed to move in skiffs up the Miami River. In the dark the rattle of oarlocks enabled the commanders to keep the boats together. At dawn the expedition reached the Everglades, where grass grew higher than a man standing on the thwarts. The channel disappeared. Oars were taken from the rowlocks and used to pole the boats. The men, used to the rhythmic thump of the oars, noticed the silence, the rasping of the grass against the gunwales. Overhead they watched countless birds – pelicans, ibises, egrets, awkward cormorants, blue herons. Officers kept their direction with compasses. At noon a lieutenant read the sextant. Meals were cooked on sand shoveled into one end of a boat. Days passed without seeing dry land. Hundreds of deer seemed content in this world of water. They were whitetails like the deer Ned had known back in Pennsylvania, but these Florida deer had a strange habit of bedding down on floating logs. The sailors saw wet places where bears had climbed out on these natural rafts to rest.

No Indian prisoners were taken (except in Ned's later accounts) but pictures of the Everglades etched themselves indelibly in his mind: hummocks of giant magnolia trees in the waste of saw grass; forlorn bark huts where an Indian family had lived in rude comfort with a garden patch, some pigs and chickens. In the cavelike gloom of Big Cypress Swamp streamers of gray moss hung from the trees. The scaly bark of submerged live-oak logs appeared like sleeping alligators. Watery trails in the green scum between big-kneed cypresses seemed to have been made by an Indian canoe, but only deserted villages were found. Judson learned that a Seminole would sometimes lie in the water with a lily pad over his face while soldiers rowed past in their boats.

Ned was very sure that the United States would be a long time conquering the Seminoles. The people up North were right. Let the Indians keep Florida. It was an unhealthful country anyway. Weren't half of the soldiers on sick call most of the time? On May 10, 1842, President Tyler formally brought the war to an end – without victory.[9] True, Chekika had been hanged by red-headed Harney, Coacoochee was exiled, Osceola had died in prison with a broken heart, and many other lesser chieftains had been shipped West with their villages but the Prophet was still free; Sam Jones, nearing ninety, had not been caught; and Billy Bowlegs, risen recently to be the greatest chief of them all, bided his time for another fight with the white men. For once the Indians could boast that they had won the war. Ned Judson went back to the fleet with a great respect for the Seminoles and all Indians. He knew that Osceola was already more of a hero than Jesup who had been sent to capture him. Many Americans liked Indians even while they destroyed them. Ned Judson never forgot that.

Ned's Literary World

THE SEMINOLE WAR was over. Sailors of the Mosquito Fleet weighed anchor, squared the yards, and their ships skimmed away. Perhaps the new leisure, back on the Caribbean, would give Ned time to put down in writing the stories in his mind. His father's bumbling quill had always irked him, but Ned learned that the Old Man had got a publisher in Philadelphia—while Ned, with all his independent talk, had not. Levi had also been admitted to the bar. Ned resolved to write a better story and show up the pater, let him see that the way to fame and fortune lay on the sea, not with Blackstone. His father's book was entitled *A Biography of the Signers of the Declaration of Independence, and of Washington and Patrick Henry: With an Appendix, containing the Constitution of the United States and Other Documents*. The preface stated that the book's purpose was to give the "common people" the whole story in one volume. Levi Carroll Judson's work could hardly be called an original composition. At best it was a compilation, poorly edited by a man unable to remember all the material reprinted in his own book. The story Ned wrote to begin his literary career was less pretentious but much more popular, and Ned claimed it was true. Thus early in life he saw the appeal of realism. Later his most impossible yarns would always be certified as "true." Ned entitled his initial effort "The Captain's Pig."[1]

The yarn was autobiographical – another writing habit Ned never outgrew. He began by saying that he had been commissary for the midshipmen on a man-of-war. At Vera Cruz he and the commissioned officers' commissary had each purchased three little pigs and stowed them in separate crates on deck. Sailing to Havana the ship encountered a squall. When the sky cleared, the deck was littered with trash and broken spars. One crate had washed away and the other was broken. All the little pink porkers but one were gone. The survivor had a black spot on one leg. Ned claimed him. The chief commissary officer insisted that the little pig belonged to the captain's mess. The argument became heated, the talk loud. The captain, with a keen weather eye for squalls, came down from his cabin, heard the evidence, noted that the pig was fat, and adjudged ownership to his own mess – an opinion dictated "from his belly not from his head," according to Ned's account. Judson, always a victim of some wrong, in his stories as well as in life, sought revenge. A few days later the officers announced a banquet of suckling pig. Ned planned a special dinner for the midshipmen on the same day, setting their dinnertime a half hour ahead of the officers' mess. The cooks in both galleys busied themselves all day with pastries and sweets. For the officers' mess the captain opened his wine locker. Ned appeared to be engrossed in his own preparations as he passed and repassed the officers' galley. He noted that the savory little pig was browning deliciously. At the appointed time his comrades assembled at their table. It was set elaborately, a meatless meal with all the trimmings. In the officers' galley the cook looked at the clock. He went into the wardroom to arrange the silver. This was Ned's chance. He disappeared and in a few moments marched breathlessly into the midshipmen's mess, carrying a steaming pig.

Half an hour passed before the captain stormed forward along the deck. He found the middies lounging at ease on the bulwarks, picking their teeth, looking idly at the Caribbean sky. All jumped to attention, responded to commands with a will: "Aye, aye, sir." But none of them knew anything about a roast pig.

Judson concluded his pig story by saying that the incident was too good to keep. With realist technique, he sensed the importance of letting the reader share the author's secret. He confided that the story had been signed "Ned Buntline" to hide his identity from the captain. A buntline is the rope at the bottom of a square sail. The famous pseudonym, Ned said later, began with "The Captain's Pig."

Ned sent the story to *Knickerbocker Magazine* in New York – considered by many the best periodical in America.[2] To have a story printed in *Knickerbocker* would put his father where he belonged in the literary world. The magazine was edited by Lewis Gaylord Clark, New York's arbiter of belles-lettres. His influence had helped bring Charles Dickens to America on a famous tour, and he acted as host for the English author. "The Captain's Pig" did not meet Clark's standards.

Ned complained about the rejection. He was sure that the story had merit. With his own savings he published it himself as a pamphlet. This method of getting into print was not new to the Judsons. Ned's father resorted to private printings of his work also, and other writers, notably the youthful Nathaniel Hawthorne, had broken into print by this expensive method.

The ship's captain chanced to see a copy of "The Captain's Pig." Ned remembered that the skipper took it to his cabin, read about the dictates of "his belly," and boiled with rage. He stamped out on deck, "steamed out his spout," and scalded the crew. By God, he'd give a hundred dollars for the name of either the author or the publisher.

The captain's request should have been easy to gratify. Ned had written the story in the first person, and his identity could not be disguised by any pseudonym. Perhaps the whole incident was Ned's moonshine. Later, in his affluent days when no copy of the pamphlet was known, Ned said he would give a hundred dollars for one himself. After it was written he thought it best to resign from the navy, and his resignation was accepted on June 8, 1842.[3] So much for Ned's explanation.

Navy Department records tell a very different story. On May 12, 1842, Midshipman E. Z. C. Judson requested a leave of absence from the United States Sloop of War *Falmouth* at Hampton Roads, Virginia, to visit his ill wife in New York. On May 14 he resigned, stating that his presence in New York was urgent; he must go, and by resigning he would escape disciplinary action. Later he wrote requesting to withdraw his resignation, but it was accepted on June 8, 1842. In August, the records disclose, Ned wrote once again to recall his resignation, but his request was turned down with the notation that the complement of midshipmen allowed by law was full.[4]

When or where Ned married remains a mystery, but the girl's name was Seberina Marin and he seems to have met her in Cuba or Florida.[5] Ned himself disappears from the record for two years after his resignation from the navy. He claimed later that he spent part of this time in the employ of the North West Fur Company at the headwaters of the Yellowstone.[6] If so, he witnessed a crucial year in Rocky Mountain history—the last of the reign of the mountain men and the beginning of the great overland migration. However, Ned did not write about the Far West until years later, and there is no evidence of his Western sojourn except his own statement. Certainly Ned had a good opportunity to learn about the mountain fur trade from trappers like Jim Beckwourth who fought in the Seminole War.

In May 1844, Edward Z. C. Judson emerges from the shadows of history in smoky Pittsburgh, Pennsylvania. That month he published, in association with his father and a man named Henry Beeler, a monthly literary journal entitled *Ned Buntline's Magazine*. The name conformed to the pattern of other serials of the day such as *Graham's*, *Brownson's*, and *Godey's Lady's Book*. Ned's choice of associates is hard to explain, but it is evident that at twenty-one he was the colorful character of the firm, for his name alone appeared on the masthead. The Pittsburgh city directory discloses that Levi Carroll Judson had practiced law in the Smoky City as early as 1841, shortly after the publication of his book and a good year before Ned resigned from the navy. Ned's sister Irene had married there. The fact that Ned followed his father to Pittsburgh and went into business with him after running away from home contradicts Ned's many assertions that his irreconcilable disagreement with his father concerned the study of Blackstone in Philadelphia. In Ned's later life his fondness for small boys and the pampering of his own son were always attributed to an unhappy boyhood which drove him to sea. Certainly Ned disliked Philadelphia, but it is noticeable that he did not begin to blame his father for his boyhood misfortunes until 1848. It is possible that the real enmity between father and son started over their unfortunate experience with *Ned Buntline's Magazine* in Pittsburgh or two years later when Ned was publicly disgraced and hanged – almost.

Ned's reason for coming West to join his father is cryptic. He admitted publishing "The Captain's Pig" at his own expense. Perhaps he considered it necessary to finance more of his own writings to build a name for himself. His father's *Biography of the Signers* was not a great success but it was certainly more notable than Ned's efforts, so the boy probably looked to his father for help. The father, in turn, plainly felt that Ned's experiences at sea had literary value. The publication they launched, *Ned Buntline's Magazine*, was printed at Cincinnati by the firm of Robinson & Jones. Editor Ned's residence in Pittsburgh indicates that he may have been living under his father's roof there. It is clear, too, that Ned's wife was not with him for he welcomed her in Cincinnati some months later.

The first issue of the new magazine contained thirty-two pages,[7] the second and last number had sixty-four. In both, Levi Carroll Judson wrote laudatory character studies of his Revolutionary heroes. However, most of the little magazine's contents smacked of salt water. One section, "Army and Navy News," was devoted to navy items, and another department, "Quarter-Deck Cogitations," reviewed current books in sailor vernacular. This and an anonymous poem, "To My Spanish Bride," indicates that Ned Buntline had not been on the upper Yellowstone. Apparently the little magazine was designed for ex-sailors or readers interested in the sea. An article by youthful J. Ross Browne satirized sea captains in general. Browne was a young man about Ned's age. Born in Ireland, he had come to Louisville ten years earlier. With an Irish flair for politics and a cartoonist's delicate touch, he made friends quickly and had gone to Washington to serve as a shorthand reporter in Congress. A year of senatorial histrionics cured young Browne and he signed on a whaler. He found sea captains as self-important as solons and wrote about them with youthful sarcasm that appealed to Ned.

In the magazine two book reviews by Buntline himself disclose his developing character. Ned dealt severely with a new volume entitled *The Cruise of the Somers*. The author, Alexander Slidell Mackenzie, was captain of the brig *Somers*, a school ship. He had hanged three of the crew from the yardarm, claiming that they planned mutiny. One of them was a son of the Secretary of War. Politicians stirred up a furor and Ned agreed with them. The other of Ned's reviews revealed another facet of his transparent character. He commented on a new book by Timothy Shay Arthur and called the author "certainly one of the best American writers of the day." Arthur had been as backward in his studies as little Ned Judson. In fact, simple addition had proved so hard for Timothy that he had been withdrawn from school. In Baltimore he had associated with Edgar Allan Poe and was now becoming well known as a temperance writer. Ned's early appreciation of Arthur's skill is remarkable and this book seems to have started Ned along the temperance trail.

Another thing in *Ned Buntline's Magazine* is noticeable. The publishers lacked funds, or, as Ned worded it, "the kind of ballast which would set us in trim, and enable us to navigate the prettiest, neatest, and *best* specimen of Magazine architecture, that ever bowed spars before the genial breeze of popular favor." [8]

Ned sent exchange issues of his magazine to the quarterlies back East and hoped for favorable reviews that might make his literary reputation. Most important would be the appraisal by Lewis Gaylord Clark in *Knickerbocker*. Clark had popularized his journal with men of letters by a special department known as the "Editor's Table," a few pages of informal reviews and gossip of the trade which made amateurs with a taste for belles-lettres feel that they were sitting in conference with the great editor. Clark prided himself on fearless criticism. His quill scourged bad writers without mercy. He had already turned down Buntline's story, "The Captain's Pig." Certainly the great critic must have picked up *Ned Buntline's Magazine* curiously. His appraisal appeared in the July 1844 *Knickerbocker:*

> "*Ned Buntline's Magazine*" – This free-and-easy title designates a Monthly Magazine, published at Cincinnati, Ohio, by E. Z. C. Judson, and edited by Edward Buntline, Esq. Your hand, shipmate, "whoever you may be, or not!" Your craft makes a right gallant appearance, and seems manned by a hearty crew, who have abundant ability, and do their work with a will:
>
> "Take with you gentle winds your sails to swell," Mr. Buntline; and if the "Old Knick" can serve your interests at any time, let him know the *how* and the *when*. That you will *deserve* encouragement and substantial patronage, is quite certain.[9]

This praise came from a high authority. Ned Buntline had reason to feel optimistic, but he had yet to learn that the market for adventure stories, even good ones, was not west of the mountains but back East. His own sea stories equaled the best of James Fenimore Cooper's – there was no doubt about that in Ned's mind – but pioneer Pittsburgh was not the place to publish them. He noticed that several publications were appearing down river at Cincinnati – Porkopolis – about which he had heard so much in the Caribbean when barrels of salt sides had been hoisted on board. Perhaps he should change his headquarters and increase his subscribers by going down there. Ned decided to investigate.

In 1844 travelers floated from Pittsburgh to Cincinnati. Two miles before they arrived, the north bank of the Ohio appeared hazy with smoke from the famous packing plants. Pens, vats, and furnaces could be seen from the decks of steamboats. Ned must have smelled the burnt hair, drying blood, and steaming soap as far out as the middle of the river; and of course fellow travelers boasted that three and a half minutes sufficed for dressing one hog, and that fifteen hundred were converted into pork daily: "If Europe would adopt some of our efficiency and division of labor they could cure their own poverty problem."

Finally Cincinnati came in sight around a bend – a beautiful city on a crescent of hills rising above moored steamboats. Prosperity screamed, whistled, shouted everywhere along the levee – no slums, no squalor. Surely Ned could be financed here for his literary venture, but would these people buy the things he wrote?

Full of hope, Ned landed and climbed the steep hill to the city proper. Every street ended in a verdant vista. Trees shaded brick sidewalks, and the houses stood back from the street on green lawns with well-groomed gardens. Everything looked new, airy and clean. The people dressed well, appeared intelligent and literary-minded. Several daily and weekly newspapers were printed in various shops. Three houses specialized in sheet music.[10] In education Ohio ranked almost as high as New York and Great Britain – Englishmen admitted it.[11] Lane Theological Seminary had imported from Boston Dr. Lyman Beecher to preach against foreigners, liquor, and Catholics. His vigorous-minded daughter Harriet drove around town in a wicker pony cart. To her the issue of the future was slavery. Ned felt no urge to join any crusade. He still wanted to be the West's littérateur – if he could finance his magazine.

Summer in Cincinnati seemed as hot to Ned as Havana, Cuba. The thermometer sometimes went up to 100° and even 106°.[12] In the sultry weather Ned found no one to help keep his magazine alive, so the little publication passed away. Left alone without ship or crew, Ned floundered desperately. Still determined to be an author, he wrote and rewrote articles which various magazines rejected. In cheap lodgings he lay on the floor with quill and paper – the way men wrote in the navy, he liked to explain. During the hottest days perspiration dropped from his chin and spattered on the writing paper. Friends warned him about drinking too much ice water. What was known as "water colic" prostrated newcomers. The cure was a stiff drink of brandy – if a man had the price. Ned learned, too, that a sudden cramp on the street usually evoked the sympathy of a passing Samaritan, but "a feller dassent" do it often unless he was really ill.

A better cure, but Ned could not afford it, was to gulp half a score of raw oysters. These expensive luxuries came by "oyster express" from Baltimore in tanks of corn meal drenched in sea water. Then, during the summer of 1844, Ned's luck turned. *Knickerbocker* accepted a story entitled "Running the Blockade," and overnight Ned became a minor literary somebody in town.

Recognized at last, Ned met a friendly law student who had both money and literary ambition. Lucius A. Hine was four years Ned's senior – big, handsome, intense, earnest, solemn.[13] Of Connecticut stock, like Judson, Hine was the son of a prosperous farmer in Erie County, Ohio, up in the New England part of the state, known as the Western Reserve. At school Hine decided that the world was out of joint. He read about the socialistic theories and experiments of his time: Brook Farm and the preachments of Horace Greeley, and Robert Dale Owen who had failed with a communistic colony in nearby Indiana. Hine became convinced that unearned increment on land (the source of his own family fortune) was the basis of human unhappiness. All that the world needed was a liberal dissemination of truth. Hine neglected his studies to discuss and consider methods of social and economic reform. Like Buntline, he was not disturbed by slavery. For months Hine had been editing a twenty-four-page publication called *The Great Valley Magazine*, with the motto "Knowledge, Virtue, and Glory." His industry had gone unrewarded. Something was necessary to get his message into the hands and minds of the people.

Ned Buntline, the recently discovered literary man, and L. A. Hine saw possibilities in one another's talents. Each wanted self-expression in his own way. Both wanted to associate with literary people. They decided to become partners in a new literary quarterly. Hine agreed to supply $1000 to start the venture. Buntline promised to furnish his name and $500 – as soon as he could raise it. Robinson & Jones acted as publishers, as they had for *Ned Buntline's Magazine*.[14] Possibly they looked forward to the new partnership as a means of reimbursing themselves for the past failure.

To the two young men Cincinnati offered an unusual opportunity for their publication. Bad communications and great distances engendered an intolerant spirit of sectionalism that seemed to be growing throughout the United States. In almost every locality people deplored competition from "outsiders." The West and South were particularly outspoken against the recognition of talent beyond their particular areas, but, paradoxically enough, this feeling of sectionalism broke down in a united opposition to European dominance over American letters. Washington Irving and the *Knickerbocker Magazine* had made Americans conscious of their own gifts. James Fenimore Cooper had scoffed at writers who copied European standards.[15] Rufus Griswold had compiled the patriotic *Poets and Poetry of America* in 1842 to remind native sons that their country had a culture of its own. Ned noted that Cincinnati looked on the Eastern seaboard with the same suspicion and jealousy with which the seaboard looked on Europe. Edgar Allan Poe had capitalized on sectional pride by starting the *Southern Literary Journal* in 1835 – a Southern journal for Southerners. Surely there was a place for a Western journal. Dr. Drake, Cincinnati physician, told a literary convention in Kentucky: "We should foster Western genius, encourage Western writers, patronize Western publishers, augment the number of Western readers, and create a Western heart." Professor William McGuffey had already made Cincinnati famous with his school readers. Lyman Beecher was making the town antiforeign. Hine and Judson determined to make the West for Westerners.

The two young men looked at their recent failures complacently. Literary magazines were no innovation out West, but their new one would be different. A half dozen others had failed in the last quarter century – journals edited by brilliant literary men, Timothy Flint, James Hall, William D. Gallagher, the last two still living in Cincinnati. Judson and Hine were not intimidated. They resolved to profit by their predecessors' mistakes. With high hearts they prepared their first number for the waiting world. Sure of victory over circumstances, Ned sent some of the firm's capital to Seberina – wherever he had left her – with instructions to come and join him in the Queen City of the West.

The Western Literary Journal

A SERIES of important events made Ned lighthearted in November 1844. He galloped downstairs from his office, blue eyes dancing. The first issue of the *Western Literary Journal and Monthly Review* was on the streets. Ned expected his wife to arrive within two months. And James K. Polk had been elected President on a platform pledging a war with Mexico and Great Britain: "The reannexation of Texas and the reoccupation of Oregon – fifty-four forty or fight." Great times were ahead. Many publishers had given more space to politics than to poetry in recent months, but not Judson and Hine. Promising that their magazine would be devoted to literature and art, they had kept their word.

In the first issue, gallant and gifted William D. Gallagher wrote the leading article, a résumé of earlier literary magazines and the causes of their bankruptcy – a subject that he knew as well as any man in Cincinnati. The bruise of his own failure still discolored Gallagher's poetic temperament.

Ned followed the Gallagher article with two sea stories, the first, entitled "The Right of Search," describing in his best nautical style a race with a New England freighter. Ned told how his own stub-prowed schooner crashed along through the water like "a dog with a bone in our teeth," a vivid simile peculiar to the sailor idiom of that day.[1] Ned's other article in the magazine was not so interesting as the Seminole War stories he wrote later. "The Last of the Buccaneers; a Yarn of the Eighteenth Century" (to be continued in the next issue) must have seemed to readers like a conventional title copied from the contemporary *Last of the Barons* by Edward Bulwer-Lytton and the *Last of the Mohicans* by James Fenimore Cooper.

The magazine contained some padding in the form of statistics and a court report. With freckled hands, Ned turned the pages and approved the copy. A few poems broke the monotony of the printed pages. Several stories were written by obscure authors, but two showed promise. One of them, "Killing a Whale," – about a "Nantucket sleighride" – was by J. Ross Browne, the young writer Ned had discovered while editing *Ned Buntline's Magazine.*

The other noteworthy contributor to the initial issue of the *Western Literary Journal* was Mrs. Julia L. Dumont. Her "A Family History" described a poor little rich boy who languished into actual illness over a frustrated love for an aunt confined by poverty to a station below him. Mrs. Dumont wrote with the style and philosophy of her time and place. She was quite a character in the Western literary world, the first woman to acquire recognition as a writer in the Mississippi Valley. Buntline was honored to get her article in the *Western Literary Journal.*

A summary of the articles in the first issue of the *Journal* showed that at least half were of interest to a casual reader. Certainly the magazine had four outstanding stories – Buntline's, Gallagher's, Browne's, and Mrs. Dumont's. It had one other feature that was believed to be the secret of Lewis Gaylord Clark's success with *Knickerbocker* – an Editors' Table and a book-review department wherein literary gossip was invited and printed. This section was conducted by E. Z. C. Judson, not Ned Buntline, a name reserved for stories. During the rest of his life Ned wrote under two names and sometimes three – a practice extremely profitable to him later, as time will disclose.

Editor Judson announced that he would accept articles for the

Western Literary Journal from Western talent only. In his Editors' Table he deplored the popularity of French novels and urged readers to be patriotic. America for Americans! Had not Ralph Waldo Emerson read a declaration of American independence before Phi Beta Kappa in Boston in 1837? Had not Willis Gaylord Clark, the poet brother of Lewis the critic, said that since the death of Byron America produced as good poetry as Europe? [2]

The *Journal's* reviews, like *Knickerbocker's*, discussed current books. Judson noted particularly the publications of Eugène Sue, whose ten-volume *Les Mystères de Paris* had made an international reputation. The French author wrote about poverty-stricken slums in the French capital. One of his characters was a little sewing girl who lived on four francs a week. Sue claimed that he drew the picture in all its realism "with a design of awakening for their benefit the sympathies of the rich." Judson, who claimed to have shot his way to the top among rich men's sons, thought Sue attributed to rich men more virtue "than is usually placed to their credit." [3] He said further: "If there are causes in operation here [in America], which will ultimately involve a portion of our fellow citizens in such wretchedness, it becomes us, while our country is yet in its youth, to remove them." Hine must have approved of such a statement from his young partner.

Zeal to be a reformer was beginning to sprout in Ned Buntline. None might dream where this passion and Eugène Sue's *Mystères de Paris* would lead the red-haired sailor boy.

Another review disclosed young Ned Judson's attitude toward literary trash. A new book, *The Midshipman; or, the Corvette and Brigantine*, had been written by J. H. Ingraham, a New England schoolteacher who had been to sea and taken part in a Latin-American revolution. Ingraham had written his first book eight years before. Since that time he had produced nine, and now in 1844 he had already written two. Ned Buntline, at twenty-one, was enough of a writer to know that no man could turn out so many books – except rubbish.

Ingraham, like other romantic-minded Yankees, had become a broad-hatted Southerner. He had taught modern languages at Jefferson College in Washington, Mississippi,[4] but resigned to devote all his time to writing. His heart was on the dueling field and the plantation; his works, good or bad, sold prodigiously. Ingraham's *Burton; or, the Sieges* was even pirated widely abroad.[5] Ingraham had dedicated this book to S. S. Prentiss, Esq., also of Mississippi. Sargent Prentiss was the beau ideal of the South, Ingraham's first friend and his standard of perfection to the last. An orator and statesman, all but idolized by the Natchez planters, Prentiss was a past master at the gentleman's code. Of him it was said that he would endorse a friend's note without looking at its face, and when his honor was affronted, he could lay down a hand at poker, fight a duel, and return without forgetting the number of cards dealt to a single player. J. H. Ingraham christened his own fire-eating son Prentiss. Buntline saw at once that the "professor's" plastic compositions lacked the rich texture of genuine ivory. In Judson's review of *The Midshipman* he complained that the author did "not know the ropes." Ned accused him of copying the popular works of Captain Marryat. Ingraham, he said, knew little of the sea, had taken but one trip – from New York to New Orleans, a sail of only twelve to eighteen days. Buntline added that he regretted to notice that this spurious author had cut another work adrift, *The Miseries of New York*, a title that seemed direct plagiarism from the French work of Eugène Sue.

After bleaching Ingraham's insipid writing in the brine of his own experience, Ned attacked another of the "trash" writers: George Lippard, a Philadelphia newspaperman who had just written *The Doom of the Poisoners*. Exalted in style, Lippard's book obviously appealed to a low stratum of society. The author championed the poor and criticized the rich. Buntline could not forgive his ornate language and hackneyed observations. He had no sympathy for cheap writers who sold their souls in paper covers for twelve and a half cents each or ten for a dollar.

Ned Buntline felt lonely after the excitement of publishing the first *Journal.* His wife had not joined him, and a whole month would elapse before the reviews of his literary effort could come in. A month was a long time for Buntline's restless disposition. Moreover, the *Journal,* to keep alive, must have more subscribers, and writers, too. Ned knew that Kentucky had a reputation for culture. Nashville also prided itself on refinement. The firm of Judson and Hine had some money left. Ned proposed that he spend it on a trip South to look for talent and subscribers. He packed his bag, donned his "best claw-hammer jacket [and] a pair of trousers which sheeted home at the bottom," then booked passage.[6] Up the gangplank strutted the small apple-checked young man, arrogant with youth, his blue eyes eager to watch the ladies, a talkative chap though fond of reading Pope and Addison.

A floating palace carried passengers down to Louisville. The lofty vessels of that day displayed deck upon deck ornately iced like gigantic wedding cakes. The lowest level was gloomy with fuel and engines, horses and wagons, kegs and casks, and lounging laborers. Slaves, in chain gangs bound down the river, were lodged with the livestock.

Up the companionway the second deck was a different world – easy chairs; women in hoopskirts round as checkers; daughters with starched ankle-pantalets showing below their knee-length skirts; gentlemen in tall hats; gamblers with rings on tapering sensitive fingers and high-heeled boots on their feet. A long saloon with chandeliers, carpets, and upholstered chairs adorned the middle of the ship. Walls and doors were painted elaborately with weeping willows, wisteria, wistful couples, flying doves, cupids, and the Seven Wonders of the World. Audubon, the naturalist, had decorated some of these spacious chambers. Occasionally a civil officer with a runaway Negro came above, chained his prisoner to the rail, and dozed contentedly in a luxurious chair while the slave looked longingly at the north bank of the Ohio where all men were free.[7]

Louisville differed from Cincinnati. It was slave territory. The English writer, Captain Marryat, who visited Louisville in 1837, was impressed by the sight of a slave child of twelve. "She was as fair as snow, and it was impossible to detect any admixture of blood from her appearance, which was that of a pretty English cottager's child." [8] The captain could not reconcile himself to a law and custom which recognized the legal sale of such a person to any man who had sufficient cash, but slavery in practice here did not touch Ned's conscience any more than slavery in theory had affected him in Cincinnati. He had got used to the institution in Cuba.

Below the Louisville Falls another boat carried passengers on down the Ohio. Ned was in a hurry to finish his trip, get back to greet his wife and read the reviews of his *Journal.* At Smithland he changed to a smaller craft and steamed up the Cumberland [9] to the thriving town of Eddyville. A cave here, under the big bluff on the right bank, was said to be two miles long. Ned resolved to explore it sometime. Now he must push on to Nashville, an insignificant young man with red hair curling over the collar of his claw-hammer coat.

In the Tennessee capital Ned noticed the famous City Hotel, scene of a murderous brawl between Thomas Hart Benton and Andy Jackson over thirty years before. The huge rambling structure had been remodeled extensively. Around the front and back of the edifice, gallery towered above gallery — a veritable jungle of steamboat ornamentation screening alcoves and entryways. Ned ventured down a hall noting unexpected turns. He came to steep staircases. Benton had fallen heels over head down one of these.[10] Oddly placed windows indicated unusual rooms and treacherous hiding places. A strange coincidence this, Ned unwittingly studying the intricate passageways that were soon to shelter him from a howling mob.

Out in fresh air again, Ned hunted the addresses of people to whom he carried letters of introduction, people interested in literature. Through them he got some subscriptions and also made the acquaintance of a young man named Hudson A. Kidd. Ned said later that the fellow had more ambition than talent. At the time it seemed good to cultivate his acquaintance. Kidd was a nephew of Felix K. Zollicoffer,[11] associate editor of the Nashville *Banner*, who was credited with keeping Polk from carrying Tennessee, his own state, in the recent election. Ned knew that the newspaper business could be violent in the South. Men had an ugly habit of carrying pistols in the tail-pockets of their frock coats. Ned learned, too, that an unpopular journalist might expect a horsewhipping, and that lynch law was a recognized code — rule of the people, by God! Ned was told that he would have to watch his editorials if he expanded the *Western Literary Journal* down here, or it might be too bad for him. Ned thought that it might be worse for some of the pistol-toting young blades. His marksmanship had won him respect in the navy and Ned looked forward to a repeat performance.

From Nashville Ned went south over the smooth limestone roads into northern Alabama and Mississippi. Ostensibly he was seeking more subscribers by plowing the money he got in Nashville back into the publishing business. The horse stage made long runs between stops — rolling for hours through the pine forest without passing a single habitation, crossing streams on flat-bottomed ferryboats. Ned made arrangements, when he could, to stop at the better-looking plantation homes. Before long he learned that a planter with a hundred or more acres of land, a dozen slaves, hogs, sheep, cattle, and horses, saw little cash in a year. Three dollars was a lot of money for a man to pay for a magazine when his property required him to spend all the hours from daylight to dark in the saddle.

Ned gained more respect everywhere for his marksmanship than he did for his literary talent. He said later that he got some subscriptions – obviously not many. His city clothes and Pennsylvania accent made him conspicuous. Upcountry Southerners dressed in homespun. Home-dyed blue trousers, tucked into boots, and orange-brown coats were popular. Many wore gray undyed suits.[12] The urban cut of Ned's clothes marked him as a Yankee and all Yankees were assumed to be tricky fellows, come to get money from the sons of the soil. Ned would start to talk about literary values to a planter lolling in his saddle. The Southerner might interrupt Ned before he got to the point by asking, "What kind of wooden nutmegs have you brought to sell?" or, "There was a Yankee in heah las' month sellin' Connecticut clocks and mahogany hams. What line do you-all carry?" Ned learned also that a great many of these upland Southerners – masters of slaves and plantations – could not read or write. A red flag over a cabin in the Southern pines meant a grocery store as it did on an Ohio River houseboat, but it was possible that illiteracy made flags necessary here.[13] Certainly the pine barrens were poor territory for promoting circulation of the *Western Literary Journal.*

On Ned's way back to Nashville he stopped at the Hermitage to see the most famous man in America: Old Hickory. Andrew Jackson considered himself and his home the property of the nation. Carriages of curious people continually drove up to the Hermitage portico. Ned found a crowd standing in one of the rooms. He elbowed through the sightseers and saw the old general sitting in an armchair before the fire, frail and wrinkled as a strip of hickory bark. The Hero of New Orleans, the brawler who had led his gang against Benton in the City Hotel, coughed feebly. His bloodless mask of a face and rheumy eyes disclosed vitality running low. Ned had just written an article on handshaking and character portrayal. With this in mind he shook the old warrior's thin cold hand. The listless pressure of the ancient general's fingers made Ned revise his recent conclusions. "Farewell! God bless you, my young friend!" Buntline heard the ex-President whisper.[14]

Ned drove on to Nashville, then north to the Ohio. The time had come for him to go back to Cincinnati, embrace his wife, and get out the second issue of his magazine. More interesting still, he wanted to read the reviewers' appraisals of his *Literary Journal*. From Louisville a palatial steamer carried him up the river and home.

In Cincinnati Seberina was waiting for Ned. So was an accumulation of mail, but as yet none of the anticipated reviews. Ned did not care. He waxed lyrical with love, refurbished a story that he had written for *Ned Buntline's Magazine* and rushed it off to *Knickerbocker*. This story did not tell about storms at sea, tropical fish, or feats of marksmanship. Instead the author described women, lovely women. Lewis Gaylord Clark read with astonishment this sudden literary aberration of his promising adventure writer. He liked the story, however, and Buntline's "Masked Ball" was crowded into the last pages of the December 1844 *Knickerbocker*.

Ned may not have intended to deceive Clark about his marriage. Certainly the great editor believed that it was a recent occurrence. In any event the reunion's tender passion awakened honeymoon visions of love and beauty that Ned could not describe with ordinary grammar. Of a feminine character in his story he said, "Her eye was like a liquid lake of night-sky, with a single-star swimming like a soul on its centre." The sister of his literary heroine Ned described as dressed in a

> short white skirt, just long enough to reveal the beauties of a foot and ankle which would have killed Venus had she seen it . . . the light blue boddice [*sic*], silken-laced and tasselled, fitting neatly to a full swelling bust; the snowy, crimp ruffle, resting far down on the transparent bosom; the arms bare up to the gently-rounded elbows, so beautiful that one could scarcely look at them without wishing them for an every-day cravat.[15]

Ned concluded his story by taking the reader into his confidence — the personal touch which Clark had found so popular with readers. He worked his story into a crisis, then ended:

> Reader, I was about to conclude my yarn; but there is a little witch looking over my shoulder, who bothers me so that I cannot write. I'll describe her. As all of the witching kind does, she appears in the shape of a woman. In the first place, she's between eighteen and twenty years of age; tall — no she is not tall, nor is she short; but she is just a VENUSIAN height; her figure like unto that which Nature modelled, and then in anger broke the mould which formed it, because it excelled herself.
>
> "Confound it, Madam! — good Lord! Mrs. Buntline! — let me alone!" There, reader, she has capsized the inkstand and pulled my ears. My tale must close: there! she has blown out the light. Good night! God bless the ladies.[16]

In the same copy of *Knickerbocker* in which this story was printed, Ned Buntline saw himself, his work, and his magazine appraised along with two new books: *The Life of Francis Marion* by W. Gilmore Simms and *Afloat and Ashore* by James Fenimore Cooper — as good company as any writer might wish. Of Buntline's work Clark said in his leisurely literary way:

> "*The* [*Western*] *Literary Journal and Monthly Review*" is the name of a new and well-executed Magazine, the first number of which has just reached us from the place of its publication, the "Queen City of the West," beloved of occidental travellers, on the beautiful banks of "La Belle Riviere." We have perused the initial number with pleasure and profit. It is in an ample degree both instructive and entertaining. Our old-time correspondent, W. D. GALLAGHER, (whose charming poem upon "August" "syllables his name" whenever we write or encounter the cognomen of that sultry month,) has an article upon "Western Periodical Literature," which deserves the attention of every periodical-publisher and delinquent subscriber in the United States. He has also a fine poem inculcating freedom of opinion and action in his countrymen:
>
> "Bold in speech and bold in action
> Be forever! Time will test

Of the free-souled and the slavish,
Which fulfils life's mission best.

"Be thou like the noble Roman!
Scorn the threat that bids thee fear;
Speak! – no matter what betide thee;
Let them strike, but make them hear!"

"NED BUNTLINE," however, is his own best contributor. There is a certain life, a *semblable* spirit, in every thing which we have seen from his pen, that renders him a most entertaining companion. Witness his "Running the Blockade" in our October number, and "The Masked Ball" in the present issue. May happiness attend him, and the beautiful bride whom he won at that brilliant carnival! Time rolls his ceaseless course, and

– "rosy lips and cheeks
Within his bending sickle's compass come;"

but long may he spare Mrs. NED BUNTLINE and her joyous, gallant companion!

"And when with envy, Time transported,
Shall think to rob her of her joys,
She in her girls again be courted,
And he go wooing in his boys!"

We shall look to the "Literary Journal," among other good things, for independent criticism. The present number has an admirable exposé of the literary pretensions of "Professor" INGRAHAM, who spawns every week something in "the cheap style" of publication which he terms a novel or a "nouvellette"; each successive pamphlet furnishing still more lamentable evidence of the furniture of his mind. From the nothingness which characterizes his later performances, we begin to think that he has solved in his diet one of the categorical problems of JOB. He must have succeeded in "filling himself with the east wind." The "Western Monthly Review" has our cordial good wishes for its complete success. It will richly *deserve* the generous support of the West, and we cannot doubt that it will *receive* it.[17]

Ned knew better. He had barely enough money to publish the second number.

Up the Rope He Goes

In the fall of 1844 a slim, blond young woman of twenty-five called at the office of the *Western Literary Journal.* She saw a redheaded, rosy-cheeked boy lying on the floor writing with a quill. The young lady asked for Mr. Buntline. Ned jumped to his feet and bowed. The slim and graceful lady laughed gaily. She said that she expected to see a bearded monster in canvas trousers and a tarpaulin hat, then introduced herself as Amelia Welby, of Louisville.

Ned knew all about her. Indeed every literary person on the Ohio did. She had come west as a girl with her widowed mother and had grown up with the country. Amelia loved nature and wrote about it tenderly. Her first poetry had been published by George D. Prentice in the *Louisville Daily Journal* and was highly praised by reviewers. In 1838 she married a prosperous merchant. In 1840 her collected poems had been published as a "gift edition" in crimson cloth with gilt letters. Poe pointed to her as a new literary star. She in turn admired Lord Byron and wrote a poem to him entitled, "I Knew Thee Not." The literary critics of her day—Caroline May, Thomas Buchanan Read, Rufus Griswold—all included Amelia Welby in their anthologies. Her house was recognized as a literary center on the Ohio. For her to call at the *Journal* office flattered Buntline no end.

Amelia was four years older than Ned, and a few inches taller.

She had a slight deformity of her upper lip. People said that it gave her an elfish appearance but in no way marred her piquancy. Without doubt she had what was known as "a presence." Ned, still soft with his own romances, later described her as "a little golden-haired thing, more like an angel than a woman." [1] Amelia Welby's interest in the *Journal* betokened success.

The second issue of Ned's literary magazine, though late in appearing, maintained the high standard of earlier publications. Feature articles ranked in popular appeal with those in the November issue. The book-review section continued to malign foreign talent and native trash. Ned called attention to a new satire, *Peter Ploddy's Dream* by Jasper C. Neal, a Philadelphia crusader like Lippard but a better writer. Neal described the slums in the manner of Charles Dickens—much better than Dickens, Buntline maintained. Always Ned exalted American writers above foreigners. Like Lippard, too, Neal had become famous for lampooning Philadelphia's unworthy City Worthies. Ned urged readers to buy Neal's new book and not send their money abroad for inferior productions. Having thus championed the superiority of American letters, Ned turned next to the trash writers at home. Maintaining his high standard of literary criticism, he played a stream of scorn on the new publications of "Professor" Ingraham. Since the November issue of the *Western Literary Journal* Ingraham had produced two "nouvellettes"—coverless "shilling shockers" selling for the usual "bit" (12½ cents), as the sum was called in the West, or a "shilling York" in Manhattan, where colonial coinage still influenced counting-house conversation. Ned assured his readers that the criticism was "a *duty* which the station we have assumed demands of us." [2]

Lewis Gaylord Clark matched the *Journal's* "independent criticism" by ridiculing Ingraham even more severely. *Knickerbocker* sarcastically quoted the "professor's" alleged work to let readers sample for themselves:

'Twas a horrible night; wild shrieked the storm-spirit above the mad waves; the foam was white; the wild lightning leaped from the abyssmal vaults of Heaven; and the tempest howled like a tiger stung by a spider. Heaven! is that a vessel upon the gloomy waste of waters!

A second alleged quotation was printed to show Ingraham's ignorance of nautical terms:

"Ho! brace the helm, there! Let go the main-sheet! Furl up the clue buntlines: Ha! ha! we'll yet baffle the storm!"

These words proceeded from the mouth of one who stood upon the main-truck of the "Phantom Clam-Sloop." Dark was his complexion, but clear; his eye keen and flashing; his teeth white and well-set; his smile was the smile of an angel, and his glance the glance of a fiend![3]

Ned was pleased to note that *Knickerbocker* agreed with him on literary values. He set to work on the third issue of the *Journal* with confidence in his ability, but funds were running very, very low. He had in mind two plans for refinancing his publication – Amelia Welby's rich husband in Louisville, Kentucky, and Hudson A. Kidd, the literary young man he had met in Nashville, Tennessee. His interviews with both prospects had to be delayed, however, until the third issue was ready for the printer. As Ned worked on his copy, a shabbily dressed young man of his own age called at the office. Emerson Bennett had a manuscript for sale. He had failed as a writer both in New York and in Philadelphia. He had failed as a lover, too, in the City of Brotherly Love. In Cincinnati, since the spring of 1844, he had supported himself in the cheapest lodgings by peddling from house to house a patent linen-marker.[4]

Ned looked over Bennett's manuscript and turned it down, but he offered the poor chap a position as assistant editor on the *Journal* – a high-sounding title. The new man was really employed to tramp through rural Ohio soliciting subscriptions. Bennett accepted the job and set off. While he was gone Ned closed a deal with Hudson Kidd. He agreed to move the *Journal* headquarters to Nashville. If the young bullies down there resented a newcomer they would have to protect themselves.

In December 1844, Ned and Seberina moved South. Their baggage consisted mainly of unpublished manuscripts. The next *Journal* announced Kidd as the new associate editor, but Hine's name also remained on the banner. The reorganized magazine called itself *The South-Western Literary Journal and Monthly Review*, and it contained the West's big literary names: Donn Piatt, wealthy politician and littérateur; Albert Pike, a New Englander who had gone Southern like Ingraham, let his hair grow long as a cavalier's, and now wrote poetry near Little Rock, Arkansas, in a white mansion with green shutters and a pillared portico on a lawn surrounded by giant oaks. Ned also included in the issue three Hine productions. Thus the reformer was getting self-expression for his $1,000 after the paper left his home town. Ned contributed two Seminole War stories of his own, and balanced them with a plains adventure by C. B. Gillespie. Yes, the third number of the *Journal* maintained the old standard, and with the field of publication extended into Tennessee the magazine might be saved from financial ruin.

In the editorials Ned proved himself the acknowledged Lewis Gaylord Clark of the West. He demonstrated his independent judgment by criticizing the weak parts of Amelia Welby's work – her husband had not financed him – and lauding the superb passages. Ned played up his new Southern surroundings by publicizing the productions of two Nashville artists and commenting favorably on a new book of Americanisms by a member of the local bar. Ned's disgust for literary rubbish appeared again in an outcry against another book by George Lippard. Like Ingraham, the Philadelphian was writing too many books, but the stuff was selling by tens of thousands. Unlike Ingraham, Lippard preached socialism. A Marxian before Karl Marx, his muscular words jarred complacent Philadelphia. Ned opposed such radi-

Fracker Library
Buena Vista College

calism. Neal's sarcastic and less vicious pictures of the Philadelphia Fathers seemed better to him, although he was impressed by the fact that Lippard outsold Neal. The horrible *Doom of the Poisoners* had been dramatized successfully as *The Quaker City*. Criticism of the well-born and the well-to-do seemed to be gaining popularity since the age of Jackson. But as Ned worked on his *Journal* word came from east of the mountains that the police had closed Lippard's play — too socialistic to be safe. No, Ned was not ready to climb down from Parnassus and write for the common herd. He dipped his quill in the inkpot and scribbled a rebuke against Lippard for "prostituting his able pen in recording, in trifling *nouvellette* shape, scenes which have already cast a sufficient blot and stain upon our land."[5]

With the third issue in circulation, Ned studied his finances and the reactions of Southern readers. So far he had found none of the dangerous truculence about which he had been warned. To save money and the time required for letter-writing Ned worked out an economical scheme for communicating with his contributors. The cost of expressing a letter was exorbitant and the express companies were successfully keeping the government from carrying mail — complaining against such infringement on private enterprise.[6] Ned surmounted the postage problem by printing a personal column in his *Journal*, in which he referred to contributors by their initials, and told them in print that he would take their articles, or explained his reason for rejecting them.

Ned appreciated the importance of printing the compositions of promising women writers but he paired their work with rugged masculine contributions. Readers could always turn from sweet sentimentality to robust adventure. Ned continued to furnish heroics on both land and sea. Always he made the most of his own adventures in the Seminole War. He called on veterans to contribute their experiences in the Everglades — the old trick of going into partnership with the reader. Buntline's own stories of personal escapades in Florida began to contain more combat than had been reported by his commanding officers in the war. Ned was learning that a story must improve on life if a reader is to give up real life for it. Another trick which Ned had first tried in "The Captain's Pig" was also becoming fixed in his stories. People wanted to believe that the narrative they read was true, even when they knew better. Scrupulously accurate accounts bored them. Ned already understood enough of the tapestry of life to make fictitious characters walk convincingly in acceptable settings.

In vivid detail he wrote about his trip up the Miami and across the Everglades. The commanding officer had reported in the official records that no Indians had been seen. Now Ned, in his magazine, described from memory the sea of waving saw grass taller than the heads of the men standing on the boats' thwarts. This much was true. Ned added that the men sighted a palm tree as they poled along. A scout, he said, waded over to it and began to climb. The men watched as his head rose above the waving grass. Quickly the scout dropped back into the swampy water. In whispers he told the officers what he had seen: five canoes filled with Indians in a lagoon nearby. The Indians were fishing, unconscious of approaching white men. The soldiers prepared for action. Guns were inspected, flints picked and changed. The gaiter-footed soldiers hitched up an extra hole in their belts and peered ahead as the boats rasped gently through the green curtain of grass.

At last they reached open water and saw the Indians fishing. The sailors dropped their oars into the locks and began to row with all their might. Terrified, the Indians grabbed their paddles and sped away. The white men's boats, with great sweeps of the oars, leaped forward across the soapy water toward the dugout canoes. The desperate Indians fired a volley over the gunwales, and when the cloud of smoke cleared they were gone. However, their dugouts left a plain trail through the swampy water.

The oarsmen followed a short distance, then stuck in the mud. Soldiers and sailors clambered into the muck and splashed off, eager as otter hounds. They came to deserted canoes. Ned saw a moccasin track in the muddy water. With drawn sword he followed it. In the distance he could hear shouts and swearing as other men plunged through the rushes hunting Indians. Ned sloshed along. An odd bundle in the water attracted him. With his sword he turned it over. A baby, choked to death with a thong around its neck, lay in the marsh. Ned hurried away, watching the tall grass ahead. Before long he came face to face with an Indian woman, mother of the dead child. She stood in the shallow water looking at Ned calmly, almost stupidly, but with wild defiance. Ned pointed down the back track with his sword. She marched away sullenly — his prisoner — back to a small hummock where a village was discovered. Other prisoners squatted here beside the naked bodies of dead warriors. At one side soldiers prepared a noonday meal, lolled behind their stacked rifles, laughed over their experiences. After eating they manned the boats and started home. Behind them vultures wheeled above the destroyed village. Yes, Ned's story was much better than the official records, and it had a semblance of truth. It showed, too, his sincere respect for Indians, as genuine as Amelia Welby's effusions, even if less sentimental.

In April 1845 appeared the last issue of the *South-Western Literary Journal.* Ned seemed to have escaped the pistol and bowie knife in Tennessee — almost. Readers might have guessed that the magazine's end was near. Ned had persistently kept a bold front, whistling in the dark, reiterating the fact that times had been bad but that he saw light ahead. Suspicious readers might also have noted bravado in the editor's exultant statement that at least four other literary journals had been born and died since the Hine-Buntline-Kidd venture.[7]

With this death song the *Journal* passed away. Ned was bankrupt and his wife expected a baby. He had written a couple of stories for *Knickerbocker* during the preceding winter and knew that he could not live by writing fiction even if he succeeded in selling a story a month, which was unlikely. While in these desperate straits he heard from his family in Pittsburgh. His father had been burned out of house and home, lost all his manuscripts, and planned returning to Philadelphia for a new start in his old age.[8] He was past forty! From Cincinnati came word that socialist Hine complained that he, Ned Buntline, had left many of the defunct magazine's capitalistic debts for his partner to pay. Ned learned, too, that poor Emerson Bennett had come back from his subscription-soliciting tour. The magazine's failure had taken even his wretched job.

Back in Cincinnati, Bennett sat disconsolately in a cheap restaurant. With nothing to do, the brokenhearted writer lingered where the least money would buy the most food. At a nearby table he heard some conversation that flushed his pale cheeks. The men were talking enthusiastically about a story recently printed in the *Cincinnati Commercial*. Bennett had written nothing for this newspaper, but the story sounded familiar. He asked if he might see the sheet. To his astonishment Bennett recognized a story he had written without success for a competition in Philadelphia. He related the coincidence to Hine, who introduced him to the editor. Bennett was put to work at once.

Ned knew Bennett's work to be second-rate – below standard for the *Literary Journal*. But now he had a good job, and Ned himself was out of employment. Discouraged with the prospect of living on the proceeds of occasional articles in *Knickerbocker*, Ned decided to resurrect *Net Buntline's Magazine* with new features that would make it the sensation of the age. At steamboat wharves he posted broadsides announcing his new publication, *Ned Buntline's Own*[9] (like *Hood's Own* in England but different). Ned's paper was to have two features not found in either of his previous failures – *Ned Buntline's Magazine* and the *Liter-*

ary Journal. One was to be an exciting continued story of his own adventurous life. The other would be a guide to help travelers evade gambling pitfalls and confidence games. Moreover, Ned promised to publish the names of notorious gamblers, the details of their crooked games and the names of steamboats on which they operated. This was dangerous business but Ned professed not to care what the gamblers might do to him. In Clarksville, on the road between Nashville and Hopkinsville, Ned rented a cheap room for Seberina. Time for the baby's birth was getting close and the prospective parents were very short of money. To get copy for *Buntline's Own,* Ned was obliged to be away from home for long periods, locating new gamblers to expose. Often he disguised himself in homespun, dressed like a farmer come to town for a friendly game of cards. At other times he posed as an Easterner looking for investments. Before long he had a notebook full of names and addresses of men willing to pay him to keep out of his paper. While building up this clientele Ned wrote hopefully to *Knickerbocker's* editor, Lewis Gaylord Clark. He wanted to sell him a serial story of his adventures at sea, to be called "Ned Buntline's Life-Yarn."

Clark wrote back from his exclusive New York office, accepting the attractive series. He liked the vivid vitality of Buntline's writing. His welcome letter assured the Judsons a fixed income and their future appeared bright,[10] but Ned knew that he would eventually run out of stories about hairbreadth escapes. Then what? His twenty-two years had been packed with adventures, but people would tire of old stories. They must have variety. Ned thought of a remedy: he would continue to do heroic deeds even while he wrote, and good newspaper publicity must keep readers interested in him between articles. His name must appear constantly in print as a fabulous hero out in the fabulous West. The first publicity stunt he tried was surprising. In March 1846 *Knickerbocker* printed a strange letter from a contributor in Natchez:

By the way, NED passed through here this morning, on his way to Gallatin, thirty miles distant. Being on a visit to Eddyville, (Ky.,) a few days since, he heard that three persons, charged with having committed an atrocious murder near Gallatin some time since, were in the woods in the neighborhood. Arming himself, NED "put out" in pursuit of them, *alone*. He soon overtook them, when two of them surrendered, after a short resistance. These he tied to trees, and then went on in pursuit of the other, who had absconded in the mean time. But the fellow had too good a start; and NED, after firing one or two shots after him, gave up the chase. He arrived here with his two captives last night in the steamer, and as I said before, went on to Gallatin with them this morning. He has entitled himself to the reward of six hundred dollars which had been offered for their apprehension.[11]

The letter came from Nashville, not Natchez, of course. Contemporary newspapers report the three criminals' capture but do not mention Ned.[12] Undoubtedly he had already assumed his lifelong role in a world of make-believe. The same issue of *Knickerbocker* contained more news from Buntline, but this time it was grim. Mrs. Judson had died. Clark promised his readers that the "Life-Yarn" would be continued in the April issue but by April affairs had gone from bad to worse. *Knickerbocker* announced: "There is great reason to fear that before the sentences which are now running from our pen shall have been placed in type, we shall have heard of the death of our frequent and always entertaining contributor, 'Ned Buntline.' "[13] Readers who believed these words to be publicity for the "Life-Yarn" soon found their error. Ned Buntline had been lynched. No mistake!

The true story was slow to reach New York. In time people learned that Nashville gossips had whispered about Ned Buntline and a married woman in the city – a woman in her teens. The affair had started during Christmas week, while Seberina was still living. Ned had swaggered around in a Spanish cloak and Panama hat – unseasonable surely, but literary celebrities were entitled to their peculiar trimmings. He sauntered into a church bazaar near the Planter's Bank. Mrs. Robert Porterfield, young wife of an auctioneer's assistant, presided over a picture gallery, charging twenty-five cents for the church's benefit. Ned, on the alert for news for *Buntline's Own*, chatted with her at the entrance. In the next issue of his little seven-by-nine paper Mrs. Porterfield read that she was "a beautiful woman with exalted accomplishments." Immediately her teen-age heart fluttered for the sophisticated literary lion of twenty-two.

During the holidays Nashville people masked and reveled in the streets. It was an old Southern custom. At Trabue's boardinghouse, where the Porterfields lived, the guests noticed that Mrs. Porterfield joined the merrymakers without her husband. Later, at a Baptist social, the game called "post office" was played. Ned sent a poem through the "post office" to Mary Porterfield and another to her husband.[14] Later he sent still another to Mary, signed El Strangero – she relished Spanish as he taught it to her. Some nights later boys found Ned with a woman in the alley behind the Episcopal church. They pelted the couple with rocks. Ned covered his companion with his cloak and escaped. The boys were not sure that the woman was young Mrs. Porterfield, but the story set the neighbors' tongues wagging. Next day Porterfield met Ned on the street up on Capitol Hill, pulled out a pistol, and accused him of improper relations with his wife. Ned denied the charge. Passers-by overpowered Porterfield, and Ned's life was spared.

That night in the Porterfield home – they had left the boardinghouse – Robert sat in the parlor with the minister of the church, the Reverend Mr. Paul. Outside in the dark they heard someone whistling a merry air. They also heard Mary's steps hurrying along the hall toward the door. Robert called to her. She stopped, and came into the lighted room. Her husband and the minister both lectured her seriously. Mary pleaded innocence, said that she had not heard the whistling outside. Her husband accepted the story and shortly thereafter purchased for her a ring with "Confidence" engraved on the inside.

This happened on Wednesday, March 11, 1846. On Friday the thirteenth, the Reverend Mr. Paul started to walk out to the graveyard. On the way several ladies leaned from their windows to call confidentially that Ned Buntline had gone ahead of him. At the cemetery the minister hid behind a tree and soon Mary Porterfield came tripping along in shawl and bonnet. She went into the lane behind the graveyard wall, a sunken roadway shaded with cedars. The minister waited for several minutes. Then he slipped after her. He found Ned and Mary standing face to face talking earnestly, quite close together but not touching one another, so he testified later. The couple saw him, turned, and walked away side by side.[15]

The Reverend Mr. Paul sauntered back downtown to the Porterfield home. Mary was there ahead of him. He assured her that he would not tell Robert what he had seen if she would promise never to meet Ned Buntline again.

Mary replied with spirit. She had done nothing wrong. She intended to tell Robert all about it herself. Buntline had not been in her mind when she went to the graveyard. The meeting was accidental. She had gone there to plant a flower on the grave of her dead baby. When she saw Buntline she told him that she intended to have nothing more to do with him. He had remonstrated, but she had been obdurate.

Mary's story sounded plausible and, true to her word, she told her husband when he came home from work. Robert believed her, but the next day a group of his friends, including his brother John, came to his house and urged him to kill Ned. The distraught husband primed his pistol and set off down the street, with the young men goading him to act.

Friends warned Ned Buntline. He went at once to the edge of town and practiced pistol shooting. Porterfield found him there. The young husband opened fire, shot after shot, with his irate companions applauding. Ned fired back, and Robert Porterfield fell face down in the road. His friends turned him over and saw a bullet hole in his skull above the right eye, but he was not dead. They carried him back to town, and Ned gave himself up to the law.

The hearing was held in the courthouse, across from the City Hotel – scene of the brawl between Benton and Jackson. Ned pleaded self-defense. Porterfield had fired first. The witnesses present knew this to be a fact, but before the court made a ruling John Porterfield and his friends entered the room, shouldered their way through the crowd of lank Southern loafers, and shot point-blank at the prisoner. Ned ducked, ran from the room and across into the quaint rambling City Hotel. A dozen guns barked at his heels before he disappeared in the gloomy passages. "I was slightly hit by three only," [16] Ned reported later with characteristic optimism. As a matter of fact he received a bullet wound in the chest, and a Negro hit him a bad blow with a stone as he scampered across the square. The mob stormed into the hotel, shouting from gallery to gallery and up and down the steep stairs. Ned had disappeared. Then from the third floor someone yelled, "Here he is."

Ned jumped out a window, reached with his strong sailor-arms for the roof coping above the portico, missed, and fell – "forty-seven feet three inches, (measured,) on hard, rocky ground, and not a bone cracked!" [17] he boasted later. Ned exaggerated. As a matter of fact he was crippled for life.

Officers dragged the stunned man to jail. That night irate people stood along the street telling one another about the fracas, pointing to the window from which Ned had jumped. Some blamed Ned for breaking up a home. Others said that he shot in self-defense. "No," replied still others, "Ned shot Porterfield from behind. The bullet went in the back of his head and came out over his eye. By God, Sir, the home-wrecking murderer should be hanged high as Haman." Gamblers who had been threatened with exposure in *Buntline's Own* seemed very bitter. They complained that Ned had deserted his wife, left her to die in childbirth alone in a miserable room in Clarksville while he was rollicking in Nashville's gaming parlors to spy on and blackmail the operators. They said that Seberina had not had enough to eat. Neighbors had raised a subscription for her and Ned had used the money to pay for another issue of *Buntline's Own*.

Zollicoffer apparently did nothing to allay the storm. His *Banner* reported the case factually. Ned's one-time colleague, Hudson A. Kidd – the literary lad with more ambition than talent – also stayed out of the excitement. Perhaps he pulled wires behind the scenes. On the other hand, he may have heard Ned's uncomplimentary appraisal of his ability and done nothing. But Ned had some friends in the crowd. That was apparent later.

At eleven o'clock at night the crowd in the square learned that Robert Porterfield had died. The mob marched to the jail and broke in. They found Ned and threw the battered man into the street. A rope was looped about his neck, and Edward Zane Carroll Judson was hanged from an awning post in the public square. Then his nameless friends smuggled him away. "The rope did not *break;* it was *cut* by a friend," Ned said in his report. Bruised but not broken, Ned wrote *Knickerbocker*, "I hope to be ready, in two or three months, to 'go it' for 'the whole of Oregon.' "[18]

A grand jury assembled and listened to the crippled man's story of innocence, his plea of self-defense. They deliberated and found no indictment against him. Ned slipped out of town quietly. He knew that the great Lewis Gaylord Clark liked his work. Why not go to New York? Without doubt the notorious Ned Buntline could make a name for himself in the literary world back East. That the sequel of his Nashville affair would unfold after he had crossed the Alleghenies seemed beyond the logical realm of probability.

New York Confounds Ned Buntline

NED STOPPED at Pittsburgh to write the *Knickerbocker* office, next at Philadelphia to recover his strength. Traveling was difficult for an invalid. Ned's fellow passengers had buzzed with opinions about President Polk's declaration of war – not for Oregon as promised in his campaign, but against Mexico. However, here in Philadelphia in the spring of 1846, Ned saw and heard little war excitement. People strolled along the brick sidewalks as though nothing had happened.

Short of money, Ned may have looked for his father, but if he did he left no record of the humiliation. Levi Carroll Judson, since the fire in Pittsburgh, had hung out his shingle in Philadelphia again and was also seeking a publisher.[1] He had written a new book entitled *The Probe: or One Hundred and Two Essays on the Nature of Men and Things.* The work contained homely Wayne County philosophy with advice on rearing boys, the importance of religion, virtue, and discipline. "Anger, like too much wine, hides us from ourselves, but exposes us to others," he observed wisely.[2]

On the streets of Philadelphia Ned learned that newspapers were arguing about his own Nashville escapade. The *Spirit of the Times* defended him and censured the *Pennsylvanian* for copying uncomplimentary notes from Western papers.

In Cincinnati Buntline had no defender. Lucius Hine and Emerson Bennett were both on the *Commercial* and they cherished no love for Ned. They maintained that he had written from Nashville boasting of his conquest of Mrs. Porterfield,[3] but they did not produce the letters. Hine, of course, was still paying the debts of the *Western Literary Journal.* The most revealing part of the scandal was yet to come.

In July, Ned was still recuperating in Philadelphia. The *Spirit of the Times* reported him able to walk again, but he limped noticeably, carried his left arm in a sling, and the bullet wound in his chest had not healed. Crippled as he was, Ned joined the staff of the *Times,* and the paper welcomed him with an introduction due a great literary personage. The editorial said: "As a contributor to the *Knickerbocker Magazine* and other standard literary periodicals Mr. Judson has already won an enviable reputation; his nautical tales and sketches are among the best in our language. We trust he may live long to enjoy and to add to the laurels that have already been awarded him." [4]

Ned learned from his colleagues on the *Times* that George Lippard had succeeded amazingly with his crusade for the common people against the city fathers. The mayor had closed his radical play, *The Quaker City,* but what of that? The *Saturday Evening Post* printed his articles, and he had more lecture engagements than he could fill. Ned did not plan to remain in a peripheral position in the new Lippard-Ingraham shilling-shocker school. He looked forward to a place with Lewis Gaylord Clark in New York. In the meantime he could accumulate a little money and convalesce. To his readers he introduced himself with a poem replying to the assistant editor's recent "valedictory to wine." Ned wrote:

> I'll bid adieu to *juleps,* John,
> Farewell to *smashes,* too,
> They ne'er shall pass my two lips, John,
> I've bade them all adieu!

This poem seemed sufficiently popular to warrant publication a fortnight later of another Buntline poem entitled "Words from an Old Sycamore Tree in Independence Square." Seven stanzas were printed in the issue of July 25 and the poem was concluded on two later days. Stanza three follows:

> I am an old-time tree! strange things
> I've seen, strange thoughts I've heard! Beneath
> The shadow of my spreading wings,
> Young love hath twin'd the rosy wreath;
> And in the circle of my shade
> Cold Death hath come and softly laid
> His hand upon his own! The spade
> 'Neath my old roots a grave hath made!

While these poems were being published, the sequel to the Porterfield affair occurred back in Nashville. Mary had moved to the country shortly after the death of her husband. The Baptist Church considered expelling her from membership and ordered a trial. Mary's uncle, Mr. Blakey, pleaded her case before the moderator. He introduced as evidence a letter from Mary asking to be forgiven. She admitted that she had been indiscreet but insisted that she had done nothing criminally wrong. She had been flattered, she said, by attentions from a literary man who was being acclaimed throughout the city. She assured the church also that her dead husband's determination to kill Judson was unwarranted. She admitted being guilty of reading and memorizing passages from Lord Byron and from Moore's *Lalla Rookh*. She realized that this was frivolous and she was sorry. She would not repeat the offense if forgiven. Her uncle read this letter to the jury, then presented evidence to show that Mary Porterfield was not the woman with Judson in the alley behind the Episcopal Church, and also that Mary had gone to the cemetery, as she had said, to plant a flower on the grave of her dead baby. Meeting Buntline there had been accidental, and she had talked to him to censure him.

In spite of this explanation the church voted to expel Mary Porterfield. Then Mr. Blakey made a great mistake – an error that ferreted out the story which might have remained permanently hidden. He published his side of the case in the *Nashville Union* and excoriated the church for its verdict. Thus the moderator was forced to reply in the same paper, to place, as he said, before the world "*some* of the facts of the case, where they will stand for ages." [5] Item by item he rebutted Blakey's charges. The incident in the alley, he said, was not conclusive, but the fact that Mary wore a white dress and the woman with Buntline was dressed in black did not prove anything. All the boys who had seen them agreed that the woman was wrapped in Buntline's cloak. So much for that. Next, according to the church's reply, Mary could not have met Ned in the graveyard by accident. None of the witnesses – and they were legion – at the windows along the way from town saw any plant or trowel in her hand to substantiate her story about going to her baby's grave. Furthermore, instead of entering the gate to the cemetery she had followed the hidden lane behind the wall.

The moderator, before he closed his rebuttal article, made one more incriminating statement to "stand for ages" and at the same time cast light on his own personality. He concluded his defense of the church's action cryptically: ". . . and on the same night she was found under suspicious circumstances in the privy – she was fond of spouting Byron, Moore and Shakespeare." [6] Whatever Mary's guilt, it was quite plain that Ned Buntline had escaped from soil where youth admired Byron and Moore, but where age was as yet unready for the *South-Western Literary Journal.*

While the newspapers gloated over the sensational story, Ned boarded the train for New York as he had planned. The *Spirit of the Times* commissioned him to represent them as a New York correspondent, to write "a letter" to the Philadelphians on anything that interested him. His meeting with Lewis Gaylord

Clark and the literati was the important thing ahead of him, however.

From the ferry on the Hudson the city appeared to be a low flat tongue of land sticking out into the water between the Brooklyn highlands and the Palisades. Ships' masts at the docks towered above steep-roofed houses. The bay was alive with steamboats, sailing vessels, and transports outfitting for Mexico. Here Ned felt the war excitement he had not noticed in Philadelphia.

New York had changed since Buntline was there after his resignation from the navy. Now a mature man of twenty-three, short, wise, and cocky, he considered himself a veteran. Confidently he strutted up the street, lame as he was, swinging his cane with the swagger of the seventeenth-century musketeer, a redheaded D'Artagnan come to the big city to earn fame and fortune with Lewis Gaylord Clark. Yes, Ned had read and enjoyed Dumas's recent historical novel – the talk of both hemispheres – and he stared boldly at every stranger as a possible antagonist. The Western man was prepared to fight by the code at the drop of a hat if anyone insulted him.

New York's Battery looked much the same as it had when Ned first saw it as a boy midshipman. Spacious walks, green grass, and shrubs invited idlers. A tempting bridge led out to Castle Garden. From the Battery, Broadway stretched along the ridge between the East and Hudson rivers. Uptown, new monster hotels – some with a hundred "parlors" [7] – accommodated guests. Fulton Street ferryboats, charging one cent a ride,[8] still splashed across to Brooklyn. The coast over there where Ned had landed his crew after being almost drowned nine years before was now unrecognizable.

The favorite resort of beauty and fashion, and also of gay duel-sensitive dandies, was Broadway. On the corner of Fifth Avenue and Ninth Street a three-story mansion situated on a small lawn behind an iron fence was famous as the Brevoort Hotel – alleged scene of a masked ball from which a merrymaker dressed as Lalla

Rookh eloped before morning. Ned knew all about masked balls and also Lalla Rookh. He heard that New York banned masked balls after this indiscretion.

Ned registered at the Franklin House with the air of a conqueror and then limped over to meet Lewis Gaylord Clark. In the *Knickerbocker* office at his desk sat the great editor, distinguished looking in white stock and black tie, a ruff of whiskers surrounding his smooth-shaven face. Ned swaggered into "the presence," looked jauntily into Clark's kindly eyes, and felt his own brash assurance waver. The great man was fifteen years his senior, appeared dreamy, abstract. The spirits of James Fenimore Cooper and Washington Irving pervaded the office, and the stocky sailor boy with a desire to display his marksmanship seemed out of place. Clark's letters had been cordial. Ned knew him to be interested in sports as well as in belles-lettres, but he found the great man's personality cold. The sailor boy had plenty to tell but he got no encouragement. Clark's aristocratic reserve paralyzed Ned's tongue. The conversation became strained, stilted, but scrupulously polite.

Soon other men sauntered into the sanctum, removing gray stovepipe hats with elegant flourishes – Charles Elliott, the artist; Lieutenant Dick Meade and his brother George Gordon Meade, who was making a topographical map of New York Harbor. The Meades, both wealthy young men from Philadelphia, seemed upset about the war. They complained habitually and showed only polite interest in Ned and his adventures. Charles Elliott had just completed a portrait of James Fenimore Cooper. He wanted to discuss his own work and was not impressed by a small-fry writer from the West like Ned. Then a tall figure filled the door. William T. Porter stood six feet four inches in low-heeled boots. The greatest sports editor of his age, he published the New York *Spirit of the Times*, an outdoor paper very different from the Philadelphia sheet of the same name. With him stood a shy young man, a newcomer to New York [9] like Ned himself and, like Ned, a man who hoped to be a writer some day. Porter introduced Dr. Alban Payne. The young man bowed formally and spoke with a soft Virginia drawl.

Then another bewhiskered gentleman stepped into the room, an eccentric chap with a shepherd's check shawl draped over one shoulder of his frock coat. Obviously timid but self-consciously aggressive, apparently on the lookout for an affront, the kind of man to be fanatic over the code duello, Henry W. Herbert was known to literary people as "Frank Forester." His mustache, too big for his face, might have graced one of Sir Walter Scott's staghounds. His dreamy eyes bespoke both absent-mindedness and egotism. He spoke with a clipped British accent and everyone recognized him as the one Englishman from whom all American sportsmen might learn the etiquette of the chase. Ned had a yen for sporting stories but this formal fellow antagonized him. What a target for his gun on the field of honor!

Someone suggested drinks and luncheon – a capital idea. The men sauntered out and lined up along a bar. Ned watched the barkeeper mix sherry cobblers, an Eastern equivalent of mint juleps except that wine instead of bourbon was poured onto the chipped ice, and an orange peel instead of mint leaves garnished the goblet. Porter towered over all the line and to him everyone aimed his remarks and banter. Even Clark became insignificant before Porter in a group of men. Known as "York's tall son," Porter was a recognized authority on all forms of sport. No editor of his time had so many records and anecdotes on his tongue's end. Ardent readers once speculated on a horse of the future that might run a mile a minute. Porter put them in their place. "Such a feat is impossible," he replied, "for it would require a horse to have a stride of 90 feet, and perform it once in every second.[10]

Ned noticed an intimacy between Porter and Herbert – a weak eccentric drawn to a strong character. He should have sensed that "Frank Forester" did not take criticism with good grace. A sensitive, proud fellow, Forester liked to pose in his shawl as a man of mystery, to be pointed out as an English nobleman. There was really much similarity of taste and temperament between Ned and Frank – too much for friendship's sake – and it was plain that Ned, shooting man from the West, faced the antagonist of his heart's desire. Had Forester listened, Ned could have told him about deep-sea fishing in Florida, green turtle catching, duck shooting in the Everglades, and a lucky shot that killed a record jaguar on Key Largo, but the two men did not reach such common ground. Ned was already prejudiced against Britishers, and Forester fanned his resentment.

At table with his new acquaintances, tough little Ned found himself outclassed. These men all talked in the leisurely language of Pope and Addison. They quoted lines of Shakespeare and Milton to express every idea. Ned had delighted in displaying his erudition in Nashville, but here in New York these men made him uncomfortable. At last Lewis Gaylord Clark, with a host's consideration, called on Ned to enter the conversation, tell a story from his adventurous past. All eyes turned toward Buntline's tousled red head.

Ned assumed the role of a navy man and told a dialect story about a French commander's "leetle breeg" that was captured by "ze John Bull natione." The British man-of-war, according to the story, took the Frenchman's cargo of brandy and then had the effrontery to offer the defeated captain a drink of it. Shortly thereafter, the victorious British man-of-war met an American ship of the line that captured her. The French prisoner, now a freeman again, turned politely to his erstwhile British captor and said, "Captain, drink a leetle of *my* brandy. It will cheer you up." The men laughed politely at the story as Ned told it and he felt that it had been a success, though a tasteless one. He did not notice Frank Forester's irritation. The party soon broke up. Ned had felt at ease only with Alban Payne. At parting, Ned asked if the Virginian knew General Walker K. Armistead, his old commander in the Seminole War. Then with a grand manner Ned handed the Southerner a card, saying, "Should you ever need a friend, call on E. Z. C. Judson, and your draft shall be honored." Alban Payne did not know then, nor later in a lifelong friendship, how near Ned was to insolvency and that his connection with Armistead was distant, to say the least.

Ned limped back to his hotel room a disappointed but still hopeful D'Artagnan. With pen and paper he began his letter to the Philadelphia *Spirit of the Times.* Down on the street the shouts of itinerant hucksters mingled with the rattle of their wagons. Ned wrote for his "letter" that Porter of the *Spirit* had been "very kind," and that he, Judson, "met Knick, Mrs. Knick and the little Knicks." Obviously he had regained his cockiness, but the briefness and finality in his letter indicated that the friendship with New York's literati was over. Ned devoted the rest of his space to conditions in the city. The hotels, he said, were "chock-full" of sailors and soldiers bound for the war in Mexico. "What the meandering brooklet is to the broad and noble Mississippi with its floating cities, so is our Chestnut street to Broadway."[11] But in spite of the greater size of New York Ned found some civic improvements less advanced than in the Quaker City. Manhattan had been slow to supply running water. At Forty-second Street a great reservoir had been constructed, but some residents still hesitated to use the water that came to their houses in wooden pipes. They preferred to run into the street and purchase water in buckets or pitchers when the water-wagon's bell announced its approach. Milk was also sold by dippers from wagons.

Ned finished his article, folded it for the post, and went to the hotel office. The city abounded in places to amuse out-of-town people, and Ned seems to have forgotten his earlier relish for fighting his way to fame. Certainly he did not know that Frank Forester bore him a grudge and was planning revenge. Ned decided to spend his first evening in Niblo's Garden, then write a story about it for the Philadelphia paper.

Horse-drawn busses clumped up and down Broadway. The fare was a "York shilling" and passengers sat facing one another in two rows, bumping, jostling, talking about husbands and sons sailing to Mexico. Niblo's Garden proved to be an amusement park and theater. The name would stick in Ned's mind for years. How strange it would be to compare the Niblo's of 1846, the hedges and fountains before the playhouse,[12] with the stage on which Ned himself appeared with Buffalo Bill almost thirty years later!

Back at his hotel, Ned was busily engaged in writing up his evening at Niblo's when a knock at the door made him lay down his pen and jump to his feet. A messenger presented him with a letter, and Ned broke the seals curiously to discover that Frank Forester's name was signed to the message. In ornate language Buntline read the Englishman's irate note:

> If Lieutenant Judson thinks Englishmen need *brandy* to make them brave, he could be convinced to the contrary by naming a friend to arrange preliminaries. . . .[13]

Ned did not finish. He hobbled over to the *Spirit of the Times* office, where Porter, like a great Dane beside the feisty red-headed Judson, read the note and grinned. He remembered how Forester had flushed with rage long ago when Lewis Gaylord Clark had turned down an article of his for *Knickerbocker*. In a few minutes the British sports writer walked in and Porter looked down on him with a kindly smile. The big American had a laughing way that soothed the touchy Forester. Buntline laughed too and explained that he had meant no insult—he had told the "brandy story" on account of the humor in the broken French. The three men went out and forgot the incident in a friendly glass, but the literary gamecock from the West was not happy. Culture had cowed him for the nonce.

During the days that followed Ned found it difficult to write interesting material for his "letter." The city had many historic places, but Ned was not a reporter. He was a writer of stories, preferably in the first person singular. Around Trinity Church he found a treasure house of historical tales. Beside graves of quaint burghers buried a hundred years ago modern heroes lay under the cool green grass. Here was the grave of Captain James Lawrence whose heroic "Don't give up the ship" was the kind of slogan Ned loved. Buntline had heard these words repeated in fun between decks during many a storm at sea. In Trinity churchyard, too, lay a slab dedicated to Charlotte Temple, heroine of one of the first books of historical fiction written in America. The author, Susanna Rawson, did not claim that the story was true, but an alert sexton had placed the gravestone, and people accepted Charlotte's fate as a good moral lesson for innocent young women. Ned himself had played the sexton's game of passing off historical fiction as fact and the technique had been successfully accepted by readers. He would keep it up. The grave of Alexander Hamilton was also in Trinity churchyard. Aaron Burr, who killed him, had died in New York only ten years ago. These men were real to Ned, thanks to his father. Ned could not remember a time when the Old Man had not stormed and orated about Whigs, Tories, and Federalists. Burr was a little whiffet of a man, like Ned himself, and also one with bright eyes for pretty girls. Burr's house was pointed out to curious tourists. The old brick building with dormer windows appeared dingy and deserted—no longer in the residential section.

Ned wrote a poem about Aaron Burr. In his letter to the *Times* in Philadelphia he discussed another character, John Jacob Astor, aged eighty-three. The immigrant boy who had made a vast fortune in the fur trade and also in New York real estate was in better health than generally thought, Ned reported. Some people, he said, believed that the ancient millionaire would never die. Instead he would "dry up and blow away." [14] Ned must have realized that his "letters" would not be continued long, but better news was hard to find.

Ned tried next to interest his Philadelphia readers in the "electric telegraph," a vastly new and unfathomable force that might change all civilization. Rogues and highwaymen, he reported, would no longer be able to escape; a warning could be clicked down the road faster than they could gallop. "I wonder," he concluded, "if we will not have *conversation wires* before long, instead of being obliged to send written communications. I believe it, piously I do!" [15] No one questioned Ned's observations, but it is plain that he was desperate for something to write about.

How did the others make a living at it: by pirating from one another and following a pattern? Edgar Allan Poe had written a great crime story, "The Mystery of Marie Rogêt," immediately after a charming cigar salesgirl, Mary Rogers, had been murdered at the St. Nicholas Hotel in 1842. Poe, with his reputation and literary skill, had marshaled all the clues and solved the mystery, but the police found no help in his deductions. Ned remembered that "Professor" Ingraham had written one of his "nouvellettes" about *La Bonita Cigarera; or, The Beautiful Cigar-Vender: A Tale of New York*, and it had proved so popular that he had written a sequel a year later. Poe, too, had followed his story with another, "The Murders in the Rue Morgue." Impossible realism was what the people wanted, it seemed, but Ned hesitated to debase himself. He would struggle along with the "letter."

One day Ned saw a familiar name in the papers. Francis Key Murray was leaving the city, transporting a regiment to Mexico. Ned remembered him as the midshipman [16] who, with but eleven invalids, had tried to help defend the settlers at Indian Key in Florida. A note of despair crept into Ned's next poem, written while other young men sailed away to war:

A feeble form, sore crippled too,
Alone has kept me back,
But were I there—*I'd do my do,*
Or die upon the track! [17]

In time Ned would say, and perhaps believe, that he fought in the Mexican War and received some of his wounds storming the Halls of Montezuma, but in the fall of 1846 he left New York quietly in civilian clothes. His own great expectations had come to naught. His old contributor, J. Ross Browne, was being hailed as the author of a great book *Etchings of a Whaling Cruise*—better than Dana's *Two Years Before the Mast,* critics said,[18] for Dana merely described a sea voyage while Browne added to his description a plea for better working conditions for sailors. Ned read, too, that his own father had found a publisher for *The Probe.* Everyone was succeeding but Ned Buntline, and he was not one to submit to fate without a desperate act.

XI

The Hub: 1847

NED'S REASON for going to Boston in 1847 seems obvious. Massachusetts was becoming the literary capital of America. An editor named Hawthorne, an essayist named Emerson, and two poets, John Greenleaf Whittier and Henry Wadsworth Longfellow, attracted readers throughout the United States. Moreover, publishers in the Hub were specializing profitably in "shilling shockers," and Ned had made a decision. Once he had wanted to write lasting literature. That dream had now faded. Next he would have preferred to write sporting stories, but he could not compete with William T. Porter and Frank Forester. Lewis Gaylord Clark, ruler of American belles-lettres, had offered scant encouragement. Good writing seemed to be a rich man's pastime. Cooper and Irving were both well-to-do. Amelia Welby, with a wealthy husband, published her own poems in an upholstered gift edition that was highly praised. Expensive embossed leather binding seemed more important than good text. Over fifty authors had embellished their work with these so-called gift editions this year.[1] Impecunious writers like Ned seemed doomed.

But in New York he had seen something that opened his eyes. Reading rooms were crowded with poorly dressed people who smelled, twisted, squirmed, scratched, and squinted at tattered, cheaply printed books. These new readers were not critical, but they were numerous. Their dimes and quarters counted.

Money paid for books had increased 60 per cent between 1830 and 1840. It promised to increase over 100 per cent in the present decade.[2] The common man was coming to the top. In upstate New York, farm laborers were waging an anti-rent war against landlords. Lippard, Neal, and Ingraham had found it popular to praise the poor and ridicule the rich. They were selling to this new market and doing well. Lewis Gaylord Clark and his companions with their flowing eighteenth-century conversation already belonged to the past.

Ned Buntline, at the age of twenty-four, made up his mind to write for the masses. In New York the Harper brothers had already become wealthy catering to the new trend. They had published some of Professor Ingraham's books. The senior member of the firm, James Harper, could be seen any day driving a fast team of trotters down the avenue. He had been elected mayor of New York in 1844. Surely shilling shockers were a legitimate field for a young writer. The "professor" had knocked off seven novels in 1843, eighteen in 1844, twenty-six in 1845, eleven in 1846, and at least one a month so far in 1847. All but seven of these had been published in Boston. Obviously the Hub was the gateway to this profitable field of literature.

In Boston Ned found several publishing houses printing sensational literature in booklets and also in weekly magazines. He presented his card first at the Jones Publishing House, printers of *Star Spangled Banner*, a weekly costing a "bit." Next he called at the Gleason Publishing Hall, which issued another weekly, *Flag of Our Union*. Ned was unable to interest these publishers in his authorship. Both firms had all the material they wanted.

Boston, like New York, pulsed with war preparations. Ned went down the bay to Quincy, an ancient hamlet perched on a granite headland above salt marshes. Sea breezes stroked the tall grass and ruffled the sparkling blue waterways. In the *Quincy Patriot* office Ned sold a story, his rattling good naval yarn,

"A Dream Not a Dream." [3] It had been printed in *Knickerbocker* last September, but what of that? This second printing seemed to change Ned's luck. The Jones Publishing House had recently declined Ned's work; now they accepted for *Star Spangled Banner* his "Race on the Bahama Banks," a revision of the story *Knickerbocker* had published in March 1845. With this encouragement Buntline sat down to write popular fiction, his initial nouvellette, *The Last Days of Calleo; or, the Doomed City of Sin.* Jones accepted this too,[4] and announced it as a seventy-five-dollar prize tale. The story proved popular. Soldiers bought copies to carry in their knapsacks onto transports in Boston Harbor. Neatly tucked between blankets, the paperbacks sailed away in clouds of saluting cannon smoke while newspapers speculated on the troops' possible landing places in Mexico – Tampico, Vera Cruz, Matamoros, or somewhere in Texas?

Ned made the most of his success. A month later the great house of Gleason announced that their *Flag of Our Union* was publishing a one-hundred-dollar tale by Ned Buntline entitled *The King of the Sea: A Tale of the Fearless and Free.*[5] Ned dedicated the story to old shipmates and friends in the United States Navy. Perhaps this might interest military-minded youths who were buying reading material for long transport trips to Mexico. The hundred-page romance was written with the stylistic realism of Defoe. Ned's impossible characters indicate that he may have read Mrs. Rawson's *Charlotte Temple* while searching for news in New York. In any event he assured the reader that the story was founded on fact.

Lewis Gaylord Clark capped the climax of Ned's minor publishing achievement by printing two more Buntline stories in *Knickerbocker*. "A Visit to Lafitte" appeared in March, and in the April issue Clark printed "Running the Blockade in the Last War" ahead of a story on the Oregon Trail by a new writer who signed his name Francis Parkman. Ned had suddenly become a literary man. One reviewer in the *Boston Daily Times* said of *The King of the Sea:* "By writing such a story Ned Buntline has wrote himself into everlasting fame, and Mr. Gleason does well in employing such writers."[6] Trashy as the story sounds to modern readers, it was printed and reprinted over and over until 1860, and British publishers pirated the text without even printing the author's name on the title page.

Ned followed his successful *King of the Sea* with a smaller work entitled *The Queen of the Sea; or, Our Lady of the Ocean: A Tale of Love, Strife & Chivalry*. In these books a reader had no trouble distinguishing the villains from the hero and heroine. Ned gave his bad people names with guttural consonants and vowels that hissed – Luigi, Lord Hawkhurst. The "Lord" alone was enough to designate a despicable character to Buntline readers. A name like "Don Benito" might be assumed to characterize a hero, and the Neds and Edwards were consistently good fellows. Buntline also understood that his readers would be attracted by short chapters. His bombast was fully equal to Ingraham's worst. In *The King of the Sea* Ned had his villain declaim:

> Go bid the mad ocean be calm, while the wild hurricane careers over its rushing waters; go chain the red lightning of high heaven; go curb and dam up the boiling lava which rolls down Elia's rocky sides, but do not stay the course of my revenge.[7]

Within a week of the publication of *The King of the Sea* Gleason accepted another Buntline nouvellette entitled *Love's Desperation; or, The President's Only Daughter: A Romance of Reality*, but the firm did not pay $100 for it and Ned seems to have been disgruntled. He went at once to the H. L. Williams Company – Ingraham's publishers – and outlined a plan to the publisher. The details are obscure but they may be readily conjectured. Williams had noticed the success of Jones's weekly, *Star Spangled Banner*, and Gleason's *Flag of Our Union.* After talking with Ned he announced that his firm was starting a third weekly, *Flag of the Free*, featuring a new story by Buntline founded on incidents that had occurred in the recent battle of

The Novelette.

NUMBER 43.

CONTAINING THE STORY, COMPLETE, OF

THE RED REVENGER:

—OR,—

THE PIRATE KING OF THE FLORIDAS.

A TALE OF THE GULF AND ITS ISLANDS.

BY NED BUNTLINE.

Edward Z. C. Judson

ILLUSTRATED.

THE ATTEMPTED ASSASSINATION. [See page 21.]

[WRITTEN EXPRESSLY FOR THIS ESTABLISHMENT, AND COPYRIGHT SECURED ACCORDING TO LAW.]

OFFICE AMERICAN UNION, FLAG OF OUR UNION, AND DOLLAR MONTHLY.
No. 63 CONGRESS STREET, BOSTON, MASS.

Courtesy of the Boston Athenaeum

One of Buntline's early triumphs in the shilling shocker field

Buena Vista.[8] Obviously Ned had the publishers bidding against each other for his work. Four days later Gleason paid Ned $100 for a new story, *The Black Avenger of the Spanish Main; or, The Fiend of Blood: A Thrilling Tale of Buccaneer Times,* and then took another from him entitled *The Red Revenger; or, The Pirate King of the Floridas: A Romance of the Gulf and its Islands.*[9] Both stories were still being reprinted forty years later, and Mark Twain, in *The Adventures of Tom Sawyer,* had his hero dream of the day when he would come back to the Missouri village, stalk into church wearing a black velvet doublet and trunks, "his crime-rusted cutlass at his side . . . and hear with swelling ecstasy the whisperings, 'It's Tom Sawyer the Pirate! – the Black Avenger of the Spanish Main!' "[10]

Gleason published still another story that was apparently by Ned, although it did not bear his name. *The Nautilus; or, the American Privateer: A Tale of Land and Sea* was signed Frank Clewline. Several explanations may be surmised for this new pen name. Had Ned signed a contract under the Ned Buntline pseudonym and found it more profitable to write for others under another name, or did he feel that the name Ned Buntline was appearing too often in print? Or Frank Clewline might have been another writer taking advantage of Ned's popularity. Patent pseudonyms were used constantly by writers of cheap literature.

As Ned marked his success with Gleason, the rival Williams house that furnished the competition which had made him continued to advertise, from June 30 to October 10, Ned's promised story about Buena Vista – a timely nouvellette – while newspapers screamed about the great victory of Old Rough and Ready Taylor. Finances seem to have retarded the publishers, and when the Buena Vista story did appear it was published in New York by a reorganized Williams firm. Ned, in the meantime, profited by their advertising, and in September he prepared for Gleason a nouvellette on the Battle of Monterrey, not Buena Vista. With a two-column spread in the *Boston Daily Times* the publishers announced their fall list, stating that they were printing a million copies to fill the demand. Light literature had reached heights of popularity unknown by the classics. Later wars would stimulate similar publications – dime novels in the Civil War, Pocket Books in World War II. Ned's book on the Gleason list in 1847 was entitled *The Volunteer: or, The Maid of Monterrey.* The story began with:

> No preface, reader, nor apology here – this is a story of thrilling scenes, daring deeds and stirring times. We will leap the breast works of reserve, and at once dash into its merits, as did the brave warriors who led the way and won the day at Monterrey.

The story opened with a barbecue in Logan County, Kentucky, in July 1846. Volunteers were being recruited for the war. Ned introduced his reader to the background with sure language, for Ned knew whereof he wrote. Then, with a touch he always loved, he gave his hero the name of Blakey, the man who had defended Mary Porterfield. Ned's characters were typical of the shilling shockers. Any or all of them might have stepped straight from the pages of "Professor" Ingraham. His villain, Captain Gorin – note the guttural *G* – of the Texas Rangers, spied the unfortunate heroine and said:

> So it is indeed she. She whom once I loved as few can love – one whom I now hate as none can hate! Yes, Helen Vicars, Your parents scorned and reviled me – *me*, and now *they* are dead. You, too, shall die, You and yours. You shall know what it is to insult a *Gorin!* Twice have you escaped me – twice as by a miracle, but now I will not fail.

This story would be reprinted in 1852, 1860, 1863, and 1865. Ned Buntline, in a few short months, seemed to have established himself in the new field as firmly as "Professor" Ingraham. For Gleason he wrote another nouvellette, "*The Tempter and the Tempted*" – *A Tale of a Western Boarding School.* Three more were taken by a New York publishing firm. Ned also sold two poems, "The Star" and "A Sleeping Babe upon Its Mother's Bosom."

These poems and stories seem to have been the extent of Ned Buntline's participation in the Mexican War. Years afterward, as has been said, Ned claimed battle scars from this war. Stranger still, two veterans, Colonel John McArdle and Colonel Michael K. Bryan, both remembered serving in the same regiment with him. Another witness, Dr. William Sewell, reported seeing Ned at the same time acting as second in a duel near Quebec. The principal in this affair of honor was Dr. Alban Payne who, according to the story, got into an argument on a St. Lawrence River steamboat with some red-coated British officers. A few drinks set the Americans' tongues wagging about Andrew Jackson's victory at New Orleans thirty-two years ago. Pistols were selected for weapons and the doctor won the passage at arms.[11] Strangely enough, Ned himself never wrote about this duel so the whole episode seems doubtful. Contemporary records do indicate that Ned moved out of the city, for the editors of the *Boston Daily Times* printed an acknowledgment of a box of smelt he sent them. The box may have contained something else besides fish – Canadian rye, perhaps, but that is pure conjecture. The editors merely said that they spent the afternoon consuming it and hoped themselves to visit "*that* fishing ground." [12] Ned also sent them a poem which attracted the eyes of a romantic-minded woman, and a duel royal of words ensued. Ned's opening thrust follows:

THINGS I'D LOVE

I'd love a little house,
  Upon a grassy hill,
Out in the country here
  Where everything is still;
I'd love a little chaise
  To drive to Boston in,
And for my comfort's sake
  I'd love a little "*tin.*"

II

I'd like a little fishing gear,
  A setting dog and gun,
I'd love a friend or two
  To help me think of fun,
And ev'ry now and then
  I'd like a glass of punch
To cheer our spirits up
  And settle down our lunch.

III

I'd like a little wife
  To comb my tangled hair
And wake me up at morn;
  And when I'd time to spare
I'd drive her up to town
  To see "the lions" there
And with her rosy cheeks
  To make the town girls stare.

IV

All these "*and nothin' else*,"
  My heart is craving for;
Though some were better off,
  I'd envy not their store.
To please a darling wife
  I'd "cut" the punch and wine
And let her love for me
  Make life almost divine.

V

I'd *never* make her work,
  She shouldn't mend my clothes,
Nor cook the food we ate,
  Nor need for other beaux
To take her out to ride,
  I'd be her "all in all"
And treat her like a queen
  If the baby didn't bawl
And she kept the critter clean!

Under a hedge—in the country. October 4th 1847

In the October 12 issue of the *Times* appeared an answer to Ned's poem. Entitled "Things You Might Have," it was signed "Laura Lovell":

Why don't you buy a house
  Upon a sunny hill,
Out in some lonely country place,
  So lovely and so still?
Why don't you have a pretty chaise
  To ride to Boston in?
You've got a gold mine in your head,
  Why wish you paltry tin?

But for the fishing gear,
  The dog and dangerous gun,
(Forebye the pleasant friend or two.)
  Dismiss them every one.
For winter's storms are coming soon,
  And by the quiet hearth,
There's many a purer, sweeter joy,
  Than in the halls of mirth.

Why don't you take a wife,
  To sooth you when you're sad;
With ever ready sympathy,
  To smile when you are glad?
What would she care for drives up town,
  Or "lions" any where?
So you were gentle as a lamb,
  Not savage as a bear?

Put by the social glass,
  Which mounts into one's head;
Cut punch and vulgar herbs *es-chew,*
  Your brains will earn your bread.
The cup that ne'er inebriates,
  Un-alcoholic tea,
A fire, a lamp, a pleasant book,
  These are the joys for me.

Your wife need never work,
Nor mend your worn-out clothes;
For you could write the poetry,
And she might write the prose.
If, as you say, you sometimes fear
Your thread of life is brief,
Why not, before another year,
Turn over – A *new leaf*.

Two days later Ned printed an answer "To Laura" in the *Times*, bemoaning the fact that his serious writing earned "so scant a sum to me 'twould scarcely buy my pony's grain" – a statement that undoubtedly reveals Ned's mental suffering. For a year he had been writing trash very successfully, but he was not happy. As a literary editor he had failed. He could not make a living writing good adventure stories. His blackmail paper – or Mary Porterfield – had almost got him hanged. Before surrendering to cheap fiction he planned one more useful experiment with his pen. Perhaps Lippard's recent marriage reminded Ned of his own erstwhile ambition to be a crusader. The Philadelphia reformer, poetic and original always, had celebrated a "natural wedding" under the dome of heaven, a rock in Wissahickon Gorge the altar. Ned wrote again "To Laura" through the *Times* and she replied with sympathetic rhyme on October 26, 1847, ending her seven stanzas:

But from this war of words, I know
I'd better have retreated;
Since, like poor little Mexico,
I'm sure to be defeated.

The identity of Laura Lovell may never be known, but shortly after her last poem was written, Ned arrived in New York with a young lady named Mary Gordon. He rented a room for her at the corner of Washington and Morris streets,[13] then set out to exploit the "gold mine in his head" – a last attempt to write above the trash level. He determined to join one of the moral crusades sweeping the country and add to it a few expert details that would make the best reformers take notice.

The change from adventure to moral-reform literature was conventional for the times, but Ned planned going the others one better. Lippard had used the shilling-shocker technique successfully in his crusade against the city fathers in Philadelphia. More recently, J. H. Ingraham had announced pompously that he had written enough nouvellettes about pirates, romantic Castilian maidens, bearded and becloaked Spanish dons. He meant to atone for his sanguinary episodes and call public attention to the evil that "menaces the stability of our institutions, and the very existence of our liberties."

With Mary Gordon safely ensconced in a room, Ned hunted up his old acquaintance Alban Payne, the alleged Quebec duelist, an ideal companion for the social study Ned had in mind. Together they would visit New York's most dangerous dives. A report written in nouvellette style, Ned believed, would surely be popular. Mary Gordon discovered that she owed a board bill before it occurred to her that she was deserted.

The most brutish part of the city, known as Five Points, furnished an ideal background for a reform story of the kind Ned Buntline planned. Foreigners had been coming to America in late years faster than houses could be built to accommodate them. Between 1840 and 1846 immigration increased from 84,000 to 300,000 annually. A potato famine in Ireland was apparently moving the Emerald Isle's entire population to New York. Ned heard people say over and over, "We must have Oregon and the Northwest to support these millions." He had helped shout this political rallying cry and it had helped elect Polk President. Many immigrants had gone to farms in the boundless West, but more remained in the slums of New York. Around Five Points old homes had been enlarged into tenements. Flimsy superstructures reached to the street across what had once been front yards. The spaces between houses were often so narrow that only small men and boys could pass through them. Guttersnipes, alley cats, and criminals knew obscure ways through tumbledown tenements, over sagging sheds, and under broken walls. In this thieves' rookery the smell of stale beer, dirty human bodies, and rotten boards permeated the atmosphere. Judson had learned that a battle royal was advertised in a dive notorious for cockpits, dogfights, and rat-killing exhibitions. Confidence men, gamblers, and bunko steerers were sure to patronize the performance.

Dr. Payne appeared eager to accompany Ned on his sociological investigation. Both armed themselves with pistols, and in the evening, after dark, they sauntered arm in arm into the area. With ostentatious nonchalance and stealthy sidelong glances from beneath their broad straw hats they watched dark hallways, scenes of past violence, murder, and desperate bestial fights. Both of them knew exactly what they were getting into. That was part of the fun — and of their service to society too, of course. At the prize ring the assembled rowdies did not seem to notice the two young men. Among Bowery toughs, who dressed well themselves at times, Buntline and Payne were not conspicuous. But one group of ruffians singled them out as strangers and whispered among themselves. At last the performance ended and the crowd jostled out into the dark street. Judson and Payne linked arms, and, holding their pistols ready but concealed in their pockets, they walked happily away. At a street intersection ahead they saw suspicious loungers. Had the fellows come around ahead by the devious labyrinth of alleys? "When within fifteen feet of them," Payne wrote later, "the rascals made a rush at us. Simultaneously our pistols were fired, three men were seen to fall, and the rest scattered in every direction." [14] At Broadway the two friends felt that they were out of the danger zone. They separated, bidding one another good night.

Ned was more convinced than ever that he must write a great social work. His father's *Probe* had gone to a third edition. The zodiac sign was evidently right for reform, but two things kept

Ned from beginning at once. He was working on a potboiler[15] romance of the last revolution in Peru, to be called *The Virgin of the Sun*, and the memory of a young woman – perhaps Mary Gordon – haunted him.

> Why don't you take a wife,
> To sooth you when you're sad;
> With ever ready sympathy,
> To smile when you are glad?

A realist in his writing always, Ned discussed her in his book and the reader may judge why he deserted her. "O woman, woman!" he wrote, "when Heaven denied thy *arm* the strength which it gave to man, it gave a double quantity to thy tongue! Let me rather meet the blows of armed men, than listen to the words of woman in her anger."

Ned signed this book, like his earlier ones, "Ned Buntline, late of the U.S. Navy." Grudgingly he gave up sea tales. Before making the final decision he tried another book, his first to be bound in boards, containing many of his old yarns, entitled *Cruisings, Afloat and Ashore, from the Private Log of Ned Buntline.* The title sounded perilously similar to James Fenimore Cooper's recent book entitled *Cruisings Afloat and Ashore,* but in Ned's day this form was as common as "Reader" would be a hundred years later.[16] The volume contained 380 pages, yet could readily be slipped into a man's pocket. Compact as a brickbat, the little work was a compilation of many old Buntline stories retold with slight variations. It included "The Masquerade"; "The Smuggler" – the dream story that he had resold in Quincy; a new version of "The Captain's Pig"; the dialect story that had elicited Frank Forester's wrath; the "Race on the Bahama Banks" that he had already printed twice; and "Running the Blockade" – indeed, all of Ned's best sea stories. To them he added a few new poems, of which the most notable were "The March-Born" (on page 34 of this book) and "Who the De'il is Buntline?" Both extolled the importance of their subject. Perhaps Ned was consciously building up his name in the minds of the reading public. More likely he voiced the opinion of a sincere admirer. As the book went on the market, Levi Carroll Judson's *Probe* appeared in the bookstalls as a fourth edition – sly testimony to its popularity. True, the Old Man had reprinted the little volume at his own expense, so the complimentary words "Fourth Edition" were slightly misleading, but nevertheless the book was a moral publication which shamed Ned's superficial writings. Buntline dropped everything else to push his great social work to a quick conclusion. He had no publisher for his ambitious undertaking, but he was not a writer to be dismayed by minor details. As usual he had a plan, and he knew that it would work.

The Mysteries and Miseries of New York: 1848

I DISLIKE prefatory remarks [thus Buntline began what he expected would be his great work] but so singular is the work I have now to write, so strange its scenes and incidents, so various and peculiar the characters which I have to delineate, that I feel bound to tell the reader that, strange as all may be, it is drawn from *life*, heart-sickening, *too-real* life. Not one scene of vice or horror is given in the following pages which has not been enacted over and over again in this city, nor is there one character which has not its counterpart in our very midst. I have sought out and studied the reality of each person and scene which I portray. Accompanied by several kind and efficient police officers, whom, were it proper, I would gratefully name, I have visited every den of vice which is hereinafter described, and have chosen every character for this work during these visits. Therefore, though this book bears the title of a *novel*, it is written with the ink of truth and deserves the name of a *history* more than that of a *romance*.

This first of the famous five volumes which as yet had no publisher was entitled *The Mysteries and Miseries of New York: A Story of Real Life*, and dedicated to the reverend clergy "with a fervent hope that they may see and remedy the evils which it describes." Buntline did not pretend that his book's title was original. Frankly it was patterned after Eugène Sue's *Mysteries of Paris.*[1]

Ned knew that he could never afford to publish the whole

story he had in mind, but he felt sure that if he printed the first installment of a continued story at his own expense, readers would clamor for more and thus solve his financial problem. To make assurance triply sure he built up horrendous suspense in not one, but three separate, contemporary stories: Francis, a gangster, working as secretary to a benevolent old gentleman in order to gain his confidence and rob him; Charlie Meadows, a merchant's clerk, being lured into debt by roulette and trying to save himself, first by embezzlement, then by sacrificing his sister, and finally by committing murder to satisfy the whims of his gambler creditors; and lastly, a poor sewing girl, Angelina – typical Buntline name for a heroine – dying of tuberculosis while being pursued by a wealthy man about town. Angelina had many narrow escapes, and was always rescued at the last moment by Big Lize, a pious prostitute, full of sermons against her own depravity. Admittedly a panel thief by profession, Lize's business was to entice unsuspecting men into her crib, where a sliding panel allowed entrance for accomplices who robbed them. Buntline made this harlot a rollicking puritan whose big fists knocked down every man who approached to "insult her."

The first of the three stories in *The Mysteries and Miseries of New York* reached a desperate crisis at the end of the first chapter. Only death or ruin for the characters seemed possible. Buntline began the second chapter with his second story, ran his characters to the verge of destruction, and then began with the third. Part I came to an end with the three strands of his narrative badly frayed and all in the air.

The most remarkable thing about the story was a poem Ned called the "Sewing Girl's Song" which obviously imitated Thomas Hood's "Song of the Shirt." Ned had sold the poem to the *Boston Times* a year before, but he used it again here as filler. No one seems to have objected to the poem's similarity to Hood's, nor had anyone complained years before when Ned followed

Hood's Own with *Buntline's Own.* It was an age of few copyrights.

Another remarkable feature in the first volume of *The Mysteries and Miseries of New York* was a glossary of "flash terms" used, the author said, by immigrants (mainly English), thieves, and robbers. Readers were warned that an understanding of these words would be necessary for a proper appreciation of the text. Among the "flash terms" were:

Bender — To go upon a spree.
Blarney — An Irishman's small-talk.
Blow-out — A feast, or a spree.
Chum — A comrade — friend, used by women and thieves to designate their companions.
Coppers — Officers of the police; also termed "pigs," "nabs," etc.
Dust — Slang term for money. [This was a year before the California gold rush.]
Flash — The language of thieves.
Jug — The prison.
Jimmy — A crowbar.
Kicking the bucket — To die.
Kid — A young or little thief.
Lifting — Stealing.
Lark — A cockney's name for a spree.
Mountain-dew — Scotch whiskey.
Pal — An assistant to a thief.
Peach — To tell.
Patter — To talk.
Swell — A gentleman.
Square — Honest. To live on the square, is to quit thieving.
Sponge — A hanger-on, who imbibes all that he can get, and pays for nothing.
Spunk — Courage; derived from the original Yankee.
Swag — Plunder or booty.
Swig — A drink of liquor.
Swell-head — A bloated drunkard.
Spot — To spot is to recognize — to mark.

Buntline promised to list and explain more terms in the next number.

This first issue, Part I, of *The Mysteries and Miseries of New York* appeared early in January 1848, with paper covers, and sold for twenty-five cents. The author assured all readers that better and more exciting parts were to come, but did not add that his money for printing was exhausted.

Ned watched the sales of his reform publication with more than common satisfaction. Small in format, it could be carried in a coat pocket. Hundreds of soldiers coming back from Mexico bought the booklet. So did railroad travelers who had found reading impossible on stagecoaches. People wanted cheap literature to read and then throw away. *The Mysteries and Miseries of New York* filled the requirements. A commercial publisher, Berford & Company, noted the publication's success and made Ned an offer. Buntline accepted and thus solved his financial problem – an old Buntline device dating back to "The Captain's Pig."

Ned felt good. Full of mischief and sherry cobblers, he mingled with soldiers just back from Mexico in formal shakos and striped trousers. One day he met an old friend, Lieutenant Potter, who was glad to be home again. The two drank together and planned a practical joke. Potter offered to introduce Ned to a young lady of his acquaintance, Annie Abigail Bennett – a real-life heroine like his Angelina, except that Annie had money. Ned beamed, suggested that he dress in cloak and sword. His curled red mustache and broad hat with an ostrich feather made him look like a Spanish grandee, his Nashville role. Potter agreed to introduce him as a Castilian count.

Young Annie was thrilled. British by birth, she had come with her father, Francis Bennett, to New York when five years old. Frugal old-country people, the Bennetts accumulated a small competence in the United States, including a residence at 16 Abingdon Place. Annie fell in love with the romantic and successful writer. On January 14 the second installment of the *Mysteries* appeared, and on January 20 Ned married the Bennett girl.[2] Money began to roll in. The *Mysteries* eventually sold 100,000 copies.[3] Reprints and translations appeared in England, France, and Denmark. Publicity stimulated sales of Ned's earlier work. *The King of the Sea, The Queen of the Sea, The Red Revenger*, and *Cruisings, Afloat and Ashore* all went into second editions.

Ned moved into his father-in-law's house. A study was set aside for the great man's exclusive use. Ned put his sword in a corner of the room, laid a dagger on his writing desk, hung pistols on the wall, and told his new family that his life was in constant danger. The villainous thieves and gamblers he was exposing were constantly after him, Ned said. This was the price a man must pay in the struggle against vice.

The Bennetts acquiesced. American customs were new to them, and Ned was their first son-in-law. Ned, on his part, forgot his aversion to Britishers. He proudly proclaimed the nuptials to his literary friends. To the editor of the *New York Mirror* he sent "a very elegant box of wedding cake."[4] Newspapers from Boston to the Mississippi announced the marital union. Ned Buntline had indeed become a prominent literary man.

Part II of the *Mysteries* contained domestic scenes much more intense than the first, with anxiety and suspense increased. Ned always put the realism of his own life into his writing. He had an avowed antipathy for extended explanatory prefaces, but he commenced with a long one glamorizing his heroics against villainous gamblers. He also indulged in his old confidence trick of taking the reader into partnership in the exciting game of publishing. He wrote:

> The unexampled and heart-cheering success of the first part of this work has given its author a hope that in the second, he will not fail to be equally pleasing to the readers of the first.
>
> He has now the satisfaction of knowing that his labors are appre-

ciated not only by the good, but by the very villains whom he had *commenced* to lash; for the first have cheered him by an unexpected and unparalled [*sic*] patronage; the second have shown by their threats, anonymous letters &c., that they *feel* the *truth* which he has uttered.

And one word of consolation to these last. The writer is one who can neither be bribed from his duty, or frightened from his course. He depends upon that Being for protection, who has before-time saved him from the assassin's hand; and whose power has upheld him in perils which he cares not now to allude to [the Porterfield affair?], but which were incurred in performing a *duty* like that in which he is now engaged. To those who may have thought that fair words and bright promises might deter us from throwing our Drummond light on their dark deeds we can only say—you are mistaken in our character. We cannot be bought.

To those who have threatened us—we have no reply, save that we are ever on the look-out for them, and are not at all principled against destroying snakes or mad-dogs, when they attempt to bite us. We have commenced *gently* with the gamblers and thieves—the future pages will show wether [*sic*] their threats will make us touch them less lightly.

One word to some of our discerning and talented city critics. Some of you in your kind reviews of my first number have expressed an opinion that some of its scenes are over-wrought and untrue. This is not so. I pledge myself, if you will take the trouble to go with me, to show you an original, or counterpart for every scene which I have described.[5]

This habit of Buntline's was fixed—always he told the reader that his story was going to be true, and then told a whopper that nobody could believe. Ned also adopted the practice of publishing letters written by readers. They liked to see their names in print, to express themselves. Sales mounted. Often Ned wrote the letters himself and then answered them. His lamp burned hours past midnight. Annie learned the patience of a writer's wife. Readers a hundred years later know that no gambler or bunko steerer wrote an anonymous or threatening letter to a man whose worst indictment against him was portrayed in Part II of *The Mysteries and Miseries of New York.* A fair sample of Buntline's description of the gambling villain pursuing the poor sewing girl, Angelina, follows:

"The kind gentleman said he'd be here to take tea with us!"

"Oh, mother, do not ask him here. Indeed he means some dreadful wrong. He would not be so generous to us if he did not expect some return."

"Tush! Child you are always so suspicious. Directly you'll begin to think that *I'd* conspire to wrong you."

"Oh, no, dear mother!" cried the young girl, bursting into tears, and throwing her thin arms around her neck, "Do not say so, dear mother, I know you well, but I cannot drive from my brain, the memory of that dreadful night, and the connection which this man had with it."

"But, child, he has said that he drank too much wine on that night; that he did not know what he was doing. He certainly apologized very handsomely."

"Yes, mother but— "

The young girl's reply was cut short, by a rap at the door, and while the mother hastened to open it, Angelina hurried into the bed-room, and closed the door.

"Ah, good evening, madam. Hope you're well, *very* well! where is your beautiful daughter, and how *is* she?" said Mr. Gus. Livingston [note the use of gutturals and hissing consonants in the name of the villain], in a free and easy manner, as he entered.

"Well—I do declare. Why the child has gone and hid herself in the bed-room. She is *so* timid, sir; you must forgive her, for it is natural to the poor child. I was so once."

Livingston bit his lip with vexation, but took the chair which the old lady placed near the stove for him, and said:

"Your daughter has no occasion to fear me. I'm sure she never had a truer friend than myself."

"I know it, sir, indeed I do.". . .

The mother went into the bed-room, and closed the door after her, while Gus remained in his chair, carelessly whistling over an air, from some opera or other.

It was several minutes before the bed-room door opened again. . . .

When Angelina entered, her face was pale as Parian marble; her eyes red with weeping; but when she met the burning glance of the libertine fixed upon her beautiful, though fast withering form, the poor girl's cheeks were in a moment covered with blushes. Her pure heart seemed instinctively to read his designs; her nature caused her very soul to close against, and shrink from him, as doth the leaf of the sensitive-plant, when touched by the rude hand of man.

He arose, and reaching out his hand, said, in a low and respectful tone:

"I had hoped that you would have forgiven my rudeness before now, Miss. Indeed, it makes me very unhappy to know that you are angry with me."

She did not take his hand, but in a faltering voice, replied:

"I am not angry with you, sir. I have forgiven you, I hope God has." [Buntline made his heroine superior to the Deity!]

"Thank you, I shall feel more happy now, but not, if you ever treat me with so much coldness."

"It is better, sir," replied the young girl, in a firmer tone – "for you know how different are our situations. We never can be intimate. You are a gentleman, a rich one, I suppose. You know that I am a poor, uneducated sewing-girl."

"You need be so no longer. You are too delicate and beautiful for such a life. . . . Yes, dear girl; I love you, and will make you mine!"

"How?" and as the young creature asked that question, she fixed her clear blue eyes on his, with an expression which would read every thought in his heart.

He could not stand that look. His eye fell beneath it, and he blushed up to the very temples while he hesitated to answer.

She noted this, and exclaimed.

"I *knew* it was so! You have sought me, but to destroy me, as the hunter seeks the game!"

"Oh, no, dear girl, you wrong me! I did not understand your question!"

"Then hear it plainly. Would you marry me – would you link yourself to me by the laws of God and man?"

"Yes – that is, as soon as I can. I am so situated with my parents that – "

"Oh, sir, you need make no excuses. Your hesitation in answering me would be proof, if nothing else occurred, of your intentions. But did you really wish and intend to marry me, you *could* not."

"Could not? Why, my beautiful – oh, why?

"Because, sir, *I do not love you.* No man living ever can claim my hand, who does not possess my heart; no, not were he possessed of uncounted gold, and I had to work the hand which I refused him, to the bare bones."

"Oh, do not speak so. You must—you *shall* be mine!!"

"Never, sir, *never!*" replied the young girl, proudly and firmly. "If it is this that has caused your bounty to my poor mother, take it back. We can return to our cellar, we can work, and earn enough to keep us alive."

"Foolish girl, you know not what you refuse. Beware how you push my love from you, for you can be made to feel that a slighted lover can become a bitter enemy."

"I care not, sir. My trust is in God! You can not harm me, for He, the All-powerful, is my protector!"

"Girl, you seem determined to defy me. Do you not know that I can go to your employers, whom I know, and cut you off from work?"[6]

And so on. Ned repeated all the clichés of the 1840's. What gambler could get very angry over such an exposure! With this moral lesson finished, Ned picked up the other strands of his story and developed them. Finally he became more explicit about the locations of gambling houses, thus leading curious readers to the climax of his righteous exposure:

The house where this scene is laid is not a mile from Astor Place. Within one of those large and elegant houses which front on — street; in the splendidly furnished sitting-room are four persons. Let me introduce you to Montague Fitz Lawrence and three members of his family, his wife and two sons. He has a daughter, but she is at boarding school. Mr. Fitz Lawrence is rich, *very* rich, for he has left off business and now lives in style. His servants are all in livery—he keeps a fine carriage, and each of his sons drive a very fast team for themselves. They are educated—that is educated for city-life. They know Pat Hisen and his set, are members of *the* club, where ere long we will see them. They can walk down Broadway and tell you the name of every woman (not lady) that they meet; they can play a fine game of billiards, smoke, drink, and swear quite *elegantly*, or, as I once heard a romantic young lady say, "divinely."[7]

Ned Buntline, who professed to hate gentlemen, who had fought ten duels in the navy to establish his right to mess with aristocrats, found thousands of readers in New York who applauded these sentiments. Obviously he was not baiting gamblers. He was writing for unhappy country boys and girls, bewildered in the big city. His audience grew with the second volume. Buntline had found something that a great many people wanted. Suppose he diverted this following into political channels, welded his readers into a great secret organization, a "mystery" like the Masons his father had admired and defended!

More than one man in the high places of New York saw the possible danger ahead. Industrialism and immigration were changing America fast. A class revolution of workers might upset all property owners. Then, again, this excitable and fast-growing population might become hysterical about slavery. Emotions would thus find an outlet in a different kind of civil war. Temperance also held the interest of zealots. The three issues – nativism, temperance, abolition – seemed to hang in the balance vying for popular favor. In Europe an agitation for democracy was beginning to bubble. Men in darkened rooms and beer cellars discussed barricading the streets and overthrowing governments. Americans already had a democracy, but the European contagion was spreading. Working people were becoming class-conscious. Hatred of aristocrats might erect street barricades in New York as well as in Paris.

Part III of Buntline's *Mysteries and Miseries of New York* reflected the social excitement. Each volume had been more outspoken in its moral crusade than the one before, and Part III gave more specific locations of gambling rooms than the previous issue. As a crusader, Ned Buntline was using the best technique of the temperance reformers and abolitionists, moral uplift and melodrama. His writing was proving as popular as he hoped – the little volume went to five printings. Some gamblers winked profoundly. "If each curiosity seeker leaves only a dollar, business will pick up."

The fourth installment of the *Mysteries* was slow to appear. Advertised for April 28, 1848, people wondered about the delay. Mrs. Judson was reported to be expecting a baby, but that was no excuse for holding up the publication. Something else must be diverting the new author. For two months an odd play, *A Glance at New York*, had been acted at the Olympic Theatre,[8] and the drama was remarkably similar to the text of *The Mysteries and Miseries of New York*. People paid a shilling for a pit stall and came away declaring that the playwright, Benjamin Baker,[9] had copied Buntline's book. The skit proved very popular, and Baker cast the same characters, Angelina, Albert Shirley, and Mary, in another play, *New York As It Is*,[10] which opened at the Chatham on April 16, 1848. The leading man, Frank Chanfrau, acted in both plays, dashing from one theater to the other during the performance.[11] Theatergoing was considered sinful by many people. What would the Great Moral Reformer say about this?

XIII

Reform Politics Beckons

ONE NIGHT Ned Buntline came home to his wife at 16 Abingdon Place with unsteady gait, pounded up the stairs and lurched into the room. Annie, shocked but dutiful, put her drunken lord and master to bed, wondering if this new trouble was the result of prosperity and fame.

If Reformer Ned, after he sobered, intended to add thespians to his sinful list of gamblers and thieves, he could do so in his fifth and last installment. But he seems to have not made up his mind, as yet. Instead he went to Cincinnati, where his old publishers, Robinson & Jones, were distributing the *Mysteries*.[1] This firm was eager to handle a Buntline book even if Hine and Bennett had turned against him. While out West, the great literary adventurer took a short vacation in Eddyville. Let his readers wait for Part V! Ned wanted to explore the limestone cave that had interested him down there in 1844.[2] With a Drummond light and a pocket full of candles Ned discovered a great underground river, at least so he said, when he returned eagerly to New York.

Baker's play, *New York As It Is*, was making a great hit. Audiences seemed never to tire of the actor Chanfrau, in the leading part of Mose, a fireman in red shirt, boots, and fashionable "soap locks." Moreover, Mose was advertised as a real person, Mose Humphrey, a typesetter on the *Sun* by profession [3] and a fireman socially — the Buntline trick of realism. Newsboys packed the gallery cheering the hero, shouting "flash terms."[4] Half the urchins knew the real Mose and had seen him roistering through the Bowery. Mose became the Paul Bunyan of Manhattan – a fabulous fellow who was said to have jumped across the Hudson, to have blown vessels back down the East River, and to have carried a streetcar with the horses dangling.[5] Chanfrau was Bowery-born himself. As a lad, working behind the scenes of New York theaters, he had made the stagehands laugh with his burlesques of Hamblin, Booth, and Forrest. Occasionally he had been allowed to take minor juvenile parts. Now as Mose in 1848 he became famous overnight.

Ned Buntline went to see the play. Instead of attacking it as he had the gamblers and the trash writers like Ingraham and Lippard, Ned added Mose in his next installment of the *Mysteries*. Ned made him a redheaded butcher-boy instead of a printer, but kept him in fireman's uniform. Mose was a male counterpart of Big Lize, always ready to take up anyone's fight, the kind of man Ned wanted to be himself. Ned described Mose and the "b'hoys" at the notorious Madam Swett's "parlour house" in his book. Ned said:

> They ordered wine – she got it for them; they kissed her girls, and cuffed them around to hear them squeal, yet no one thought of resisting their innocent familiarities.

Baker and Buntline, playwright and novelist, both claimed their characters to be real, so neither could well accuse the other of plagiarism. Ned complimented Baker and Chanfrau, too, as depicting the characters with "abler hands than ours."[6] The playwright and the actor forthwith produced a third play starring Mose and Lize, entitled *Mysteries and Miseries of New York.*[7] Thus Ned got advertising for his own work. The concluding part of the book, *The Mysteries and Miseries of New York*, hinted that Ned's social research was leading him to an exciting activity. He wrote:

There are more than one thousand *criminals* nightly and daily permitted to openly break the law of the land . . . and these wretches are nightly dragging into their nets hundreds upon hundreds of the young men of the city, not only robbing them of gold, but of their decency and morality, making thieves of them, encouraging clerks to rob their employers; enticing the married man from his family, robbing his children of their bread, and his wife of her rights.

Why is this permitted? . . .

In our last number, as a *trial*, we named the location of *four* "hells" kept open every night. We sent marked copies of that work gratis to several Aldermen; a copy was sent to the Mayor, twenty-five copies were sent gratis to the police. And yet not one of these gambling houses has been disturbed – not one of these law-breakers has been even frowned at by the law-protectors.[8]

Thus did Buntline, the crusader, begin to slip into politics. The hundreds of thousands of immigrants who landed yearly in America were being organized by Tammany Hall into a great political machine. Buntline's followers were bound to oppose a Democratic Party based on foreign franchises, but the Whigs had nothing better to offer. Ned's followers considered them aristocratic – bankers and commercial men. In the election of 1844 the Whigs had tried to get the common man's vote by affecting coonskin caps in a hard-cider campaign, but they had failed. The time was now approaching for another election. The Buntlinites were poor people, suspicious of the Whigs and opposed to the foreign hordes accepted by the Democrats. Whether Ned would ever be able to weld them into a political party was anybody's guess.

The number of Buntline's readers was increasing beyond all bounds. Newspapers in Boston, New York, Philadelphia, Cincinnati, and even as far away as St. Louis mentioned him and his crusade. In Kentucky one of the most influential church members in Logan County reported that Ned's works were sought after by everyone "and read by persons who never before took a novel in hand."[9]

Buntline stepped up his tempo in the final issue of *The Mysteries and Miseries of New York,* multiplying horrors in his three-ply story and drawing suspense to the snapping point. He sometimes even changed the tense of his verbs to the historic present. One of his characters, Charlie Meadows, the clerk who had embezzled to pay gambling debts and was now hopelessly in the toils of the gamblers, coaxed his sister Isabella from her home with a false promise of marriage. The fake ceremony was being performed by a gambler in preacher's weeds when Big Lize burst into the assemblage looking for Angelina. (Note the strands of the story becoming entangled for the finale.) A melee followed. Isabella Meadows almost escaped, but not quite. A trap door opened in the floor, swallowing Big Lize, while a fiend in human form carried Isabella away insensible. Now let Buntline carry on:

When poor Isabella Meadows came to herself, she found that she was in a small room, well furnished, but hung around with licentious and obscene pictures. She shuddered as she judged the character of the place from this; but she felt some relief, on finding herself alone. She arose from the couch whereon she had been carelessly thrown, and going to the door, tried the lock. It had been fastened outside. She glanced around the room, and saw that there was a window in front. She quickly tried the shutters of that, and found that they, too, had been fastened – apparently nailed from the outside.

"No hope, not even the means of death!" she murmured. She looked at the small toilette table where the single light burned, which illuminated the small, close room. Several books were upon it. She glanced at them, and read the titles: – "Ernest Maltravers," "The Mysteries of Paris," "Byron's Works," "Moore's Poetry," "Tom Jones," "Charlotte Temple" were the titles she looked at, but, at last – strange place and company for such a book, she found a BIBLE! . . .

Poor girl – her prospect was indeed dark, and yet how many cases are there in this city, precisely similar to that. . . . There are at the very least *fifteen thousand* of these wretched creatures in this city – counting up the white and black, and of these probably *five* thousand are poor country girls, who did not enter willingly into the life they lead – but came here poor, yet innocent, and have been *forced* into their present misery through ignorance or helplessness.

How long shall this continue? It is left with the people of New York to say, for that they can put a stop to it, no one who possesses sense will doubt. Let them elect officers who will do their *duty* – and the city would soon present a far brighter and purer picture.[10]

Always Buntline would interrupt his story to remind the reader that he was conducting a campaign which might become political – might be the forerunner of a nation-wide movement. Then he resumed his story. The usual sinister tap on the chamber door came all too soon for entrapped Isabella Meadows. The villain entered:

"By Jove, . . . I'll have a kiss if I die for it!"

"Wretch! Fiend! *dog!* . . . Back, sir! stand back, if you value your life!"

Then bounding against the shuttered windows Isabella cut her arms on the shattered glass, and the villain, hoping for a more auspicious time, departed. But the hour of delivery was nigh. Isabella looked at her lacerated arms. She had an idea. Quickly she plucked a pin from her dress, dipped it in her bleeding wounds, and wrote:

"I am kept a prisoner, against my will. For the love of Heaven, come to my aid and rescue me while I am yet pure and innocent, or send the police to my aid! . . . I write in my own blood – I have no ink!"[11]

This note Isabella slipped between the boards of the shuttered window. It fluttered down into the hands of a passer-by – our hero Mose. The rest of that scene is easy to imagine. But in the meantime other characters in the book fare badly. Charlie Meadows, still in the power of the gamblers, commits murder at their bidding. A harrowing scene discloses how his mother becomes insane when she hears the news. Now only Big Lize, sweet Angelina, vicious Francis, and his employer the philanthropist, remain to be accounted for.

Buntline weaves the last strands of his story deftly. Through five volumes Angelina has fled from both the villain and galloping tuberculosis. Now finally she seeks refuge in the home of the philanthropist! Here mortal illness lays a cold hand upon the hapless sewing girl. The reader knows that she must die, but the fates of Francis, Lize, and the philanthropist still hang in the balance. Francis, it will be remembered, planned to get his patron's confidence in order to lead the gang to his treasure. In the fifth book this comes to pass. On the tragic night the kind master sends the turncoat on an errand of mercy to bring Big Lize to comfort the dying sewing girl.

"You're a good boy, Francis – but now hurry away, and try and find her cousin!"

"Yes, sir," said Frank, but as soon as he got out side the door, he added "*in a horn.*"

The meaning of that very popular phrase may not be understood by all our readers, but Frank meant by it, that he should not trouble himself much in the search for Lize.

"Things are coming to a head!" he muttered, as he stood upon the landing at the head of the stair-case. "Jack's men'll be here to-night. I think I better mizzle now. With me, to go or not to go, is the question. Whether it would be better to stay and see the fun out, or make myself scarce. If I stay I'll have a scene – but there's precious little romance in a night-row, as Byron said of sea-sickness!" [12]

In spite of the perfidy of Francis, Big Lize was not kept from the scene. By other means she learned the whereabouts of Angelina and set off in truculent mood. It becomes plain to the reader that the Amazon and the gangsters are going to arrive at the philanthropist's home simultaneously. Then, to hold the reader off from the kill, Buntline digresses with a few pages of moral discourse against gangsters and fortunetellers.

Finally Big Lize arrives at the philanthropist's mansion just as the robbers are leaving, not in time to save the good man or his fortune, but instead to receive a dagger in her breast. The wound is not instantly mortal, but the doctor attending the expiring

Angelina says that the weapon cannot be extracted without fatal hemorrhage. Thus Big Lize has time for an eloquent deathbed scene before the dagger is snatched from her bosom. All the characters, except Isabella, are now dead or ruined, and the book ends.

Reader, with the appendix which follows this chapter, we shall close this work. If you would follow the fate of Isabella Meadows, and see what a desperate, crime-hardened being a once pure and virtuous maiden may become, when driven to the very verge of madness, by ruin and wrong; and if you would see the terrible retribution which followed the crime of Albert Shirley, and read a new and strange history of Constance, his lovely daughter, you must read

"THE B'HOYS OF NEW YORK"

The author has also secured the copyright for another novel of exciting character, "The G'hals of New York."[13]

Having thus drawn the big-top performance to a close, Buntline continued with his side show. His appendix was the real *bonne bouche* of the fifth and last installment. Sociologist Buntline backed his statements in scholarly fashion with statistics. In 1845, he said, the population of New York was 371,223, and of these over one third were foreigners. The population in 1848, he stated, was probably 450,000, with the same ratio foreign.

[Of these at least 18,000] are courtesans,[14] and connected with these, are five thousand thieves, pocket-book droppers, burners, watch-stuffers, hack-bucks, mock-auction men, gamblers, dance-house keepers, grog-shop keepers, pick-pockets, &c. There are over one thousand *known* houses of ill-fame, and some of these have from ten to forty inmates. Besides there are at least one hundred assignation houses, supported by a more secret and select class of people, who carry vice into high life.

This is a strange and a hard story to tell of the great Metropolis of the Union, but there is more *truth* than poetry in it. Church street alone, from Chambers to Canal street, contains near fifteen hundred women of ill-fame, with whom are connected the other characters alluded to above. . . .

To judge from the places of nativity of at least two thirds of the criminals, immigration must be one great cause. All of the large gang of burglars, whom with their real names and characters, we have introduced in our work, are foreigners, mostly Englishmen. The denizens of the horrible circle known as the "Five Points" are principally Irish and negroes; some few Dutch, are also living there, but not one *American,* to a hundred foreigners, can be found there.

Our Alms Houses are occupied, at the ratio of about fifteen to one, by foreigners, the overflowings of the poor-houses in Europe. The street beggars are principally Irish, Germans, and Italians. . . .

We have plenty of room in this country for immigrants, if they would seek the unsettled parts; but it is to be regretted that most of the new comers lack the means or the inclination to go to the interior, and thus become a burden to the inhabitants of the sea-port towns. . . .

There are between thirty and forty Societies here, which can properly be termed "Benevolent Associations." Among them we can name, The "New York Hospital" which was founded in 1771 by the Earl of Dinmore; the "Bloomingdale Insane Asylum" (which is getting rich, and of course less charitable); "Lying-in Hospital" for destitute females (an excellent and praiseworthy institution); . . . "Asylum for aged and *Respectable* females," into which we understand there is great difficulty of admission.

Ned noted, too, that many of the so-called charitable societies were in reality speculating corporations profiting from the unearned increment on their tax-free city lots. Then, without relevance, he summarized a recent report of the New York State Asylum. Among the many causes for insanity Ned recorded the following:

Intemperance, 50—47 males and 3 females.
Disappointment in love, 39—23 males and 16 females.
Abuse of husbands, 24 females.
Political excitement, 6 men.
Disappointed ambition, 7—5 males and 2 females.
Seduction, 3 females.
Remorse, 3 men.
Anticipation of wealth, 3—1 male and 2 females.
Excitement of law suit, 1 female.

> But to return to the causes of crime. It is not for the lack of *laws* that crime increases so rapidly. . . . We have no political prejudices, and belong to no party, but will at all times give all the little influence which we may possess, toward supporting and retaining those men in office who will firmly, honestly, and fearlessly do their duty, regardless alike of interests, threats or bribes.[15]

Always Buntline disclaimed connection with any existing party, either Whig or Democrat. He wanted reform, like so many other unorganized and dissatisfied members of both parties. If enough voices all clamored for the same thing, a new political party – and a big one – might develop. This time the party might not break up as had the Anti-Masonic Party in Ned's youth. Dissatisfaction was attaining remarkable proportions. It seemed probable that the coming election of 1848 might witness some exciting things politically.

XIV

Ned Buntline's Own

NED DECIDED to start a great newspaper. Advertising posters announced that his first campaign would expose the employers of sewing girls. Every sweatshop, Ned promised, that paid the miserable existing wage of six cents per shirt would be posted in *Ned Buntline's Own* – an old name for a new paper. This brave and commendable project was lauded in *Godey's Lady's Book* by Sarah Josepha Hale, writer of stories for women and poems for children, including a famous one beginning "Mary had a little lamb." Mrs. Hale's son had gone on the antarctic expedition which Ned had missed so narrowly back in 1838. She may have felt some sentimental urge to encourage the new and virtuous sailor writer.

To inaugurate his newspaper, Ned refurnished the study in his father-in-law's house by rearranging the cutlasses and daggers and bringing in a new set of murderous-looking pistols. Then he ordered the windows barred for a siege.[1]

Optimism glowed in Ned's ruddy complexion. The small man had a really big idea. James Gordon Bennett, a foreigner and a Catholic, had built the *New York Herald* from nothing to an income of over $130,000 annually. A native-born Protestant like Ned Buntline should attain an even more signal success. In 1835 Bennett had opened an office in a basement, with a board across two kegs for a desk. He published news without political bias, clipped exchanges, and sold his own papers. Within three months he was able to hire a cheap police reporter. Within fifteen months he had a circulation of 30,000. Three years from his beginning he employed correspondents abroad. After four years of success he built his own plant and moved into sumptuous quarters.

At the start Ned had two advantages over James Gordon Bennett. *Ned Buntline's Own* did not have to begin publication in a cellar, and the editor had a moral purpose that was already popular. He intended to add to the usual news a crusade for reform in the city of New York – then later, perhaps, in the whole nation. Ned's room at 16 Abingdon Place served as his first editorial office. Notoriously carefree in money matters, Ned let his father-in-law manage the firm, keep the books, and deal with the delivery boys. At 2 Astor Place he maintained another office near the presses.[2] Ned had learned that it was convenient to have two offices as well as two names.

In July 1848, the first issue came from the press on schedule. Readers found no names of victims posted, but Ned had fearlessly taken his fellow journalists to task. James Gordon Bennett read that his *Herald* was an accessory in crime by carrying an advertisement of Mauriceau's *The Married Woman's Private Medical Companion*,[3] and Ned promised to continue assailing the great editor until the "base born Britisher" stopped aiding the sale of illegal books. Ned also attacked the editor of the *New York Sun*, Moses Y. Beach, for printing the addresses of houses where libertines might find mistresses and to which "gentlemen of resources" might bring *boarders*.[4]

Ned's scandal sheet sold well. He sent sample copies to Boston, Philadelphia, Albany, and Honesdale, Pennsylvania, near his old home town. He added a theatrical critic to his staff, and soon had subscribers in outlying cities, especially in northern and western New York. To interest these new readers he extended his purity campaign to out-of-town newspapers. The *Binghamton* [New York] *Courier* was censured for carrying advertisements of Dr. Weisselhoff's book on abortion. Ned posted the *Camden* [New

Jersey] *Gazette* for the same offense, and watched his paper's circulation grow. He hired reporters who shadowed prominent citizens or made friends with housemaids and picked up gossip. People paid well to keep some of their escapades out of print. In his columns Ned warned certain young ladies not to walk to a specified house at regular hours as had been their custom. He asked pointedly why a certain gentleman in a gray beaver hat was seen so frequently at someone else's residence.[5]

Then suddenly he dismissed his theatrical critic, announcing that *Ned Buntline's Own* was discontinuing theatrical news on moral grounds. Ned also stated that he was receiving letters from blackguards who wanted employment as spies for his gossip columns. He printed one from an H. G. Brady and announced that the original was on exhibition at his publishers', at 2 Astor Place, but could not be seen long: "Barnum has made us an offer for it." "If this person had really undertaken his labors with an honest desire to do good," Ned said, "he would have found us, not an opposer, but a friend. . . . There is vice enough in the city to employ many people in rooting it out, but we wish no 'devil upon two sticks' . . . peeping in through window-blinds, and corrupting chambermaids." An editor, he said, who was not motivated by the highest moral principles might extort large sums from people who feared exposure. As an example Ned published another letter to a woman from a man who signed his name as Harrison Gray Buchanan, a fellow who had recently written a work like Ned's *Mysteries and Miseries* under the title *Asmodeus or Legends of New York*. In this letter the blackmailing author requested "the small sum of $1000" to refrain from exposing "your ladyship."

A half dozen sensational newspapers began to attack Buntline. With jealousy, righteousness, or for simple sport they tossed Ned and his paper in blankets of ridicule. Ned, they said, was a blackmailer himself. The alleged letters he had printed were his own handiwork.

A hundred years later it seems quite obvious that H. G. Brady and H. G. Buchanan were the same person. Harrison Gray Otis, the famous New England statesman, had died in October 1848. James Buchanan was Secretary of State. How natural for a busy journalist to make a pseudonym of the two familiar names. Ned then must have written the *Asmodeus* volumes too, and the blackmailing letter was undoubtedly a copy of one written by himself. This becomes more apparent after consulting contemporary city directories. Ned is listed, but there is no H. G. Brady or Buchanan.

Opposition papers exposed Ned to constant derision. They claimed that he resorted to all the tricks he complained about in others. He had a long list of subscribers, they said, who paid regularly lest Ned write unfavorably about them. As for his benevolent campaign for higher wages for sewing girls, that was a fraud. Ned had tricked the boss printers of his own paper to sweat the girls employed to run their presses. Starvation wages for women indeed!

The notorious Dr. Weisselhoff, one critic complained, was none other than Buntline's theatrical editor. Ned had dismissed him, not because theaters were immoral, but because the doctor refused to split the profits of his illegal book.[6] As proof of Ned's attitude toward the theater, the critic showed that Ned himself had written for Chanfrau a sequel of Mose's further adventures in a new play entitled *Three Years After*,[7] printed also as a book. The *Scorpion* – a scandal sheet like Ned's – offered a reward of $10 for any spy information about "a red mustached libertine" who keeps a mistress at Fanny White's.[8] Ned's wife and father-in-law must have looked at Ned's red mustache, read the dispatches, and wondered. Could the new member of their family be guilty?

Ned struck back at his maligners with redheaded fury. He had one man sent to the Tombs for libel, and challenged another to make his statement sufficiently clear to be a subject for prosecution.[9] Constantly threatened with personal violence, Ned seldom left the house undisguised. When necessary to go to another part of New York he drove in a hack with the curtains closed.[10] His enemies railed at him for hiding behind petticoats every time he ventured out for a short walk with his wife – now well along with child.

The election campaign of 1848 gave Ned his first opportunity to make a political issue of his principles. Four years before, the Democrats had won on a platform promising a war with either England or Mexico. Now in 1848 the Democrats tried a war platform again: Cass, Canada and Cuba. To counteract the appeal of military conquest the Whigs put up a war hero, General Zachary Taylor, Old Rough and Ready, a Southern man of no party. Underneath the shouting, men argued sullenly about the slavery issue. Politicians begged people not to discuss such an incendiary subject. Abolition of slavery meant government confiscation of millions of dollars' worth of property. But, in spite of the politicians, the issue would not quash. Slavery overshadowed the crusades against intemperance and immigration. David Wilmot, a boy who had gone to Beech Woods Academy when Ned's father taught there, had become a representative in Congress from Pennsylvania. A Democrat, he insisted that the vast territory gained from Mexico in the late war be kept free from slavery. Southern members of his party considered this an insult. Northern members threatened to form a new Free-Soil Party. Another disaffected bloc of Democrats – radical workmen known as Locofocos – opposed the recent aristocratic trend in Jackson's party. Even another foreign war did not seem sufficient to reunite the dissolving Democracy, and herein lay the opportunity for *Ned Buntline's Own.*

Ned had disliked practical politics since the Anti-Masonic excitement in his youth, but the temptation to get into the looming political contest tugged irresistibly. He knew that the desperate Democratic leaders were trying to hold their majority by enlisting thousands of immigrant Irishmen who had fled from the potato famine. The Democrats appealed also to immigrant radicals who had escaped from Europe after their recent unsuccessful revolutions. These foreigners eagerly accepted low wages and usurped the jobs of American-born workers. The Democratic Party of Andy Jackson, alleged friend of the common man, ignored the native American workers' predicament. Whigs had never been their friends. Ned Buntline resolved to champion their cause to the death. A new, so-called American Party devoted to workers' interests had held a national convention in 1845. Now in 1848 this new party promised to upset the old two-party contest, and Ned determined to jump into the maelstrom. The Democratic Party might not survive against a coalition of Whigs, Free-Soilers, and Americans.

The political uncertainty ahead was enhanced by other parties – various brotherhoods of mechanics, cherishing rituals like the honored Masons yet open to people of moderate means. Ned decided to make his party a brotherhood with secret ceremonies. The knowledge of Masonry and of redcoats and bloody tracks at Valley Forge which Ned had gained from his father served him well at last. Why, Ned asked pointedly in his paper, should America's traditional enemies, British immigrants, be given the franchise by Democrats after only three years' residence in America, while all native-born sons had to live in the country twenty-one years before they were allowed to vote? The columns of *Ned Buntline's Own* announced rallies of the Order of United Americans and the Order of United American Mechanics – O.U.A. and O.U.A.M. Political issues were added to the usual exposures of gambling dens and the locations of houses of ill fame. In no time Ned became an acknowledged local leader, Generalissimo of the American Phalanx of the O.U.A.[11]

Election day came at last. The broken Democratic Party lost to the Whig candidate, Zachary Taylor, hero of Monterrey and Buena Vista. The diverse labor, idealistic, and humanitarian parties had captured the independent vote and cut holes in both old political organizations. The new Free-Soil Party had attracted Northern Democrats, including many of Buntline's mechanics, who complained that the American Party had no national organization worthy of the name. Although Ned's Americans were badly beaten, he was too familiar with slavery to consider abolition a political issue. He intended to bide his time and get a real following on the principle of "America for Americans." Perhaps, like the patriots of '76, he might even lead a revolution, but this must be kept secret at present. In the meantime, female temperance societies beckoned him to regale their cause with his oratory. Ned forgot his party's defeat momentarily and turned his furious energy into the new channel.

Ned had heard temperance preached as long as he could remember, and he had been impressed by Timothy Shay Arthur's prose. Under Jackson a new temperance society had waxed strong, established auxiliaries in every state and got a million pledges signed, then split and decomposed, arguing over total abstinence versus moderation, and the achievement of temperance by education or legislation. One bloc of reformers had insisted that the society also denounce the growing antislavery movement. Thus the moral crusade had disintegrated in a dispute over morals.

In 1840 the temperance movement had revived and sailed to success on a new tack. The strange procedure began by accident on April 2, 1840, when a few convivial friends sat in Chase's Tavern, Baltimore. One of the men suggested that they attend a temperance lecture advertised in the town. They all went and after the performance returned to the tavern, pledged total abstinence, and organized what they named the Washington Temperance Society, in admiration of the character of the Father of his Country "rather than by a desire to imitate his practice regarding the use of intoxicants."[12] The founders called themselves reformed drunkards. Other alleged drunkards were invited to speak at their meetings. By Christmas, 1840, more than a thousand Washingtonians were attending crowded "experience meetings." Religious revivals had lost favor recently, but something of their emotionalism appeared in the new temperance crusade. By the spring of 1841 the missionary impulse spread to New York. A year later the contagion had taken Indiana, Illinois, Tennessee, and Ohio, where, Ned remembered, Lyman Beecher had preached against liquor and liquor-drinking Catholics. The antiliquor agitation flourished in Maine, too, where Neal Dow, cold, cautious, and conservative, got a law passed in 1846 against retailing intoxicants.

As a temperance lecturer Ned faced two established methods of selling prohibition: cold logic or warm evangelism. Neal Dow represented the former school, and a new temperance speaker, John B. Gough, attracted immense audiences with the other method. Gough out-Washingtoned the Washingtonians. With magnetic voice he alternately pictured the pleasant path to perdition and the horrid debauchery at the bottom. Gough drew vivid drama from the temperance writings of Timothy Shay Arthur – especially his famous *Six Nights with the Washingtonians: A Series of Original Temperance Tales.* Ned had predicted Arthur's future greatness long ago in Cincinnati, and now his prophecy came true. Within five years Arthur was to rewrite his *Six Nights* as *Ten Nights in a Barroom and What I Saw There,* a best-seller that would hold its own in print and on the stage for fifty years. Ned realized the importance of arousing an audience's emotions, but he knew, too, that Gough was accused of being a hypocrite; that he occasionally disappeared to get howling drunk. In the columns of *Ned Buntline's Own* [13] he scoffed at Gough for his tippling as well as for his romantic imagination and histrionics. Neal Dow's cold logic was good enough for Ned Buntline!

Ned announced boldly – if not truthfully – that reason would be master of his paper, and that *Ned Buntline's Own* would walk with temperance and the American Party as its handmaidens. He saw clearly that a lecture crusade on the double track of these popular principles might readily be switched into a political terminal. In halls crowded with auxiliary organizations Ned boomed to attentive ears that American-born women should be above menial kitchen tasks fit only for foreigners.[14] As he talked he forgot his derision for Gough's emotionalism. Instead, he wooed female audiences with sentimental stories about his boyhood sweetheart. For her sake, he said, he had never touched tobacco. For her he never tasted rum, as she would not kiss lips that did. For her, he reiterated, he had abstained from robbing birds' nests on Dyberry Creek in Wayne County, Pennsylvania. For her he had gone to sea.

Once when the United Daughters of America assembled in the costumes of their Order to hear Ned, he did not appear on schedule. He had written his speech for them beforehand and, with it in his trousers pocket, had stopped for stimulation at Palmo's, then at Madam Pastor's, next at Florence's. Finally Ned remembered his lecture. Laughing girls dosed him with soda water, flopped cold towels on his flushed face and ruddy mustache.[15] Breathless, but with the dignity of a great editor, he arrived at the meeting and delivered his message.

At another time, when Ned was invited to address the L. N. Fowler Society of Daughters of Temperance, the assembled ladies were disappointed to see a short, heavy-bodied young man step to the center of the stage. His shoulders stooped to the verge of deformity. Ned was aging fast. But when he talked, the audience forgot his tousled red hair, his unkempt mustache. The ladies heard only his flattering words. Each one felt as though she, and she alone, were Annie, Mary, or Seberina. His tales of storms at sea made temperance maidens' eyes dance. Dramatically he closed by saying, "I am a man of deeds rather than words. I write better than I speak and therefore I sign my name to your pledge." [16]

Ned marched out of the hall with feminine applause rippling above his grotesque figure. On the way home he pushed open the door at 77 Lispenard Street, a low brothel where he ordered a drink and sat behind a table with eyes half shut but watching stealthily over his rough mustache. Some of the best stories in

Ned Buntline's Own—and handsome fees for keeping them out of print—could be acquired here. Men of prominence and plotting gamblers ignored an inconspicuous ruffian asleep in his chair.

At home Ned's wife, expecting her baby, waited through the night, peeping through the shutters for the first glimpse of her staggering husband, whom she knew a dozen men threatened to thrash or kill on sight. He came at last, lurched through the door, mumbling about a gambler, Samuel Suydam. Yes, Ned had caught Sam. The scoundrel would have to pay.

In the morning Ned sent Suydam word to deliver $250 for the benefit of his reform crusade or have his name posted in the next issue of *Ned Buntline's Own*. The gambler did not send the money. Instead he came himself to 16 Abingdon Place, stood in the street, and dared Ned to come out and be killed. Buntline laid out his guns, cutlasses, and daggers. He stormed from room to room cocking great pistols, breathing awful vengeance. His wife prayed and her father marveled at "these Amurricans." A crowd gathered. The police arrived. Suydam was taken to jail. Then the officers entered Buntline's house and took him too.

Annie pleaded with her father to bail Ned before her baby was born. Timid Mr. Bennett finally consented, went down to the city jail, and signed a bond. Ned, penitent and dejected, returned home in time to comfort his wife in childbirth. The baby was a boy, and, horror of horrors, he had a strange mark on his breast. A dagger! [17] The mother became hysterical. Ned knelt beside her and swore he would never take another drink. Father Bennett ran in from the sitting room with a pen, ink, and pledges. Ned wept and signed. He was so upset he stepped outside in the air to clear his head. At a saloon he took a bracer, became interested in an argument. Two days passed before he staggered home to inquire about his wife and newborn son, but he had gathered salacious copy for his paper.

Ned's domestic life could not be called happy, but his business prospered. In December he employed an associate editor, one

Thomas Paterson, a Scotch newspaperman who eked out a meager living coaching students for examinations at Columbia College. Paterson had been imprisoned in England for the liberality with which he expressed his opinions in the press. In America, land of the free, he welcomed an opportunity to be unrestricted by government.

Ned announced proudly that in January he would increase the size of his paper.[18] He would continue to persecute gamblers and illegal liquor sellers. He would fight foreign immigration and make America a land fit for Americans. He did not hint that he might resort to revolution after the fashion of the patriots of '76 and trust to the unrest in America to support his banner, but he did affix at the top of his paper a picture of himself in sailor costume with a drawn sword. Beneath his heroic form the paper carried an alleged command of Washington's: "Put none but Americans on guard." Of course Washington had said no such thing—but if an innocent misquotation be treason, let Tories make the most of it!

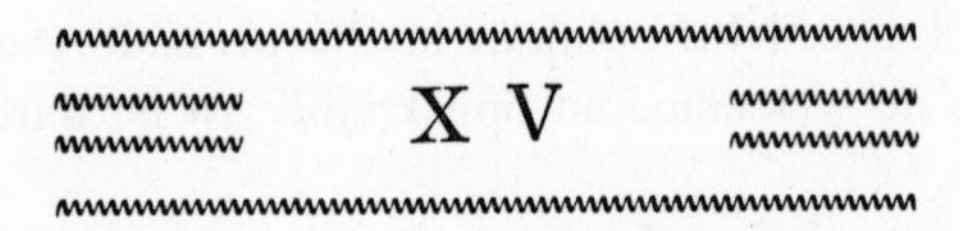

XV

Come the Revolution

NED BUNTLINE decided to grow a full beard like the patriarchs and apostles. This seemed altogether fitting and proper for a second Father of his Country who championed temperance, despised vice, exposed gamblers, and intended to keep America safe for Americans. *The Mysteries and Miseries of New York* had honored Ned with fame which he might turn to good account for the American Party in the coming campaign. To publicize himself and his cause, Ned announced that he was building a yacht as fine as any of the ships in New York Harbor, a trim little gem of a craft to be manned by a crew of eight. The model, he said, had been awarded a medal by the American Institute.[1] The design was drawn by a skilled member of his United American Mechanics. Ned planned to christen the craft *Buntline's Own*. His enemies rubbed their hands covetously and promised themselves to attach this nice bit of property for damages the next time Ned libeled them in his scandal sheet.

In February 1849, Ned took pity on a poor and bewildered nineteen-year-old sewing girl named Nora Janes. He hired a room for her at Fanny White's, paid her board, and called once or twice a week.[2] Scurrilous newspapers continued to attack him. The vicious *Scorpion* kept the public posted on Buntline's private life. The editor knew so much that it seemed probable he might be working incognito on the staff of *Ned Buntline's Own*. Whoever he was, he brazenly published details about Ned's affair with Nora Janes.[3] The mysterious editor's vocabulary indicated that he might be the Columbia College tutor. He called Ned "this miasmic hecatomb of abominations and distorted plagiarisms," and he accused Ned of intimidating his employees, spying on them constantly, having case histories on file to keep married workmen in his power. Ned's boldness and his willingness to lie, said the *Scorpion*, cowed innocent employees and made them afraid to quit.[4]

Before long, Ned's enemies announced that the great reformer supported six mistresses in New York and also a mysterious Mrs. Ned as first mate on his yacht.[5] A spy dug up the information that Buntline had deceived one Mary C. Thompson of Jersey City into a sham marriage, using a fake parson, Robert Henshaw, to conduct a counterfeit service.[6] The only flaw in these stories – if a flaw – was the fact that Ned had written about such escapades in *The Mysteries and Miseries* before he was accused of practicing them. It was also reported that a notorious woman, Fanny Ettling, followed Ned from Boston where he had gone to get subscribers to his *Own*. Fanny conferred with Ned and henceforth her name was not mentioned in his paper. Employees around the publishing house whispered to one another that she had contributed to Ned's fund for the suppression of vice, and pledged support to his political organization. Ned's old enemy, Samuel Suydam, furnished a rich item against virtue's champion. On April 4, 1849, Suydam said he saw Ned Buntline, the Great Reformer, keeping cases in a faro game at 3 Park Row.[7]

Scandals accumulated around the successful newsman, but Ned was unprepared for his next misfortune. He had given up his habit of walking in the street with his wife to protect him. One day[8] he strolled debonairly along Broadway with Mike Walsh, a rowdy to be reckoned with in New York politics. Champion of the "b'hoys," Mike's political influence threatened Tammany Hall. Here was just the man to ramrod Ned's plans for the American Party. At Duane Street a carriage pulled up to the gutter and stopped. A fashionably dressed woman bounded out, her face flushed with anger. She grabbed Ned Buntline by the coat collar, spun him around and hissed, "You dirty, mean, sneaking, paltry son of a ——, how dare you publish me in your paper?" The woman drew out a whip from her voluminous skirts and beat Ned over the head and shoulders. Ned warded off the blows with his arms and ran. People on the streets hooted. The woman, known as Kate Hastings of Leonard Street, walked away proudly trailing her whip, and Ned's plans for an alliance with Mike Walsh were postponed.

Ned swore out a complaint against Kate for operating a disorderly house. At the trial Kate presented Judge Charles P. Daly with a blackmail letter. The judge read it, reprimanded Buntline, and dismissed the case. James Gordon Bennett reported the incident in the *Herald* with apparent satisfaction. He printed Judge Daly's censure and added that Ned was soon back in Kate's house buying liquor as though nothing had happened.

Ned read Bennett's account in the *Herald*, stuffed the paper in the pocket of his frock coat, and strode to the office of *Ned Buntline's Own*. Time had come for a showdown with the baseborn British upstart! Ned stamped into the editorial room where his assistant, Tom Paterson, was reading proof. He reached for pen and paper, saying, "I will rip up the character of the whore of a sister of that cockeyed villain Bennett next week." Ned scratched a reckless slander about Georgiana C. Crean and sent it to the printer.[9]

James Gordon Bennett, already a power in New York City, read in *Ned Buntline's Own* the disparaging remarks about his sister-in-law, and handed the article to his lawyer. Ned was arrested and held for $2000 bail. His enemies crowded, called him a "strumpet fondled — cow-hided; and well-thrashed mountebank."[10] His friends quickly offered surety for the $2000. Ned walked out of jail fuming against the Britisher who had wronged him. Surely the American Party would give all such public enemies their just deserts.

Ned's opportunity to get even with British Bennett and improve the prestige of the American Party was close at hand. Two actors, William Charles Macready and Edwin Forrest – one English and the other American – had been quarreling bitterly since 1844. That year Macready had toured America as Polk ran for President on his platform threatening to fight England: "fifty-four forty or fight." Everywhere Macready had played, he was insulted – on account of his nationality, he thought. American audiences claimed that the fault was with his acting.

A century ago plays were limited in number. Theatergoers saw the same ones over and over. Like spectators at a Spanish bull-fight, they judged the merits of different actors in parts known to them almost word for word. Edwin Forrest was considered by many Americans to be the ideal Macbeth. He had a perfect form. Straight as an arrow, elastic as a circus rider, he walked the boards with haughty mien. New York's Bowery "b'hoys" idolized him. Macready, symbol of England, elicited their scorn. Yet intelligent Americans preferred Macready to Forrest. Walt Whitman said of actors of that day: "If they have to enact passion, they do so by all kinds of unnatural and violent jerks, swings, screwing of the nerves of the face, rolling of the eyes, and so on." [11] These faults were Forrest's to a marked degree.

Mechanics, workmen, Bowery "b'hoys," all Buntline's people, classed Macready, Britishers, and aristocrats as common enemies of their America. Didn't rich people want immigration from abroad to supply cheap labor, which took bread from the mouths of American workers' children?

Forrest followed Macready on his American tour, often playing in the same towns on the same nights. Then he crossed the ocean and repeated the performance in the British Isles. In 1848 it was announced that Macready planned a return engagement in America. The year had been one of violence abroad with revolutions threatening established governments. Ned read about embattled citizens barricading the streets and a great idea dawned in his active mind. He had just returned from exploring the Kentucky cavern when Macready arrived in America, to be greeted everywhere with near riots. After touring the country Macready turned his course toward New York – the curtain bell for the last act with Forrest. *Ned Buntline's Own* screamed for the people to give the Englishman what their ancestors had given the redcoats at Lexington. "If they mean to have a war, let it begin here!" James Gordon Bennett's *Herald* warned that trouble was imminent,[12] a class struggle. Macready and Forrest had ceased to be actors had they but known it. Instead they were class symbols like the tricolor and the fleur-de-lis. In New York, supporters of Forrest and of Macready seemed equally determined.

Advertisements announced that Macready would play Macbeth in Hackett and Niblo's Astor Place Opera House, New York, on May 7, 1849. The theater stood close by Ned Buntline's office. Two other Macbeths – Forrest at the Broadway and Thomas S. Hamblin at the Bowery – promised to open on the same night. James H. Hackett was an impoverished Knickerbocker, a broken-down aristocrat of the class Buntline disliked. William Niblo was Irish born. His fashionable theatrical garden described by Ned in 1846 had burned to the ground shortly thereafter. Both men's backgrounds warranted the scorn of the American Party.

On the opening night the opera house filled quietly. The orchestral overture was accompanied by a chorus of "b'hoys" in the gallery. The pit seemed friendly to the Britisher. If Buntline was present he had good reason never to admit it.

The curtain rose. White handkerchiefs fluttered like snowflakes over the pink faces and white shirt fronts in the gloom of the parquet. Ominous boos and hisses mingled with the polite demonstration.

Macready winced in his dressing room. "They are about 'arf and 'arf, sir," his hairdresser reassured him. Upon the stage the witches began their chant. The gallery "b'hoys" sang with them.

People looked at one another and said knowingly that Forrest had paid for their tickets. The American actor, some whispered, had even rehearsed them in the song. Macready, in the wings, heard his cue. Dressed in tights and doublet, he strode out before the audience. Shrill jeers roared over the footlights. Above the tumult a great voice boomed like Buntline in a hurricane, "Take off the Devonshire bull."

"Nine cheers for Edwin Forrest," bawled another voice. The house rocked with huzzas. Macready went through his familiar part in dumb show.

"Three groans for the English bulldog," someone shouted. The house responded.

"Huzza for native talent!"

"Down with the codfish aristocracy!"

Placards appeared. From the upper tier of boxes a sign announced: YOU HAVE BEEN PROVED A LIAR.

Macready was outwardly unmoved by the thunderstorm, even when it began to rain eggs, oranges, and rotten apples. The footing under the Scottish conspirators and their consorts became slippery. Several direct hits were greeted with cheers. A broken bottle of asafetida diffused a repulsive stench throughout the house.

The next day the *Morning Star* reported that the first act was one of "shouting, fun, frolic and drollery." The second act was more serious. Spoiled fruit began to find the target. Macready "was also hit with a penny, thrown by some infuriated person, who could get no other weapon." [13] During the third act, according to the *Star*, Bill Wilson – trainer for the prize fighter Yankee Sullivan – threw a chair from the gallery. It landed in the orchestra and "caused a prestissimo movement . . . not set down in the original music for Macbeth." Rowdies laughed. Three more chairs hurtled from the gallery. One of them landed with a crash of splintering wood at Macready's feet.

The Britisher ordered down the curtain. He had had enough.

Exultant rowdies surged down the stairs, across Astor Place, past Buntline's office chanting:

> When shall we three meet again? . . .
> When the hurly-burly's done,
> When the battle's lost and won.

At the Broadway Theatre they stopped and cheered Forrest to the echo.[14]

Most of the New York newspapers censured the rioters. Some were amused. *Ned Buntline's Own* praised the patriots' inalienable right to express their opinion of public men — the triumph of democracy. Let the British Bull dare appear again.

Leading citizens circulated a petition for a repeat performance. The name of Washington Irving headed the list.[15] The Lewis Gaylord Clark clique, Buntline's enemies, sympathized with art and Englishmen. May 10, 1849, was the date selected for the performance. New York's "best people" purchased tickets and appealed to Mayor C. S. Woodhull for police protection. In politics Woodhull was a Whig, like so many of the "best people." He promised to maintain law and order. Buntline's Americans had just two days to organize their demonstration. The Democrats, with their Catholic foreign voters, were sure to oppose them as strongly as the Whig codfish aristocrats. But Ned Buntline intended to show his party's strength. Hadn't his Americans drawn enough working people from the Democrats in the last election to let the Whigs win?

May 10 came. Ned, in blue frock coat with gilt buttons and tall hat, drove furiously around town in a light wagon. A boy rode with him to hold the horse when Ned bounded over the wheel, with coattails flying, to run into an office for a hurried conference. In the evening, before the theater opened, Ned rushed home to change clothes. He put on a short, light-colored "monkey-jacket" and Tom Hyer cap,[16] ideal for action as well as a disguise. Ned's wife wept and begged him, on her knees, not to join the crowd that was already gathering around the Astor Place Opera House. Ned brushed her aside, snatched a sword from its scabbard, and ran down the stairs into the dark streets, which had been freely posted since early morning with great bills:

WORKINGMEN,
Shall
AMERICANS OR ENGLISH RULE
In this city?

The Crew of the *British Steamer* have threatened all Americans who shall dare express their opinion this night, at the *English Aristocratic Opera House!!*

We advocate no violence, but a free expression of opinion to all public men!

WORKINGMEN! FREEMEN!

Stand by your
LAWFUL RIGHTS.

AMERICAN COMMITTEE[17]

At seven o'clock 180 policemen marched smartly into the square before the theater.[18] By squads they were detailed around the building. Two regiments of militia – infantry, cavalry, and artillery – assembled at their armories.[19] Ned, to his way of thinking, had become one of the Revolutionary patriots ready to resist Tory tyranny.

A police captain noticed tickets to the performance being distributed among the crowd. The Americans, no doubt, planned a disturbance inside the theater. He ordered a strong detachment to enter the opera house and barricade the windows. At last the main entrance opened for admission. Two thousand people filed in and took their seats in orderly fashion. Were many of them rioters in disguise? Policemen stationed throughout the house noticed only seven women in the audience, two of them in a box. This looked suspicious.

The orchestra played the overture — no interruption. The witches' scene finished without a repetition of Monday night's mockery. Buntline's mischievous face was nowhere to be seen in the audience. Macready in his dressing room appeared calm but more irritable with his hairdresser than usual. Then the great man's cue came and he strode out before the footlights. With assurance he boomed the first line of his part: "So foul and fair a day I have not seen."

A thunder of applause rocked the house, then silence, and the act progressed. Heckling and catcalls began to punctuate the performance. The disturbers all seemed to be scattered among the occupants of the first two rows in the parquet. Policemen patrolled the aisles and marked the offenders. Macbeth, ostensibly scheming to bring the king to his castle to be murdered, in reality pointed with his truncheon at the disturbers,[20] thus adding new italics to the Shakespearean lines.

At the end of the act police arrested the miscreants and marched them out amid applause from the audience. Doors swung shut behind them. The theater became silent — a menacing silence. A few curious onlookers had seen something unpleasant outside the great doors. Ten thousand grim, angry men stood in Astor Place. Many of them wore firemen's uniforms — Mose multiplied ten thousand times. Such reckless and popular fellows were known to be organized as well as the militia. Far away, in the direction of the office of *Ned Buntline's Own*, a voice shouted earnestly. The soggy little editor was flourishing a sword and exhorting the mob. "Workingmen, shall Americans or English rule? . . . Shall sons whose fathers drove the baseborn miscreants from our shores give up their liberty?"

The speech ended and the crowd turned toward the theater with exultant determination and long scaling ladders.[21] Stones shattered the street lights. Glass tinkled to the sidewalks and crunched underfoot. The lights flared up for an instant, illuminating fanatic faces. Pitch darkness followed. Men shouted arrogantly.

The curtain rose for the second act. Before long, rocks began to beat a tattoo on the barricaded doors and windows. Broadway was paved with cobblestones the size of goose eggs – unlimited ammunition for rioters. Soon the pelting changed to regular volleys. A familiar voice commanded, "Ready, aim, fire," and an avalanche of cobbles shook the walls. People said Ned Buntline had organized his firemen into a semimilitary revolutionary army. Some rocks penetrated the barricade and landed in the audience. One hit the great glass chandelier and "caused a good deal of scattering." Musicians in the orchestra retreated beneath the stage. The audience took shelter under the balcony and the players spoke their parts resolutely through the second and third acts.

A great crash of glass, followed by a wild cheer from the mob, told the audience that one of the barricaded windows had given way. The police outside were obviously overpowered. Inside, the officers of the law rallied at the breach, a handful against ten thousand. Shouts of "Burn the damned den of aristocracy" could be plainly heard in the theater. Members of the audience looked apprehensively over their shoulders toward the exits. Could it be that the mob had reached the lobby below? Then quiet returned! Outside, the rattle of muskets and sabers and the heavy trundling of cannon over the cobbles distracted the audience.

The militia had come!

Act five progressed without disturbance.[22] People who knew Buntline suspected him of being up to more devilment, but Macready strode the boards with confidence. In the fifth scene he waved his sword and shouted – true to his script:

> . . . our castle's strength
> Will laugh a siege to scorn . . .

The pit cheered. Macready had regained his audience. Henceforth he played the remaining lines for all they were worth.

The curtain rang down amid deafening applause with laughing theatergoers crowding the aisles, proclaiming *Macbeth* the greatest comedy of the season. The patter of cobblestones pelting the building had stopped, but men who peered out into the dark street beckoned their companions and pointed to the fireflies among the soldiers' gun barrels down yonder – rocks striking sparks on the steel. Now and then a soldier collapsed, his gun rattling on the cobblestones.

An officer's horse became unmanageable. Eyes knocked out, a hip broken, the desperate animal plunged blindly through the crowd. Major General Sandford of the militia turned to Colonel Abram Duryee and ordered him to have the men fix bayonets. In a twinkling the blades were in place. A charge was ordered, but the mob pressed too close to the ranks. Guns were snatched from the soldiers. General Sandford became desperate. Then a rock knocked him down. From the ground he ordered Duryee to shoot a volley over the rioters' heads.

The militiamen raised their guns. "You dare not fire, you d—— sons of ——," a voice taunted.[23] Macready in his dressing room heard a volley.

A voice in the mob scoffed, "They have only blank cartridges. Give it to them again." Another storm of cobblestones hailed on the soldiers, but they reloaded.

"Fire low," the militia officers ordered.[24] Again the guns spit red fire in the darkness. This time men collapsed on the sidewalks. The mob faltered, then turned in panic. Policemen who had been standing nearby made quick arrests. Ned Buntline and a few others were collared, hustled across to the theater, and locked up in the barroom.[25] The dispersed crowd clotted angrily behind the shelter of walls and building corners. Rocks continued to click viciously on gun barrels and here and there they knocked a soldier to his knees. A third volley convinced the rioters that the militia meant business. With no leaders, the angry men stopped fighting.

Inside the theater barroom the crash of breaking furniture indicated that the prisoners were still rampaging. Soon thin wisps of smoke issued from door cracks. Had Buntline set fire to the opera house? [26] Upstairs groups of apprehensive men stood in the aisles and at the doorways. Two, evidently personages of importance, hurried back to see Macready. Stagehands let them pass. One was David Colden, a friend of Dickens's and a sympathizer with British art. The other man was of Irish descent, but also in sympathy with the British actor. Robert Emmet, nephew of the Robert hanged in Dublin in 1803, was now a resident of New York. His father, as much of an Irish nationalist as his martyr uncle, had escaped the noose. Young Robert, a successful lawyer, had eloquently championed a recent revolt in the homeland, but in New York he opposed the Patriots. With Colden he invited Macready to come to his house at once, but first, before leaving the theater, to put on the best disguise of his career.

The three men entered the parquet from the stage before the audience had all left the theater. Mixing with the crowd, they sauntered into the dark streets. On Broadway the disguised men noticed that the throng had dissipated. Sullen people stood at street intersections. Swearing stretcher-bearers carried prostrate men on boards and shutters. The fugitives glanced at the wounded men as they passed. Macready mumbled imprecations in his best stage manner against "codfish aristocrats." In a drugstore dead men lay in a row on the floor. How far had this disturbance spread in the great city?

The fugitives entered Emmet's house. At this late hour they thought it best to sit quietly in dark rooms, an atmosphere of conspiracy familiar to Robert Emmet. Loyal servants brought word from the outside. The armory had been captured by the mob, they whispered. Come daylight, the rioters might turn the artillery on City Hall — re-enact the fall of the Bastille.

At four in the morning Robert Emmet called a carriage. He took pains to tell the driver that the passenger was a doctor who must be hurried to New Rochelle. Then Macready with cloak and satchel, entered the vehicle, and drove away. From Boston he sent back word that he was safe and sound.

The total casualties in the riot will never be known. Newspapers reported 34 killed and 141 wounded.[27] The names of the dead show plainly the origin of the Nativists. Among them are Owen Burns, John Jones, Mathew Carhart, Washington Taylor, and George Lincoln – men of the old America. In the *Herald*, British-born Bennett deplored a civilization that put nativity above talent. "Do we now really see the beginning of socialism in America?" he asked.[28]

Ned's friends plastered the upper wards with a new poster:

AMERICANS!

Arouse! The Great Crisis

Has Come! !

Decide now whether English

Aristocrats!!!

and

FOREIGN RULE!

shall triumph in this,

America's Metropolis,

or whether her own

SONS,

whose fathers once compelled the base-born miscreants to succumb, shall meanly lick the hand that strikes, and allow themselves to be deprived of the liberty of opinion – so dear to every true American heart.

AMERICANS!!

Come out! and dare to own yourselves sons of the iron hearts of '76!!

AMERICA [29]

Meanwhile, Ned Buntline issued an extra of his *Own* from jail – a little broadside five inches by nine, stating that he had been imprisoned for fifteen hours without a hearing. Miscreant authorities under the influence of "gratuitous lies of the *Herald*," the broadside stated, had refused bail for his release. At the moment of his arrest, Ned continued, he had not been five minutes on the ground and was turning to go home. "If the wife of my bosom," the broadside concluded, "who is now on a sick-bed, dangerously ill, should die from this shock, there shall be more than one man held responsible for her murder!"

Aroused by the poster, thousands of New York workingmen assembled in the park. A platform was erected for speakers, and local notables took seats before their constituents. Democratic malcontents – the Locofocos or Barnburners – seemed to be in the majority. They disliked the city's Whig administration as much as the Americans did, and they had a much better organization, for their leaders were not in jail. Captain Isaiah Rynders of the Empire Club called the multitude to order. Mr. Manerstock was elected chairman. He mounted the platform and announced that resolutions against the recent massacre of unarmed women and children were in order. A shiver vibrated across the platform on which he stood and the entire structure collapsed like a heap of jackstraws. Underneath, a spying newsboy was crushed to death – the last casualty of the great riot.

Out of the wreckage a table was trundled. Edward Strahan and Captain Rynders, both Democrats, climbed aboard, denounced the Whig codfish aristocrats and pleaded for support from the now leaderless Americans. Then a voice called for Mike Walsh, Ned Buntline's friend who had been with him during the Kate Hastings cowhiding. Mike stepped forward in a mussed black frock coat. He handed his plug hat to an associate and, like his colleagues, began a furious harangue against the sins of the City Fathers, their whole administration, and especially the shooting down of "unarmed women and children." [30]

Then the assembly dispersed, promising to express themselves at the next regular election. Thus the revolution terminated. Ned Buntline remained in jail, and Annie applied for a divorce.

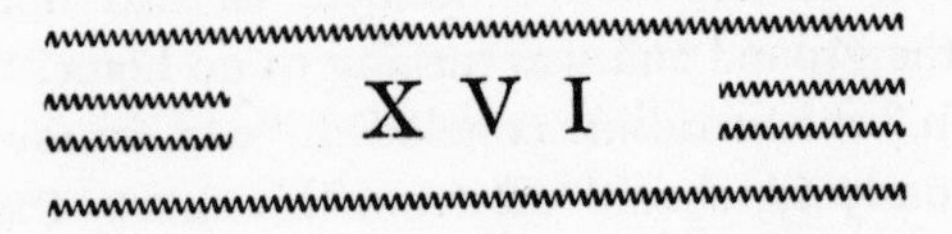

XVI

Pirate of the Hudson

NED WAS RELEASED from jail under bond to appear for trial in the riot case. An officer immediately served the liberated man with summonses to appear as defendant in a slander suit brought by James Gordon Bennett, and in Annie's divorce suit. Then the firm of Dewey & Graham, ship chandlers, clapped him in jail for a three-hundred-dollar debt he owed for provisioning his yacht. Imprisonment for debt had been illegal for years, and Ned resented the court's evasion of basic law by incarcerating him for fraud.

In this crisis Ned's assistant editor, Thomas Paterson, the Columbia College tutor,[1] decided that Ned's newspaper was insolvent, and quit. Having learned the Buntline technique from every angle, Paterson resolved to go into business for himself and publish a scandal sheet of his own. Ned was safe in jail, so Paterson picked him for the first victim to be exposed – a great error. Paterson should have known his employer better. The tutor's first act was to plaster walls, *à la* Buntline, with a great announcement of a proposed book to be sold at twenty-five cents a copy:

The Private Life, Public Career, and real Character of that odious rascal Ned Buntline!! as developed by his conduct to his past wife, present wife and various paramours! Completely lifting the Veil, and Unmasking to a Horror-stricken Community, his Debaucheries, Seductions, Adulteries, Revilings, Cruelties, Threats and Murders!!

From jail Ned appealed to his yachting friends [2] and was soon a free man – with riot, slander, chandler debt, and divorce suits pending. He went first to the police court and demanded the arrest of his erstwhile editor, Tom Paterson. Then he notified all printers, publishers, and dealers that he would sue each and every one of them who produced, bought, sold, or offered for sale Tom Paterson's malicious work. Next, in large letters, he posted his wife for being a Britisher who illegally held his newspaper property to prevent him from publishing information against the activities of foreigners.

The *Police Gazette* whooped with glee over Ned's suit against Paterson – a thief caught red-handed shouting "Stop thief." Bennett, waiting to get his lick in court at Buntline, pointed at him through the *Herald's* columns as a sample of what might be expected from socialism, unlicensed liberty, and irresponsible freedom. This, said Bennett, is what Horace Greeley advocates in his *Tribune;* this and that other horror, the liberation of the slaves.

Ned was too busy with his own countersuits to appear in the ship chandler case, and a judgment was entered against him. The sheriff attached his yacht. Ned protested, but the officers ordered his crew ashore and towed the vessel to the Atlantic Docks. Advertisements announced that *Buntline's Own* with all her rigging would be sold at auction to satisfy the judgment. A New York merchant came at once to the constable's office. He appeared to be outraged. What was this he read about selling his yacht? What authority had the officers to take her from her crew and tow the craft to the Atlantic Docks without his permission? [3] By God, sir, if the officers did not take that yacht back where they got her they would be sued for a damage claim that would ruin them for life.

The officers looked at the merchant's title. It seemed to be good. There was no evidence that Ned Buntline owned a stick in the vessel. The officers apologized and towed her back in haste. Ned met them at the mooring with his crew, boarded and sailed out into the bay. Everyone knew there was something crooked, but nobody could unearth it.

Ned had a comfortable home on board, but without his newspaper he had no means of making money. He asked for a contribution to his reform campaign from the notorious Mary Fowler. She refused to pay and Ned reported her to the police. At the trial she claimed that Buntline had threatened her with blackmail. Judge Daly dismissed the case and gave the reformer another tongue-lashing from the bench. Buntline realized that his crusade was threadbare. Even the law courts seemed in league with wayward sisters.[4] Thoroughly disgusted with the morals of the administration, Ned returned to his yacht and ordered sails unfurled. The craft was well found with food and drink. Barometers forecast fair winds. Why not leave the vile city for the pure air of the open sea? Moreover, a cholera epidemic in town threatened to spread during the coming hot weather. Yes, the place for Ned was far away on the wide ocean with no locks, bonds, or bars to bind his spirit, or, as Ned had worded it, "free; free as the glad albatross that . . . sleeps . . . on the bosom of the wave that feeds it."

Ned, at the wheel, guided *Buntline's Own* across the lower bay, skimmed around Sandy Hook, and plowed the blue waters along the Jersey coast. He had reveled in the name of Pirate of the Hudson, but was glad to get away — slow, lazy days with no worries, no officers pressing lawsuits, no bills, no sultry city streets. Pearl-gray evening faded into velvet night and Ned slept, water lapping along the yacht's smooth side. At dawn the little crew watched the western horizon for a telltale thread of land. With the dawn, too, came sea gulls to follow the yacht's wake — gulls that appeared black as crows against the dawn sky, and white as cotton once the sun was up.

At the old Cape May lighthouse Ned steered into Delaware Bay. Watching the wind on the water, he eased the yacht up the Delaware River. Soon he recognized the mouth of the Schuylkill, and in a few hours moored before Quakerdom, as he liked to call Philadelphia.

Ned walked up Chestnut Street and turned on Seventh. The side streets, always muddy in wet weather, were inches deep in dust during the dry, hot summer. Ned limped along. He appeared very old for twenty-six, a warped and twisted little young man with long beard and hair hanging over the collar of his frock coat. A few doors from the corner he stepped into a saloon, ordered a drink, and bragged that he was Ned Buntline, hero of a hundred fights. "Set 'em up again!" Ned soon had plenty of drinking, admiring friends, and word passed out onto the street that the great man was in town. His scandal sheet was well known in Philadelphia, having some fifteen hundred subscribers.[5] Ned's drinking friends asked whether people cowhided him constantly for the things he said. Ned became arrogant. "If anybody in Philadelphia wants to see me particularly, send him word that I am here. Draw us another drink."

A man walked insolently in the door. "Are you Ned Buntline?" he asked.

"Yes, that's my sobriquet," Ned replied.

"But are you sure that you are Buntline?" the fellow said.

"No mistake about it."

"Well then," said the stranger, "I'm going to whip you." He reached out his hand, slapped Ned's face, pulled his beard, spun him around, and kicked him out onto the street. "I guess he did not know that I am the real Ned Buntline," the stranger said, "Now, gentlemen, have a drink on me."

Ned picked himself up from the gutter. In the drugstore on the corner of Seventh and Chestnut he got liniment and bandages. The clerk said that the rowdy's name was McGowan.[6] Bandaged and refreshed, Ned hobbled back to the yacht. His crew made sail and the vessel drifted down the Delaware to Cape May and turned north. With the sea breeze blowing his long hair Ned recited snatches of poetry:

I like to *see* a pretty girl;
I used to love to kiss them,
When I was young (I don't know as I'm much changed, either by the nearly seven-and-twenty years of care and trouble which have sobered me). . . .[7]

Ned had acquired a bad habit of wandering in the middle of a poem or a thought. Certainly the mind of any man might be distracted by the court trials pending in New York. He would have to face three suits – the Bennett libel, the Astor House riot charge, and his divorce – if they had not already been lost by default. In any event the sunny days at sea were glorious. Surely his sins would be forgiven, unless some irate bondsman had had to pay heavily for Ned's nonappearance.

West of Sandy Hook, Ned sighted the steep roofs of Manhattan. Ocean liners, coastal schooners, and fishing smacks dotted the lower bay. Ned helmed his craft toward the city, tacked through the busy harbor traffic and hauled up at dock. So far, so good. Nobody paid any attention to him at first. Then officers bounded aboard – arrested again, by God!

Ned greeted the law officers meekly, and, as they talked, *Buntline's Own* drifted out into the Hudson. Across the water Ned saw the surface ruffle and darken with an approaching breeze. To amuse his unwelcome guests and kill time, Ned mustered his ragamuffin crew. Suddenly the gust of wind filled his sails. The yacht heeled to leeward and raced across the Hudson channel with the officers clutching deck cleats and belaying pins to prevent being swept into the water. On the Jersey side Ned asked the minions of the law where they wanted to land. Having left their bailiwick, he explained, they were without authority. At Fort Hamilton Ned docked, and the crestfallen officers of the New York law went ashore. The crew of *Buntline's Own* laughed derisively at them walking up the wharf.[8]

Late in August billboards announced that Ned Buntline intended to give the city a real treat. A British merchantman had anchored in the East River. Ned promised to give her a salute suitable for her nationality. On the day set, he hoisted sail and started around Manhattan – far enough from shore to be safe from police interference. On the mainmast he carried the American flag and beneath it floated the British jack upside down. He was pleased to see the Battery black with a crowd watching him. Ned saluted the crowd with his brass cannon. Then with a steam whistle he outscreeched all the pilot boats in the harbor. At last he came to the British steamer. Heaving to under her gigantic stern, *Buntline's Own* fired salutes to all the states in the Union. Then he hauled down the British jack, rammed it into the cannon's mouth, and fired a parting blast at the looming hulk.

People on the New York shore laughed, but the city papers scoffed at Ned for taking such great pains to insult his wife.[9] Ned heard the laughter only. Cocksure that he had re-established himself as a hero, he landed in the city and was promptly taken into custody. In the city jail, he heard about the sultry terror in New York's sweltering streets. Five thousand people had died of the Black Plague.[10] Survivors looked ahead for relief after cold weather came. Ned's constituents had been hit hard. What was left of his party seemed thoroughly demoralized.

Ned's bondsmen showed no sympathy as various cases against him came to docket. Annie, in her divorce proceedings, testified that Ned was a drunkard, that he had signed the pledge and broken it within twenty-four hours, that he had lived with other women since their marriage, that he continually frightened her with his cutlasses and pistols, that she had worried constantly lest he be assassinated by some gambler, and finally, that when drinking he had threatened to take her "where the sun never shone, and the devil couldn't find her." [11]

The court did not give a verdict at once. In the meantime Ned stood trial for taking part in the Astor Place riots and was found guilty. Judge Daly sentenced him to one year at hard labor on Blackwell's Island. On the same day Annie received her decree for divorce together with custody of the child. Ned appeared incredulous. His friends had always come to his rescue, but this time they left him alone. Ex-employee Paterson and ex-father-in-law Bennett both appeared incredulous also. They had seen Ned get out of the clutches of the law too many times.

Ned himself turned for help to the doctor at the city prison, and persuaded him to write the physician on Blackwell's Island to hospitalize the important prisoner. James Gordon Bennett's reporters got wind of the transaction and gave it due publicity. Other papers joined the shout of fraud. The island physician examined Judson when he arrived and pronounced his health excellent. Next Ned appealed to the warden for permission to publish *Buntline's Own* from jail. This, too, was denied.[12] Ned was given a prisoner's garb of striped clothes. Ex-father-in-law Bennett and ex-employee Paterson must have sighed with relief. The bane of their existence was incarcerated at last. Paterson dared to publish a second edition of Ned Buntline's *Private Life*, which he concluded with an advertisement for Columbia College students who needed to be coached for examinations on Homer's *Iliad* and *Odyssey*, Virgil's *Aeneid*, and Tasso's *Jerusalem Delivered*.[13]

With endless time and no worries, Ned became interested in a new craze sweeping the country – spiritualism. On the night of March 31, 1848, a strange thing had happened in an old house in Hydesville, New York. The full significance of the gruesome event was just beginning to be felt. Neighbors had said that the old house was haunted, but a poor family by the name of Fox had moved into it. In the Fox family there were two daughters, Margaret and Kate, aged fourteen and eleven. On the notorious March night, they lay in bed in the same room with their parents. Suddenly a tremulous knock shook the girls' bed and made a chair in the room quiver. John D. Fox, the father, lighted a candle and saw his daughters sitting bolt upright in bed, their eyes round with excitement. As he watched, the strange knocking came again. Little Kate piped with childish audacity, "Mr. Splitfoot, do as I do." Then she clapped her hands. Instantly the same number of knocks replied. "Now, do just as I do," Margaret said. "Count one, two, three, four." Four knocks replied.

The two children enjoyed the mysterious visitation, but Mrs. Fox appeared serious and frightened. She asked the spirit to knock the age of each of her children, and heard with awe the correct number of thumps for each. "Is this a human being that answers my questions so correctly?" she asked. There was no answer. "Is it a spirit? If it is, make two raps." Two thumps responded. By this method of question and answer the knocks disclosed a horrible story. Here in this house, according to the knocks, a poor peddler had been killed for his money and buried in the cellar. His restless spirit had been trying to tell the world of his fate ever since.

Ned Buntline had heard about the cult of spiritualism as he dodged the law in the summer of 1849. Now in jail, Ned talked with the prisoners about its dangerous growth. On the night of the first historic visitation Mr. Fox had hurried to a neighbor's house and soon citizens of Hydesville were flocking to the Fox residence. They stood attentively, asked questions of the "spirit," and listened to the answering raps. People remembered the peddler who had not come back. So this explained it: murder. Wondering townsmen came to the Fox house the next night and again the next. The strange manifestations excited everyone. Before long the Fox girls visited their sister in Rochester. The knocking spirits followed them there, and the whole city became interested. A peculiar formation of Kate's toes was examined. Eminent authorities announced that the unusual joints could not produce the strange noises. Several Northern cities bid for an opportunity to investigate the eerie exhibition. Soon the girls were the talk of New York. The great novelist James Fenimore Cooper, the poet William Cullen Bryant, the historian and statesman George Bancroft, with his English guest William Makepeace Thackeray,[14] all attended séances. Spiritualism became a craze.

Ned remembered an impostor he had exposed in 1848 — before the Fox sisters' fame. That old rascal, no doubt, gloated now over Ned's imprisonment. Ned had caught him taking money from a grief-stricken mother. The cheat had made her dead son appear in a mirror and wave cheerily. The ghostly figure appeared and disappeared before the weeping mother's eyes. The trick was very simple to understand after Ned explained it to the readers of his paper, but before he did so a score of women had wheedled hundreds of dollars from their husbands to see once more their dead children. The mysterious mirror, Ned explained, was plate glass backed with white wax instead of quicksilver. On the floor under the glass an ingenious set of small tubes connected with a steam boiler in the basement. Heated air or steam could be played upon the glass to render the wax transparent. Another set of tubes from a bellows above an ice-box could blow cold air on the waxed surface of the glass and thus make it opaque. To a spectator in the darkened room the waxed glass looked like a mirror. The operator placed a child of the correct age behind the glass. When the wax melted the child appeared, indistinct but lifelike, in the "mirror." Alternate currents of hot and cold air made the image appear and disappear in a ghostly fashion.[15] Ned had warned all bereaved parents to beware of the humbug. Now look where benevolence had got him!

Ned felt better when his jailers supplied him with paper and he began another book, *The Conspirators' Victim,* himself the hero as usual. He determined to publish the work as soon as released, then start a campaign against spiritualists and their cohorts. One curious thing about the spread of spiritualism must have impressed Buntline. Spirits seldom visited people south of the Mason and Dixon line. By and large it was plain to any man that spiritualism flourished best in the areas where reformers, socialists, "new thoughtists," and abolitionists dwelt. Ned had prospered in a "reformer" atmosphere. He had failed in a slave country, but he did not hate slaveholders. George Washington had tolerated the institution, and Ned's party professed to accept the Revolutionary Fathers' definition of right and wrong.

Spiritualists were organizing congregations – to protect the people from charlatans, they said. Ned Buntline called it fraud combining against fraud, precisely as the *Police Gazette* had called him a thief yelling "Stop thief." Worst of all for Ned, the new cultists had developed an expert showman's performance far superior to his own. Moreover, charming women were appearing on lecture platforms recounting experiences with the evils of polygamy, and the degradation of intemperance, and the mysterious manifestations of spiritualism that they had seen with their own eyes. Gossip of this kind appealed to an audience more than the boisterous antics of Big Lize in *The Mysteries and Miseries of New York.* Ned Buntline faced a technique much more attractive than anything he had yet devised, and every day he remained in jail these competitors entrenched themselves more firmly in popular favor. Moreover, his own political colleagues, the Americans, could not be expected to await his return indefinitely.

XVII

St. Louis Riot

On September 30, 1850, a crowd of rowdy men and boys congregated at the landing where ferries from Blackwell's Island docked.[1] They had heard that Ned Buntline's time was up. Soon the boat came in and bumped against the green mossy pilings. A bell rang, the gangplank clanked on the dock, and a little, scarred jockey of a man stepped ashore, free again. His friends fired a cannon and escorted him to a gorgeous barouche. Ned Buntline drove away behind six white horses, with a band playing "Hail to the Chief."[2]

The martyr was dined by patriotic orders, and justified himself – at least to his own satisfaction – with his new book, *The Convict's Return or Innocence Vindicated.* He revived *Ned Buntline's Own*, began his long-promised serial, "B'hoys of New York," and viciously attacked Judge Charles P. Daly, who had sentenced him. Gossiping with printers and publishers, Ned learned that his old friend, ragged Emerson Bennett – the fellow who had worked for the *Western Literary Journal* – was now a rich man. He had made a name for himself with a book entitled *Mike Fink*, and in 1849 his *Prairie Flower*, a tale of Indian captivity, had sold 100,000 copies. Its sequel, *Leni Leoti*, repeated the sales performance.

Ned found it hard to settle back into the New York life he had known. Jail had taught him a lesson about crusading against gamblers and libertines. Spiritualism seemed to have become too popular to warrant an attack; besides, charming women speakers championed the new cult, and the manifestations were becoming complex. The American Party offered the best opportunity for Ned's energy and ambition. Surely he could organize it before the next election.

In 1848, when Ned wrote *The Mysteries and Miseries of New York*, he had thought English immigrants the root of unemployment. Now, in 1851, he saw plainly that the Irish were the dangerous element – fine reward for bringing them from their potato famine! In New York they controlled Tammany Hall. In Philadelphia outraged Americans rioted against Irish domination. With proper organization the Irish could be put in their place. First the Americans must control the cities. They must send representatives to Congress. In 1852, with good management, they might elect a President.

The immediate need of the American Party was Western converts. The political balance of power lay in the Mississippi Valley. Ned went to Cincinnati in April 1851, organized a mass meeting in the hall of the Mechanics' Institute, and lectured "in the full Regalia of Five American Orders." [3] His itinerary from here is hard to follow. In all probability he floated on one of the lofty Mississippi steamboats all the way to New Orleans.

The date when Ned arrived in the Crescent City remains uncertain, but in 1851 he published *The Mysteries and Miseries of New Orleans* [4] – sure indication that he tried his old New York technique for a livelihood in the most cosmopolitan city in America, a city that prided itself on a European way of life. It is easy to imagine Ned limping through the Vieux Carré sneering at ostentatious displays of wealth, watching a gorgeous coach stop before the cathedral while a brilliantly dressed Negro footman let down carriage steps for the master to alight.[5]

Here indeed was fertile soil for planting seeds of protest against Whig aristocrats, for organizing honest workmen into the American Party – but Ned's nativism failed to germinate on the

Gulf.[6] If he was able to collect an audience and declaim against foreigners the newspapers gave him no lasting publicity. Poor people in New Orleans were mostly French, although American-born. They possessed little money and less desire to fight foreigners or to purchase Buntline nouvellettes. Gamblers, Ned's natural prey, flourished amid the luxury of excellent restaurants where sea food was served with exotic sauces, and Ned apparently found none who cared to pay him for omitting their names in his scandal sheet, or to buy the publication if he ever printed it. But Ned, as always, found a way to live by his wits. He noted a filibustering craze which excited the Southerners, and Ned turned this to his own advantage.

A dark-skinned adventurer from Venezuela, Narciso López, preached revolution in Cuba to annex the island as a new slave state like Texas. Here was a political opportunity for Buntline to unite proslavery Northerners and the South in their common desire for new territorial expansion. It also offered a money-making scheme for Ned. He began selling Cuban scrip at ten cents on the dollar, to be paid at par in case of victory.[7] Ned moved North selling scrip and lecturing on "Liberty in Cuba" and "Americanism at Home." In September he visited Baltimore and Philadelphia. Then a dispatch from Havana ended Ned's latest effort to unite North and South against foreigners. López had been caught and garroted. His second in command, W. L. Crittenden, nephew of the United States Attorney General, had been shot while attempting to escape from Cuba in a small boat. The revolution was over, and Ned's friends were still holding worthless Cuban scrip. Ned decided to go West again – St. Louis perhaps. No one out there had invested in his now valueless paper.

Once more he crossed the mountains and boarded a river steamboat bound for the West to organize his American Party and, incidentally, raise his own campaign funds within the year. Mingling with frock-coated planters and ladies in hoop skirts, he watched the never-ending panorama of silver-gray water and treetopped shore.

Passengers loafing along the boat rail talked about the great future of St. Louis, which had already surpassed Cincinnati. Hundreds of foreigners came to the city every year – surely a great place to build up the American Party. Ned listened eagerly when traveling companions said that fifty steamboats were moored every day at the St. Louis levee, loading and unloading – yes, some three thousand tied up there yearly. Besides the Great Lakes and New Orleans trade, St. Louis attracted Ohio River traffic and was also the terminus for overland routes from the Far West. The Santa Fe Trail and the Rocky Mountain fur trade brought the city almost a million dollars a year. Gold seekers and emigrants, heading across the plains for California and Oregon, added to the prosperity. No wonder St. Louis was outstripping Cincinnati. Passengers bragged that St. Louis would be the packing center of the West[8] and take that crown from Cincinnati, too. In 1844–1845, St. Louis packers had killed a scant 16,000 hogs. By 1848 the slaughter had quadrupled. Now that number of only four years before seemed small. The city itself had doubled in size every four years.[9] No place in the world promised such an opportunity. Surely campaign funds would be ample here.

Ned heard people boast about the lawlessness that went along with opportunity in St. Louis – very different from New Orleans. Rioting and lynching had been common since the days of statehood. The French and the Irish, the Jacques and the Mikes, fought periodically with clubs, rocks, and pistols. In 1844 the city election had been a battle royal. In 1849, the year of New York's Astor Place disturbance, St. Louis had staged two riots. In one of them firemen and rivermen had finally brought out cannon to settle their differences. Since then, cannon were considered essential for street arguments. Here was the right atmosphere for Ned's devices.

At St. Louis the steamboat stopped under a broad sloping levee crowned with imposing public buildings and a church on the skyline. Gangplanks were thrust ashore. Passengers landed among a motley crew of hack drivers shouting and waving toward their vehicles. Ned trudged past them up the slope toward the city. He picked his way around piles of freight covered with tarpaulins, and dodged drays that rumbled across the cobblestones with teamsters cracking their whips and ragged children hanging on behind.

At the top of the levee Ned noticed that the city was built on low rolling hills. He limped up the street watching for an opportunity, any kind of congenial employment. A print shop sign interested him. Here was Ned's chance – an easy way to make expenses in a new town. Soon a weekly, *Ned Buntline's Novelist*, appeared on the streets. Next Ned turned his attention to the social and political needs of the metropolis and the proper time for organizing the American Party here. St. Louis was a city of over eighty thousand – booming, as Ned's fellow passengers had said. Yet on every hand Ned saw evidence of the frontier town – occasional Rocky Mountain trappers in buckskin shirts, emigrants outfitting for Santa Fe or the Oregon Trail. The *Novelist* did not sell well in front of stores offering saddles, tents, bedding, and guns. Overland travelers preferred to purchase guidebooks. They did not expect leisure hours ahead as had train travelers or soldiers embarking for the Mexican War. Ned must find some other means of making a living until election time. He decided to organize a concert troupe and play the country towns across the river in Illinois.

Ned trained a quartet, designed a few costumes, printed some playbills, and led his little company on board a steamboat – a cheap way to tour the villages on the Mississippi, Missouri, and Illinois rivers. In rural towns Ned practiced a fixed advertising routine. First he placarded the main street, inviting all working people to his show. Next he announced that admission tickets sold for fifty cents, ladies free. With the assembly hall filled, "Colonel" Judson stepped on the stage dressed in the uniform of a Cuban insurrecto and lectured on "Cuba and Her Martyrs," adding a few excoriating remarks about the filthy rich in America. Next, the quartet rendered national selections while Ned changed to the costume of a Seminole chief, came out again, and delivered an oration on "Wrongs Done the Indians of America." Then Ned declaimed against foreigners, explained the advantages derived from joining the Patriotic and Benevolent Order of the Sons of America, offered to take initiation fees, and reminded the audience that election day was less than a year away.

The little troupe visited many towns, including Springfield, Illinois,[10] where a lawyer named Abraham Lincoln was beginning to make a name for himself. Returning to St. Louis, Ned began to organize for the spring elections. He planned first to take advantage of native-born Americans' dislike for the large German population, many of them revolutionists who had fled to save their necks after the collapse of the 1848 uprisings in Europe. The Germans' leader, a newspaperman named Henry Boernstein, had served five years in the Austrian Army. An intellectual and a university graduate as well as a man of action, Boernstein had managed grand opera in Paris and had written plays that attracted audiences in all the capitals of Europe. In St. Louis he edited the sensational *Anzeiger des Westens*. Ned Buntline had met no English or Irish immigrant of his caliber in New York. Boernstein preached unity for all German Americans. Voting by bloc, he said, would win the lawful rights of all Teutons in democratic America. And this was not all. He had stolen Buntline's thunder by publishing a book entitled *The Mysteries of St. Louis.*

Ned learned that the Democratic Party was split into two factions here in St. Louis – supporters of Thomas Hart Benton and of Sterling Price. Both men were candidates for governor of Missouri – the former antislavery, the latter proslavery. Boernstein and his Germans backed the Bentonites. Whigs controlled the city with Mayor Luther M. Kennett. City elections were due in April 1852, and the state and national elections in the fall. In this political chaos Ned Buntline saw his first real opportunity to establish a strong party in the heart of the Mississippi Valley. For the spring election both Whigs and Democrats organized long parades of marching men with brass bands and fire-engine companies. Boernstein boasted that he would carry the city: "Conway, Benton and Democracy." The Whig partisans shouted back that they would hold the offices they already maintained. Once or twice rival demonstrators met in the streets. Crushed stone, piled along a new macadam improvement, furnished admirable arguments to hurl back and forth—repartee which Ned understood.

On the morning of April 5, 1852, the polls opened. Voting started without interruption. The town appeared to be quiet around City Hall. Then word came that a Whig carriage had been assaulted and broken to splinters in the German district. Boernstein was making his threat good. Another Whig carriage drove away from headquarters with banners on each side advertising "Kennett and City Improvements." [11] Like the first, this carriage never came back. A muddy and bleeding coachman, trembling and swearing vengeance, stumbled up the City Hall steps. He had been pulled from the box and pelted with mud, he said, at the Soulard Market polls. The Germans had mauled and beaten him and stampeded his horses.

The courageous mayor called for his own carriage. He drove straight to the scene of the trouble, stepped down, and sauntered into the polls. A crowd gathered around him. Someone tried to start an argument, "I heard you abuse the Dutch in the ferry-boat." Several angry voices shouted: "Hang him; drown him." [12]

Kennett climbed back into his carriage and ordered the coachman to drive away. He had not been touched, but it was no safe place to linger. Back in City Hall one of his constituents, David

Robinson, burst into his office. Robinson complained that he was not allowed to vote in the first ward and he wanted his rights. Two other men came in with similar complaints. Precinct workers crowded around the mayor, talking, giving advice. They said that no Whig ballots were available at some polling places. The Democrats had destroyed them all and left only Democratic ballots. At other polls bands of Germans stood in the doorways and prevented all voters except Democrats from entering. That man Boernstein had achieved the German unity he wanted.

The mayor looked out the door and down the hall. Angry politicians and their workers, who should be at the polls, stared at him with desperate, beseeching eyes. Four or five hundred more stood in the streets outside. The mayor delivered a short address, said that he would not interfere in the election. The people must maintain their own right to vote. For a moment everyone stood in silence. Then a small man on a big horse rode forward. "Come with me," he shouted to David Robinson. "I'll see that you get a chance to vote." Behind the heels of Ned Buntline's charger a local politician, Robert O'Blenis, followed in a buggy with a keg of whiskey. These two men led the way down Fourth Street toward the Soulard Market polls. The crowd followed, men and boys packing the street, curb to curb – five thousand, it was estimated.

The Germans saw them coming. Veterans of street barricades in recent revolutions in Europe, they advanced toward the Americans. Buntline, on horseback, and a few fast pedestrians were far ahead of the City Hall crowd. The Germans waved their pistols. They threw rocks. Ned was knocked from his horse. His companions fell beside him. The horse galloped back with an empty saddle, bridle reins dangling. Buntline, bleeding and angry, whooped to the mob to come on: "Rush the lop-eared Dutch." In short order the rabble – buggy, whiskey and all – swept exultantly upon the enemy. Hopelessly outnumbered, the

Fracker Library
Buena Vista College

Germans disappeared. The invaders took over the polls, placed Whig ballots on the tables, arranged tumblers around the keg of liquor, and invited all who felt patriotic to come and vote. Drinking friends called on Buntline for a speech. Someone brought up his horse. Ned mounted and rode back and forth in front of the polls reciting the Revolutionary oratory which his father had taught him.

The mob prowled into nearby saloons. Across the street, in a coffeehouse, an old man told inquisitive rioters that he had been whipped because he was a Whig. The Americans offered him a drink. In another saloon some muskets were discovered behind the bar. The rioters threw them clattering into the street. Buntline, pistol in hand, rode up to a large Democratic poster on a house front. From the saddle he reached up to tear it down. A hail of stones pelted him, spattering on the wall. Germans were throwing from second-story windows across the street. A shot rang out. Men ran from the polls. Someone pointed to the house of a German saloonkeeper named Niemeyer, and said the shot came from there. The mob surged up in front of the drawn shutters. A young man in a fireman's uniform, Joseph Stephens, pounded at the door with a club. A panel gave way. From the inside a gun appeared through the shattered door – a whiff of smoke and a dull report. Stephens turned, staggered down the steps, faltered across the street, and fell dead, his head on the curb.[13] Cursing men gathered about him. Others rushed into Niemeyer's saloon, upset the stove, piled wood upon it, and ran upstairs. The fire alarm sounded. Shots boomed from windows and hallways. Ned Buntline shouted above the din.

Niemeyer was found in a room with his sick wife. Another man sat with them, nursing a wounded leg. Smoke from below began to billow up the hall. The Americans snatched four corners of a mattress and carried Mrs. Niemeyer out of the burning building. Her husband and the cripple followed. Out in the open a shower of stones knocked Niemeyer down. He got up, staggered forward, and was knocked down again. Behind him the fire crackled viciously.

A Phoenix engine gonged down the street and unrolled its hose. Men in red helmets ran toward the blaze with a nozzle. The captain shouted through his trumpet, "Water! Turn on water!" Nothing happened. The mob milling across the hose had cut it in a dozen places and the building burned to the ground.

Some men's rage cooled with the useless conflagration and the sight of the sick woman. At the trial, later, several witnesses testified that O'Blenis said with shame, "When it comes to fighting I'm in, but when to burning houses I'm not there." [14]

Darkness settled over the city and the crowd increased. Germans came out from behind fences, piles of lumber, the shadows of houses. They stood sullenly, mean and menacing. What did these professional revolutionists intend to do next? Then a word of warning went through the American throng. The Dutch were bringing up their cannon.

Things looked bad for Buntline's men, packed between the houses and at the mercy of trained foreign street fighters, but a shout of exultation showed the Americans to be undaunted. With cheers they greeted a party of hoodlums bringing two brass howitzers. Cannon would be met with cannon. At the corner of Park and Carondelet avenues the big guns were unlimbered. Men loaded them with elaborate gestures – a threat to all foreigners.

An officer in the uniform of a captain of militia elbowed his way through the American crowd. He appeared angry. He demanded that his cannon be returned, threatened to call out his company and disperse the mob. Whigs or Democrats or free elections did not concern Captain Almstedt. He was a military man and he wanted his ordnance. No one seemed to have the guns in charge and the crowd melted away from the heated captain. The fight, however, was not finished. True, the polls were closed, the election over, the captain had regained his ordnance and all issues seemed to be settled, but at 10:00 P.M. men and boys congregated again, shouting, "On to the *Anzeiger* office!"—crush once and for all time the press and the power of the German bloc and the man who dared write *The Mysteries of St. Louis.*

The mob was too late. The militia captain with his men and cannon stood deployed before the newspaper office. Nothing for the mob to do now but go to bed or to some sheltered barroom and wait until the morning papers printed the result of the election.

At dawn newspapers announced that the Whigs had carried the city. Democratic editors blamed their party's loss on an unholy alliance between the Whig minority and the Americans, but none mentioned Ned Buntline's name. All the papers deprecated the riot. The *St. Louis News* announced: "Radicalism in its worst form has gained the victory—European radicalism." [15] The *Times* editorial reported "scenes . . . enacted . . . in the course of yesterday's charter elections, which would have disgraced the capital of France. . . ." [16]

On April 7 Joseph Stephens was buried with due formality, his fireman's belt and hat on the coffin lid. The funeral procession, half a mile long, carried a great banner with typical Buntline language: AMERICANS WE BEAR A BROTHER TO HIS GRAVE. FORGET NOT HOW HE HAS BEEN SLAIN.[17] A committee sent a letter of condolence to Stephens's parents in New York.

Before long, newspapers from outlying communities began to arrive in St. Louis. These sheets mentioned Ned Buntline as the leader of the mob. How had such news got out of town? An investigation was made at the telegraph office. Three mysterious telegrams had been sent on the day of the riot:

April 5, 4 P.M.

A party of Dutch gathered around 1st ward polls. Firemen went to drive them away, etc.

ST. LOUIS RIOT

5 o'clock

Ned Buntline had a horse killed under him – he acted like a man – fired several times and each ball took effect. Bob O'Blennis scattering the Dutch blood like dew.

11 o'clock

Great riot – Anzeiger office mobbed – military ordered out – number St. Louis Fire Co. killed – Stevenson – Neiermeyers house on 7th & Park ave. burned – 250 Germans gone to Illinois.[18]

Did Buntline send these telegrams? The second one sounded like him. No one will ever know. Both Buntline and O'Blenis were arrested and led off to jail.

XVIII

The Know-Nothings

NED BUNTLINE looked for a bondsman. He soon found two with sufficient property to be accepted by the court, Robert Major and Leverett F. Hastings, the latter a tinner. Both signed sureties for $500, to be forfeited in case Buntline failed to appear daily in court and on the first day of each session thereafter until his case was disposed of – an impossible requirement for one of Buntline's temperament. On June 14, 1852, Buntline's case was postponed to the July term. In July it was postponed again. Ned, in the meantime, loafed around Bragg's patent medicine advertising company, making suggestions and reading about his American Party's national convention back in Trenton, New Jersey. For President and Vice-President the Americans nominated the great Daniel Webster and a George C. Washington, respectively – good vote-getting names, surely, for Native Americans, but not good enough. Washington was a congressman from Maryland and he declined the new honor. Webster, unsuccessful candidate for the Presidential nomination in the Whig convention the same year, died before election day without committing himself concerning the nativist ticket.

On September 9, five months after the St. Louis riot, Ned's case was called for trial. With his companions, Ned stood meekly at the bar of justice. One of the culprits could not afford an attorney, and the court appointed defense counsel for him. All swore that they were not guilty. Endless examination of jurors and cross-examination of unwilling witnesses followed. Then a juror became ill. For a time it seemed that the whole expensive business of impaneling a jury would have to be repeated. Fortunately the man recovered. The case was heard, and eighteen days after the opening of the trial the jury retired to decide its verdict. Five days later, with costs mounting constantly, they signified that they could not agree. The court dismissed them and ordered a new trial.

Ned grunted his disgust. He had missed the American Party convention, and now he would have to remain in the West until after the election. The two top posts on the nativist ticket were vacated, one by death and the other by resignation, and the positions were filled by Dr. Reynell Coates and Jacob Broom, both well-known names back East. Coates belonged to a prominent Quaker family and claimed to be one of the founders of the Patriotic Sons of America. For campaign symbols, coats and brooms were displayed. Election day disclosed a pitiful following—only 1670 votes in Pennsylvania, 831 in New Jersey, and 184 in Massachusetts.[1] Something was wrong. Ned knew perfectly well that he could raise more men than that at any of his rallies. However, there was nothing to do now until the next election two years hence, and in the meantime his own case remained unsettled.

Buntline's patience snapped. He moved across the Mississippi to Carlyle, Illinois, where two local politicians wanted to establish a newspaper.[2] The first issue of this venture bore the elaborate title, *Buntline's Novelist and Carlisle* [sic] *Prairie Flower.*[3] Ned's old friend, Emerson Bennett, had made a fortune with the name "Prairie Flower" but for Ned it proved a complete failure, pleasing neither the electorate nor Ned's backers. He moved away, destination unknown. In January 1853, his case was called for trial in St. Louis and the court ordered Major and Hastings to pay their forfeit for Ned's nonappearance. This was the case which plagued him twenty years later when performing with Buffalo Bill.

Buntline's route, after leaving Carlyle, is hard to trace. No doubt he supported himself with lectures on Americanism, the wrongs done the Seminoles, or some of his other patent procedures. Probably he crossed into Kentucky. Years later there came to light a package of letters to him from Mary Porterfield, dated 1853.[4] If Ned visited the widow of the man he had killed, he did not stay with her long. In July he had a residence at Chappaqua, Westchester County, New York. There he met the twenty-five-year-old "widow Swart" – a name to remember. For the next thirty years Lovanche Swart would be Ned's Nemesis. Time and again he would escape her, but never for long. Lovanche's late husband, a former resident of Eleroy, Illinois, had been foreman on *Ned Buntline's Own.* During that time Ned and Lovanche had never met, but now in 1853 gallant Buntline told the widow that he had promised her husband, before he died, to be a father to his three-year-old son.[5] Lovanche was pleased. It seemed like old times to her when, in August 1853, Ned revived *Buntline's Own.* On the twenty-fourth of September, the couple were married in West Hoboken in Palisade House, which Ned told his bride was theirs.

The newlyweds lived happily in their home until spring, when Ned suggested that they go on the road lecturing and creating nativist lodges, building an organization of influence before the American Party's national convention in the fall. Although 1854 was not a Presidential year, the meeting must not be another fiasco like the 1852 conclave in Trenton. Lovanche said later, "We went to all the Eastern states, had good times and enjoyed life in all its pleasures."[6]

Events were developing favorably for the nativists, but in spite of everything slavery continued to crowd aside the moral issues that Ned championed. The Democratic Party seemed on the verge of cracking wide open, North from South. Surely, in time, peace-loving people who saw the threat of war over the Negro would find nativism a safety valve for the increasing pressure of abolition steam. Some nativists also counted on a permanent alliance with the prohibitionists, whose cause had been growing steadily since the days of the Washingtonians more than a decade before. Nativists and drys would make an aggregate to be reckoned with. Up in Maine, the successful, cold, and cautious Neal Dow had been elected mayor of Portland on a prohibition ticket in 1851. The state went dry the same year. Prohibitionists were derisively called "Maine-iacs," [7] but their principles were spreading as relentlessly as the spiritualists'. The prohibitionists – unlike the spiritualists – were in politics. Both Wisconsin and Indiana had adopted the Maine Law. Ohio, Illinois, and Michigan were soon to follow.[8] The nativists, with their opposition to foreigners, who were notorious drinkers of wine and beer, might unite successfully with the drys and form a party of power.

So much for the bright side of the prospect. Handicaps against the new nativism increased daily. Shortsighted greed and jealousy of powerful factions hindered national amalgamation. Moreover, the drinking of hard liquor was not confined to foreigners. Yankees, backwoods Westerners, and Southern planters might dislike foreigners, but many of them indulged in an occasional swig. Both foreign-born and native sons evaded the prohibition laws jocularly. Enterprising Americans, some of them descendants of Revolutionary patriots, opened public rooms where a visitor was charged twenty-five cents to see a striped pig and was given a drink for nothing. Pigs with any deformity, even blind pigs, became valuable as exhibits. In Maine, heart of the prohibition area and lungs of the nativist movement, a saloon man had the effrontery to operate an omnibus in which passengers were charged fourpence for a ride – drinks free.[9]

The Democrats tried to save themselves from the impending crackup with a bold move in 1854. They passed what was known as the Kansas-Nebraska Act, to permit Kansas, located in free territory, to enter the Union as a slave state if the settlers so willed it. On the surface the act seemed innocent enough, but underneath it lurked an obvious concession to the South—an irritant to the slavery issue. To the amazement of many old-line Democrats, the act split the elements of their party instead of cementing them. In short, the slavery issue amounted to more than the politicians had calculated. In the chaos of re-crimination and threatening party bolts, both nativists and anti-liquor parties hoped to recruit enough followers to control the next election. Could they enlist enough voters who were more interested in nativist principles than in abolition? Of the forty-two Northern congressmen who voted for the Kansas-Nebraska bill, only seven were re-elected. The seats of the others were filled with new men. Ned and his party workers claimed that most of them were nativists—who could tell? An even worse land-slide from the established parties became manifest as local elections were reported. Indeed, party lines seemed to have dissolved altogether.[10] Only Americans, or Know-Nothings as they were now called, and anti-Nebraska men won at the Northern polls, and the two were often indistinguishable. Then the papers announced that Philadelphia had voted for a complete Know-Nothing ticket,[11] and in New York nativists convened a mass meeting to contest the election of Mayor Fernando Wood.[12]

For leaders in the Know-Nothing movement the sun now shone. With local members of their party fighting for control of all anti-Nebraska meetings, they looked forward to the national convention of nativists at Cincinnati in November. A properly balanced national platform might serve as a lifesaver to the myriad disorganized voters who had abandoned their own ships and now bobbed desperately in the tossing political waters.

The name Know-Nothing for the new party was attributed to Ned.[13] His years of practice in organizing secret societies and the interest of his father in Masonic orders made Ned a man full of ideas for the new organization. To get all loose voters—North and South—the party dared not have too strict a platform. Members were instructed, when asked their principles, to reply,

"I know nothing." How Ned loved that cryptic answer! He wrote the party's ritual, and introduced a mysterious form for calling meetings. Small pieces of paper, he said, should be scattered secretly along the streets. All loyal men would recognize them as a call to meeting that night. When the little papers were colored red the members should come armed.

The perplexing thing about the new political party was the fact that no one could be sure how large it really was. Old-line politicians saw definitely that their men were not winning elections, but were the winners anti-Nebraskaites, prohibitionists, or really Know-Nothings? Certainly the nativists claimed all newly elected men.

Ned's old enemy in New York, James Gordon Bennett – a tremendous power in the newspaper world now – put all his influence into a fight against the antiforeign movement. So did Horace Greeley with the *New York Tribune*. Out West the newspapers carried on a similar battle, and in Cincinnati, where the Know-Nothings planned their convention, the *Enquirer* barked sarcastically, "We suppose we shall see *Chief Buntline* . . . in full Know-Nothing toggery, parading our streets!" [14]

Ned knew of but one reply – shout his doctrine louder than the other fellow. With a crackpot known as the Angel Gabriel, he began a series of incendiary speeches in July and August.[15] The *Cincinnati Enquirer* warned readers to prepare for the Know-Nothing convention as an invasion of "Buntline church-burners." Then, to the delight of the Democratic press, Buntline and the "Angel" were both reported in jail.[16] The Angel had been arrested first in Charlestown, Massachusetts, then later in Philadelphia, the new Know-Nothing city. How the conservative press crowed! – radicals in office arresting their own kin out of office.

Ned's offense was worse than Gabriel's. He was charged with bigamy,[17] with marrying a charming actress named Josie Juda, and the complaint had been filed by Lovanche Swart Judson [18] –

first bolt from the Goddess of Retribution. The *Enquirer* asked pointedly if Ned's friends intended to break jail and bring him to the convention, or would he give orders through the bars? [19] With glee the Know-Nothings were called the "Buntlinites," but in spite of much jeering the party seemed to be gaining converts from both Democrats and Whigs.[20] The Democratic press pointed out that Jefferson had welcomed immigrants. According to his lights it was sufficient for foreigners who wanted to vote to declare only that they intended to stay permanently "with us." Surely no loyal and thoughtful Democrat could now turn away from the founder of the party. As for disaffected Whigs, consider Henry Clay. He, too, had been liberal in his ideas of the requirements for citizenship. "What an exchange of leaders," the *Enquirer* concluded, "the world-renowned orator of America, Henry Clay, for the convicted inmate of Blackwell's Island Prison, the notorious Judson." [21] Then word came that Ned had been released by the governor of New York.

Almost three months would elapse before the Cincinnati convention, so he headed for New England with two things in mind – to organize the American Party locally up there, and to work for temperance at the movement's source. From his new field of endeavor a story of violence came back. At a temperance meeting in Portland, Maine, Ned was reported to have tossed a heckler into Presumpscot Inlet.[22] Then more dismaying news arrived. In November, only two weeks before the Cincinnati convention, newspapers announced that Ned had been arrested again, this time for shooting a man.[23] The ruckus occurred near midnight on the Kennebec road between Bath and Augusta, Maine. Ned the loyal nativist, claimed that he shot at an offending Greek, who, on investigation, turned out to be a Negro with an ancestry as pure American as Ned's own. The error in identity was due in part to the blackness of the night. Shortly before dark, Ned had called at the *Mirror* office in Bath. Reporters noticed that he was red faced, full of organization plans and hard liquor, but they considered him in control of himself. He said that he must drive most of the night in order to be in Richmond the next morning to begin organizational work there. The October night was chilly, so Ned wore a coonskin coat. The newsmen watched him climb into his gig and wrap a buffalo robe around his knees. Then Ned clucked to his roan horse and disappeared in the dark. At the edge of town, beyond the poorhouse and in the tough dockyard section, he met an oxcart with four or five men walking, riding, and also drinking. A quarrel ensued. Ned fired two shots and whipped away. At the Bay Bridge he stopped, paid toll, and reported to the drowsing gatekeeper that he had been held up by twenty-five or thirty Greeks and had shot his way through. One foreigner, Ned said, had grabbed his horse's bridle. "I shouted, 'Stand by, Greek, and let me pass.'" The fellow, Ned said, did not let go the bridle. "I took a *document* out and shot, and he fell. Another one jumped, I shot and think I missed him. Couldn't say whether he was dead or alive, should probably hear in the morning."

The tollgate keeper replied that the road was dangerous after dark. He himself kept well armed. Then he paid Ned the change due him and watched the gig enter the bridge. A short distance down the way Ned's vehicle struck a pile of lumber and one wheel broke. The doughty little driver jumped from the wreck, spread his buffalo robe on the roan horse's back, bounded aboard, and rode off regardless. On the east shore he turned north, recrossed the Kennebec to Bowdoinham, and got transportation to Richmond, where he arrived in the morning after traveling twenty-five roundabout miles. Here he was arrested and taken back to Bath.[24] On the way Ned told the sheriff that he had planned to come back anyway to enter a complaint against his assailants.

The warrant for Ned's arrest was based on a complaint by Telemachus Freeman, a Negro who testified that Ned had fired at him without provocation, the bullet lodging in his right thigh.[25]

Judge Smith put Ned under a thousand-dollar bond and set a day for his trial. Ned supplied the bail from his own pocket, and said that he would employ no counsel but would defend his own case. Then he set out along the road he had traveled, asking questions about the Negro he had injured and gloating, no doubt, over the histrionics he would display in the coutroom. The trial began in the Bath city hall on October 25, 1854, and lasted just three days.[26] The Negro claimed that he and a group of young men had met Judson on the road. The white man, Freeman said, had almost run them down, and they had yelled as he dashed past. Twenty yards down the road Buntline had stopped and called, "Boys, if you want anything come back."[27] Freeman testified that he had walked along the road toward the gig, and Ned had shot twice, the second ball hitting his leg.

Freeman's companions corroborated this statement, and things looked bad for Ned – but the courtroom was full of Know-Nothing friends, and everyone waited to hear Ned's side of the story, for his cross-examination of the plaintiff, and also for the testimony of the witnesses for the defense. The presence of several Negro girls, subpoenaed by Ned, added to the suspense. Ned opened his case by drawing from Freeman and his companions the admission that they had started the eventful night by dissipating in Harrison's wine cellar as early as 6:15 P.M. In this den of iniquity they had decided to go to a dance, had met a man with an ox team, and gone along with him. Having established this, Ned called the Negro girls to the stand. Each testified in turn that Telemachus Freeman and his companions had thrown rocks at their houses, tried to gain admittance, and urged them to come out. Soon the character of the wounded Negro was thoroughly discredited. Then Ned called on others, including the town's "night watch," to testify that the edge of Bath, where the attack occurred, was dangerous after dark. Finally the toll bridge keeper was called to the witness chair.

He, too, said that the road was unsafe, that he himself kept his house bolted and his gun loaded at all times. As for Ned's being drunk: the toll collector thought him well able to take care of himself. The hotel proprietor in Bath also testified that Ned was sober when he left town. He had paid his bill, torn up the account, and thrown away the pieces. With this, Defense Attorney Judson terminated his case.

The judge acquitted Buntline. Know-Nothing friends cheered the decision, and the *Bath Mirror* announced that Ned would speak the next evening at Corinthian Hall "by request of the Guard of Liberty." [28]

Ned moved triumphantly up the Kennebec once more to Richmond. In the newspapers he read complaints about the judge's decision. The *Democrat* of Lincoln, Maine, called Ned a modern Don Quixote. Without doubt, the editor sneered, Ned thought the Negro workman a Popish troop and the lumber pile on the Bay Bridge a Romish arsenal. Ned read further that Know-Nothingism was growing tremendously in the South, for it opposed immigration the same as slaveholders did. "Oh! for some Mrs. Stowe," the *Democrat* moaned, "to expose the connexion and support which Know-Nothings give to slavery." [29]

Ned knew the "connexion" of slavery and Know-Nothingism very well. He had worked for years to strengthen it, to make nativism more important politically than abolition, and the test of his party's ability to hold North and South in an antiforeign crusade would be met in Cincinnati on November 15, only two weeks away. But Ned did not attend. Instead, he solicited recruits for the Guard of Liberty – a secret military order to protect the parent Know-Nothing organization, so Ned claimed.[30] Perhaps Ned knew that his repeated arrests had marked him as undesirable for any political preferment. Perhaps he had become an out-and-out mountebank, living on subscriptions to his so-called degrees.

On November 15, 1854, the Know-Nothing convention was

called to order in Cincinnati without Ned Buntline, although the opposition press still insisted on calling them "the Buntlinite conspirators." A large attendance was present. For the first time in the party's history, representatives came from all states. Ned's ritual was affirmed,[31] but his three degrees were altered radically. A so-called "Union Degree"[32] was added to satisfy members both North and South and sidestep the slavery agitation which had raged all summer over the Kansas-Nebraska Act. With the oath, party members swore to vote for no one who favored disunion and to dismiss from office anyone who did.[33] Then the members adjourned, with high hopes of holding Northern workingmen, many Southern Democrats, and practically all the Whigs.

Ned labored in New England without regard to the national party. He organized chapters of the Guard of Liberty on Rutherford's Island and at Round Pond, Maine. He opened his own headquarters at the Spaw Spring House – a resort of Southern planters – and he chartered a bark, which he christened *Buntline's Own.* In her he cruised up the Pemaquid Inlet and ventured out to sea past the lighthouse on the point. All members of his Guard wore brass badges cut in spread-eagle pattern. They held military musters, but mysteriously refused to tell about the organization. On certain afternoons small pieces of paper appeared on the streets – a Know-Nothing device. Always alert, these minutemen stood ready to scurry patriotically from shop and workbench for every "war alarum." One day early in December, as Ned's bark appeared off Rutherford's Island, his Guard turned out to greet him in full regalia, a great mistake. The abolition press announced with mock solemnity that Ned's modest craft had been mistaken by his own Guard for the Papal fleet, that Judson and his crew had appeared like the Supreme Pontiff and his cardinals, and that His Eminence Ned Buntline had had to cry for quarter. Every man on Rutherford's Island with a brass eagle on his coat felt ridiculous under the local paper's sarcastic praise for saving America from invasion. The editor concluded by paying high tribute to the patriots of his town, who could always be relied upon when their country's liberties were endangered.[34] At Richmond, Ned succeeded in organizing another chapter, but the town's golden-voiced minister, Isaac Kalloch, branded him from the pulpit as a jailbird and a murderer.[35]

Ned moved north to Bangor, where the raillery followed him. A new order, the press sneered, had been formed. This one was called the Knights of the Star Spangled Banner, or "Guardians of the Tail Feathers of the American Eagle." Its purpose was announced as "devotion to the bottle and hostility to everything else." [36] The *Thomastown Journal* suggested that wide popular support of Buntline's Guard of Liberty would assure security to America for many years to come.[37]

Ned had no good reply for the banter. In April he wrote a solemn letter to the *Bangor Journal* stating that the old American Party of 1843 and 1844 was no more. Not a single paper in the country, he moaned, but misrepresented the party's principles. Not one of them but would work more faithfully for the demagogue than for the true patriot like himself. "In this State, more than any other, has the Native American party been misrepresented and its intentions been misunderstood." [38] Thus Ned read himself out of the party on the dawn of its greatest year, for in 1855 the Know-Nothings claimed eight of the thirty-two governors in the United States. In the national House of Representatives a majority of the members were either anti-Nebraska men or Know-Nothings; the two were as yet not distinct. Obviously the old parties had dissolved, in acid arguments over slavery or in the fluid fear of foreign immigration—which? Politicians were still not sure.

The 1855 Know-Nothing convention told the story at last. A slavery plank was introduced in the platform and the party split, North and South, precisely as the Democrats had done. Thus slavery proved to be the paramount political issue of the day. Ned, out of a job, looked for some new quixotic windmill. His old rival, "Professor" Ingraham, had also come to the end of his tether. Ned had unwittingly copied Ingraham, changing from adventure stories to reform crusades. Now Ingraham went one step further. In his best shilling-shocker style he wrote *The Prince of the House of David, or, Three years in the Holy City*, a work destined to be printed and reprinted for half a century. Ingraham had got religion – joined the priesthood of the Protestant Episcopal Church and become rector of St. John's in Mobile, where he conducted 343 baptisms and converted 117 new members, including his son Prentiss.[39] Ned Buntline could not follow his trail there.

Ned returned to temperance lecturing, but he found that the spiritualists had usurped the "experience technique" which had proved so successful with the Washingtonians. It was discouraging, too, to discover that scientists accepted spiritualism. Some people even went so far as to prophesy that a political party would form around this cult. Spiritualism was strongest in areas where a new antislavery party, called "Republican," had sprouted, and the spiritualist creed assumed many of the planks of Republicanism, even the Western plank for free homesteads.[40] Sharp Know-Nothing arguments had snipped members of the old Whigs and Democrats loose from their political moorings, making it easy for them to join the new Republicans. Could the growing excitement over spiritualism dissolve the cartilaginous Republicans and make way for a still newer party?

Spiritualism cut particularly deep into church congregations. Perhaps these citadels of conservatism might be splintered as the Whig and Democratic parties had been. A British writer, noting the magnitude of spiritualist belief, asked:

> By what known process can hundreds and thousands of people, of all classes, and under all circumstances, be so hallucinated, that they would testify under oath to things that never happened? Of what

value is any amount of human testimony, to any fact whatever, if such hallucination is possible? [41]

Then a strange news note appeared in the spiritualist press. Ned Buntline, so the note said, had joined their ranks. At a séance he had knelt on the floor, sobbing that he believed.[42]

XIX

The Adirondacks

IN THE MIDDLE 1850's Ned was a lost soul, at his wit's end. He did not admit conversion to spiritualism – that was all newspaper talk – and the cult did not seem to be breaking up the Republicans. Ned's present wives, Lovanche and Josie Juda, had proved to be liabilities he wanted to forget. His American or Know-Nothing movement lay dead, punctured by antislavery crusaders. Right or wrong, everybody admitted that the moral issue of slavery, not the religious issue of papism, was paramount. The temperance movement alone remained, but Ned's strong constitution was being undermined by the alcohol required to stimulate him for prohibition lectures. He decided to bury himself in the woods, become sober, and devote his time to hunting, fishing, writing, and the contemplation of nature. The Adirondack region was a fabulous game country in northern New York, like central Africa or Alaska a hundred years later.

Ned Buntline hired a guide. With rod, gun, and camp outfit he entered the great forest's cathedral gloom.[1] An old road penetrated the country from Johnstown past Lake Pleasant, around the south shore of Raquette Lake, and across to the St. Lawrence. Tales of the heroic days so close to Ned's heart could be found in every cabin.[2] Tradition said that Sir John Johnson, son of a famous British Indian agent, had raided the Mohawk Valley from Canada by this route during the Revolution. Decaying spruce logs, six feet thick, lay where they had crashed to earth, sometimes directly across the road. Windfalls made an almost impassable jungle into which the sun never penetrated. Game and fish abounded, and Ned renewed his boyhood joys. A small part of the Adirondacks – about one fifth of the area – was roofed with dancing leaves of deciduous trees.[3] At every marsh and lake, deer leaped away, graceful and airy as thistledown. Black bears, round as hogs, stood on their hind legs to see the intruders and then fled with incredible swiftness over logs and through the tangled tops of fallen trees.

Ned found the guides to be picturesque fellows in woolen shirts and homespun butternut trousers. A limp felt hat with unkempt hair protruding at the top was fashionable in the mountains. People dressed and looked like the hillmen Ned had seen in northern Alabama and Mississippi, but there was one difference. Adirondack mountaineers read Horace Greeley's *New York Semi-Weekly Tribune* with conviction. They were positive that Southerners were rich, slave-owning aristocrats bound to rule or ruin. James Gordon Bennett had mocked Greeley by picturing him as a countryman in boots and white linen duster – a costly ridicule. Real countrymen from New England to the Mississippi immediately accepted Old White Coat as one of themselves. The *Tribune's* word became their gospel.

Camp life appealed to Ned. With moccasins on his feet and cocked gun in hand, he enjoyed walking on the spongy black earth, watching for game along trails mottled with sunshine. He liked the damp fungus smell of cool deep forest, and the dry hot smell of sun-drenched hillsides where bears came to feast on fragrant berries. He amused himself calling the trees by name: maple, oak, witch hazel, spruce, pine, beech, silver and white birch. Deep in the forest he listened to the murmur of breezes passing overhead in the treetops. Guides showed him how to build a bark lean-to in the woods. He learned to make wet wood burn by using shredded birchbark for kindling. It was snug in a forest shelter when the rain pelted down and a pan of frying fish sputtered on the coals. Ned adopted the ways of the people quickly. Maple sugar he found to be a good substitute for the cane variety, and he learned to whittle it into his tea like an old-timer. Moreover, he soon discovered that he was as good a shot as the best of the guides. Before the summer passed he decided that he was a seasoned woodsman. The life differed only in degree from his Pennsylvania boyhood in the Pocono Mountains. Ned wrote:

Finding a hunter's cabin, evidently long unused, near the head of Indian River, I made up my mind to test a Winter there or as much of it as I could stand. I had an old guide who could pack his hundred and twenty pounds at a time, and by his aid I had such stores as I needed packed in before the snows were deep. The cabin, built against and partly under a rocky ledge, was made of spruce logs, covered with hemlock bark, and had a door, rude, but sufficient, made of a couple of split slabs, standing upright. Windows were not needed—there were air holes enough between the logs despite the moss stuffing we put in.

Inside I had a small sheet-iron camp-stove, which could be made red-hot with a double handful of birch bark. Outside, old Birch, my guide, cut and piled about twelve or fifteen cords of birch, beech and maple wood of large size for a camp-fire when I wanted it. There was plenty of dead timber lying around loose on the banks of the little lake near camp, so I had no danger of a freeze-out. I had snow-shoes to travel with when I desired, and when he left Birch was to come in every two weeks to bring my mail and carry out manuscript, for I *worked* there, as I always do wherever I am, *penfully*.

For the first six weeks after Winter set in I had a glorious time. Hermit life just suited me. I had plenty to eat and drink, good reading matter, and all of out-doors to myself when I wanted exercise. Writing sketches and stories filled up the intervals.

Almost every night I had a concert. A gang of wolves played the principal part. A panther solo made the variation. I was happy. No temptation to deviate from the rules of health and morality appeared. I was at church every day. The blue arch of heaven was its dome, the great pines and maples and birch trees formed its columns, the lofty hills, the voiceless lake, the singing rills which never froze, its lessons — the contemplation of the God-created forest its sermons.

But I went to sleep and pleasant dreams one night at an early hour to wake at or near midnight under a light as brilliant as a salamander could desire. Some spark from my slender stove pipe must have fallen on the half rotten roof back of the straw covering in front, under the rocks. A fierce north wind that was blowing most likely fanned it to life, and when I woke fire was above and all around me, for fire had dropped from above on my bedding, and it was ablaze as I sprung to the door.

I had only time to snatch my rifle, ammunition, clothes and snow-shoes from a corner not yet afire and get outside, when the hut was all ablaze.

I dressed out on the crust, with the themometer [*sic*] away below zero, but did not feel the cold in the excitement. After I was in my thick woolen clothes, and my moose-skin moccasins on, I began to think of many things inside that I might have got out and needed. But it was too late. . . .

Sadly I looked on the fire till it smouldered down, keeping warm as I sat on my unconsumed wood-pile, and then by the early light of the morning star I laid my course for the little hamlet of Lake Pleasant, about thirty miles away. I *was* traveling "light" on an empty stomach, snow-shoeing was fair, and I got there to dinner.

I never tried complete hermit life since. I was then and there cured of all desire for it.[4]

The experience did not destroy Ned's love for the Adirondacks. In the fall of 1856[5] he was still rusticating there when Chauncey Hathorn, an eccentric guide, brought a hunting party to Blue Mountain Lake — Tallow or Ragged Lake it was called at that time.[6] Hathorn was the nephew of a state senator who owned a handsome resort at Saratoga. The hunters left the hotel with several newspapers in their duffel. At noon and night rests they read about the murder and mutilation of five proslavery men, out in Kansas, by a fellow named John Brown. The atrocity made political capital for Democrats as well as Republicans. It fanned hot talk against slavery throughout the North. Moreover, the thousands who had broken allegiance with Whigs or Democrats to join Ned's Know-Nothings now looked hopefully for a new party, and the Republicans appealed to them. The sportsmen, warming their fingers around their campfires, discussed the political uncertainty ahead. They talked about this fanatic John Brown. The guides said that the desperado had a farm in the Adirondacks. He had got it from the millionaire landowner Gerrit Smith. Both were zealous champions of abolition. The two men had tried a free Negro colony near North Elba, New York, but it failed. Old Brown's comings and goings were always mysterious. He seemed to be away from home most of the time. Perhaps the Kansas murderer might be hiding now in the paradise of lakes and mountains ahead. The prospect added a tingle of excitement to the hunters' vacation. None suspected that they might meet, instead, the notorious Ned Buntline.

Below Blue Mountain Lake, where the Marion River spreads out into another body of smooth water, the sportsmen discovered a deserted cabin. November had come, and with it snow and cold weather. The hunters moved in with the mice and enjoyed the scant luxury of a dry dirt floor. Some of them began to make plans for going home. They must start at once to reach civilization by Christmas or New Year's Day. But Hathorn, an educated and talented young man, decided to forego civilization and remain. Two woodsmen would stay with him until spring, to make a little money trapping. Living expenses would amount to nothing, for they could kill plenty of venison after the deer "yarded" in the deep snow.

Hathorn and his companions helped the homebound hunters pack their duffel and go. Then the three men settled down to hunt, trap and loaf until spring. Late one afternoon when long purple shadows of bare trees lay on the snow, the trappers returning from a hunt looked across the clearing at their cabin. A thread of smoke reached up from the chimney and a strange sled stood in the dooryard. The mountaineers hurried across the clearing, and as they approached their house the door opened and disclosed a squat figure dressed in woodsmen's togs. He introduced himself as Ned Buntline and said that he had come with some friends from Glens Falls, a sawmill town on the upper Hudson famous for a cave that James Fenimore Cooper had used for a dramatic incident in *The Last of the Mohicans*. Ned said that he had brought plenty of groceries and hoped that he was welcome. Hathorn treasured for the rest of his life the memory of this, his first meeting with the famous author.

Ned liked the cabin and its surroundings. In the spring he hunted up the owner and purchased it, rebuilding the camp into what he liked to call his shooting box. Frank Forester had bragged about such hunting luxuries in the bygone days when Ned first went to New York. Ned's camp, however, looked more like a squatter's farm than a gentleman's resort. Two stacks of swamp hay showed plainly that the first builder had agriculture, not sport, in mind. Ned tore down all vestiges of the early farm and burned the hay.[7] His retreat must be a plaything for a man of leisure, unmarred by the utilitarian. To keep his playhouse, Ned employed an eighteen-year-old girl, Eva Gardiner, from a Troy beer hall.[8] Hathorn had recommended her. The nearest post office, at Lake Pleasant, was a good twenty-eight miles away, and the woodland road down there coiled across brushy ridges where wagons jolted over great granite outcroppings. The swamps along Cedar and Miami rivers were sometimes impassable even for a man on horseback. Such isolation seemed to be just the thing for Ned's writing. From the door at dawn, after the first cool night of fall, Ned looked down on a pool of fog covering the lake. At sunrise the mist dissolved and the water lay before him, blue as a bit of inverted sky. Ned named it Eagle Lake. He also named the next lake down the Marion River toward Raquette Lake, the Utowana.[9] His home he called Eagle's Nest.

Soon Ned found that his idyllic existence was interrupted by the necessity of going to town for groceries and the mail. The trip out consumed a whole day, and a hard one at that, especially during rainy weather when water stood high in the cattail marshes at Cedar River and a long detour was necessary. Ned liked to celebrate his arrival in the post office by getting moderately drunk. After a day or two of relaxation he bought a bottle "to sober up on" and started on the long trip home. Thus the better part of a week was consumed in getting the mail, and it was almost time to go again. Ned could do little writing under such a routine, so he employed a man to bring the mail weekly.[10] Then he married Eva Gardiner and the contented couple settled down in solitude.

Literary success and the sylvan life stimulated Ned into new heights of romantic poetry. From his pen came rhymes that would be published in circulars advertising summer resorts in the Adirondacks for the next two generations:

> Where the silvery gleam of the rushing stream
> Is so brightly seen on the rock's dark green,
> Where the white pink grows by the wild red rose
> And the bluebird sings till the welkin rings;
>
> Where the rolling surf laves the emerald turf,
> Where the trout leaps high at the hovering fly,
> Where the sportive fawn crops the soft green lawn,
> And the crow's shrill cry bodes a tempest nigh –
> There is my home – my wildwood home.[11]

One frosty morning in 1857 Buntline rowed down from Eagle Lake through Utowana to the portage around the rapids of Marion River that carry the overflow of Blue Mountain Lake into Raquette. The season was too early for flies, much too cold. Ned had filled his tin bait box with white grubs he had chopped from a rotten log. At his favorite pool he waded out in the icy water. Wearing wool socks, he felt cold only where the surface made a ring around his legs. Ned cast his grubs into the smoking water. The fish were hungry. In an hour Ned caught – or claimed he had – a basketful and a good string besides. He turned to wade ashore.

"Hallo," someone called. Ned looked toward the portage used by campers to get around the rapids. A guide, Bill Wood, was carrying a boat up the way. Behind him trudged a short, thick-set man with a long beard. Ned drew in his line, reeled up the slack, and joined them.

"Got any?" the venerable fisherman asked. Ned showed his catch proudly.

"Yes; pretty fair for this time o' year," said the stranger.

Ned was nettled. "Pretty fair," he snorted. "Can you do better?"

"Yes," the grizzled beard replied. "Bill, set down your boat. I'll show this youngster (the stranger was forty years old; Ned thirty-four) how to lure the big 'uns." The strange man took Ned's lancewood rod. He put on a double leader. Evidently he expected a big fish. Then he looped on a single hook. With his knife he cut the bright red belly-fin from one of Ned's best trout. He attached this on the hook and waded out into the rushing water. The veteran cast into the swiftest current. Ned watched the tiny red fin skip across the white riffles. In a second a trout, big as a mossy log, struck the lure and raced away. Ned saw his precious rod bent almost double. The trout rushed upstream, then down, the taut line cutting the water. The stranger played the fish with a master hand. In ten minutes he reeled it in exhausted, gasping on its side, a five-pound trout, lacking one ounce.

Ned looked at the fisherman with awe. "And now, have the kindness to tell me who you are," asked Ned in his best Victorian manner.

"Me? Oh, I'm only Seth Green." [12]

No man in New York equaled Seth Green with rod and line. Known as the Father of Fish Culture, his articles in outdoor magazines had awakened sportsmen to the importance of stocking mountain streams. He experimented with hatching fish eggs artificially, discovered that different species of trout spawned at different seasons. Thus hatcheries could be kept busy spring and fall hatching brook, rainbow, and brown trout. Eventually Green became Fish Commissioner for the Empire State.

In the Adirondacks, fishermen a half century later would tell tales about Seth Green's magic skill. He could cast a fly into the wind. He never whipped his line. "Watch him next time," admirers said. "His flies don't snap on the back cast like the popper on a whip. He knows how to wait until the fly is all the way back before he lashes it forward – split-second timing." Seth Green said that he learned to cast by holding a book between his arm and body – made a feller use his wrist, you know.

Ned claimed that his best catch came in the summer of 1858. Trolling in Blue Mountain Lake, he gaffed a salmon trout weighing twenty-four pounds and nine ounces. Ned wrote the experience into an article. He had success, too, selling hunting stories, but the fees were small. Then the editor of the *New York Mercury*, a weekly devoted to sports, came up to Eagle's Nest and urged Ned to sign a contract to send serials regularly, not hunting stories but historical fiction fitted to the masses, something on the level of *The Mysteries and Miseries of New York*, but less sordid. Clean outdoor romance was what the editor wanted.

The proposition was too good to refuse. Thus Ned Buntline slipped back once more into his old role of writer of cheap historical fiction. He entitled his first story "The White Wizard; or The Great Prophet of the Seminoles. A Tale of Strange Mystery in the South and North." Ned wrote about a country and a time that he knew, but his writing was cut to pattern. Osceola, Coacoochee, Billy Bowlegs, and Sam Jones all appear as counterfeit characters. The scene opens melodramatically with the villain resting his trusty rifle across a cypress root for a long shot at a deer. Behind him a wild boar prepares to charge. The reader is supposed to be caught by the suspense of this situation. It is indeed critical, for when the villain shoots he will be unarmed and the boar may then kill him and permit all the good characters in the story to live happily ever afterward.

The villain shoots. Then, defenseless, he spies the boar rushing at him with horrible champing tushes. The helpless man turns to run. A distant tree promises asylum if he can reach it ahead of the infuriated brute. The race is exciting. The man is almost within reach of the tree and the boar has almost overtaken him. Suddenly the man falls, tripped by a palmetto root. In another instant the boar's tusks will rip into the villain's flesh and the hero's happiness will be secure. But no! A rifle cracks in the distance, and the boar falls dead beside the prostrate man.

Soon an Indian trots into the scene with a smoking rifle in his hand. The two conspirators slink off together, plotting mischief. First they plan to kidnap a nearby white family's baby girl, Ona – a typical Buntline heroine's name. On the way the villain is bitten by a giant water moccasin, and the reader sighs with relief to know that little Ona has been saved from worse than death. But the reader has not reckoned with the villain's Indian friend. Versed in the mysteries of herbs, the red man poultices the snake bite and again saves the villain's life.

Other harrowing experiences come to the miscreants, but at last little Ona is kidnaped and taken to the Indian village, where the chief holds a nice white man prisoner. He is a West Pointer named Febiger, and his superior intelligence has won for him a place of high honor in the Indian council, but our hero (for such he is) pines for a sweetheart back in civilization. The chief tries to tempt him with the loveliest of his Indian maidens, but Febiger replies: "The breast whereon Ione has pillowed her head, can never support another."

Little Ona grows up with surprising rapidity to be captured and recaptured by the Indians every few pages. Always she is rescued by the same hero, Febiger, a West Point Mose, who only once loses his patience over his sweetheart's continued misfortunes. In that one instance Febiger hears that Ona is in the

Indians' clutches again, and remarks in Mose-like language: "The old man will be madder than a stump-tailed bull at fly-time." [13]

Ned used bloodhounds in his story also. He understood the hold these animals had on popular imagination. Politicians had tried to defeat Old Rough and Ready's Presidential aspirations by accusing him of hounding the Seminoles. More recently, Harriet Beecher Stowe had used bloodhounds with telling effect in *Uncle Tom's Cabin*. Ned could not resist the temptation to have savage dogs bay the trails of his distraught heroine, but in the end, of course, Febiger comes out of the Everglades with Ona as his bride. Hero, author, and reader too seem to have forgotten Ione.

Ned concludes the story by giving his readers the usual lecture on bad millionaires and their "ill-gotten gold." Then after this tirade against wealth Ned inconsistently ends the book with his happy hero and heroine possessing all the luxuries of the vile rich:

> Wealthy, honored, respected by all who know them, the Febigers, either at their splendid home on Fifth Avenue, their summer cottage up the Hudson, or at their beautiful residence in Florida, are *happy*. . . .
>
> Reader, my story is told. I hope you feel as if you had got your money's worth! It is my private opinion that you have.
>
> THE END

The nouvellette was a potboiler – not so good as Buntline's hunting sketches, but more profitable. Trash had lured Ned from good sea stories. Now it enticed him from good stories about the backwoods. Forced to write for the profitable market, Ned dashed off another Indian serial, "Thayendanegea, the Scourge; or, The War-Eagle of the Mohawks: A Tale of Mystery, Ruth, and Wrong." The first installment appeared in the November 1858 *Mercury*. This work was a story of the Revolution and the part played by Joseph Brant, an Indian who fought on the British side. Ned told his story with the usual hero, heroine, and villain. He introduced a new character, Hon Yost, a humorous drunk, who under the influence of liquor "up set the bowl of caution" and floundered through the underbrush "like a wounded moose."[14] This clumsy inebriate seems to have been the only tangible benefit Ned got from his years on the temperance platform.

Ned's next serial appeared on February 19, 1859. The plot of "Seawaif; or, The Terror of the Coast: A Tale of Privateering in 1776" seemed as improbable as that of "The White Wizard." The Seawaif began his adventures as a child when he was cast ashore on the southwest corner of Nantucket shoal.[15] As a man he had miraculous experiences, sailing through an enemy fleet in disguise, slipping unseen into a neutral Spanish port, saving the ship's surgeon from a boa constrictor. The humorous drunk, so appealing in "Thayendanegea," is introduced once more, but Ned found no place at sea for the useful bloodhounds.

In the last chapter the Seawaif turns out to be Lord Egerton. He marries the pretty country girl back in Salem. "Reader, I hate to end a story so well!" Buntline concluded. "But I am inditing a historical matter, and must stick to the truth."

Misfortune soon overtook Buntline in his Adirondack retreat. Eva died in childbirth on March 4, 1860, a fortnight before his own birthday. The snow had not yet melted from the clearing at Eagle's Nest. Long dirty drifts lay in the hollows, and snow water gurgled down the gullies. Ned buried Eva with the baby in a rude coffin under the wet ground behind the log house. When the roads opened he went down to New York for a change of scene. Unkind friends said that he went for a new wife – certainly not Lovanche. At Blue Mountain Lake a tradition persists that he seduced a settler's daughter, and descendants of the clandestine union were pointed out as recently as 1947.

The New York to which Ned went back in the summer of 1860 throbbed with tragic gossip concerning his friends and acquaintances. Politicians were agog over descriptions of a "long-armed ape" named Abraham Lincoln who had been nominated Republican candidate for the Presidency. If Lincoln were elected,

New Yorkers prophesied a civil war. The great commercial city, dominated by Irish Tammany Hall Democrats, might secede along with its planter customers. Ned had given up all interest in politics. Let the abolitionists and the foreigners ruin the country if they must.

Ruin of another kind had already come to many of the classic figures in literary New York. Washington Irving and James Fenimore Cooper were both dead, and with them had gone the gentle school of letters in which Ned had been unable to make a living. A new writer of sea tales, Herman Melville, had become famous since Buntline's time, but he was not of the old school. Fine writing's arbiter, Lewis Gaylord Clark, always so elegant and aristocratic, had failed with *Knickerbocker.* His friends had published an elaborate gift edition of *Knick's* treasures to buy a cottage for him. Ned Buntline was now much better off financially than this once great man. Clark's old associates, those successful sports writers, giant William Porter and British Herbert, were both dead. Touchy Herbert, the "Frank Forester" of sporting sketches, had shot himself dramatically while standing before a pier glass. W. T. Porter, in poor health at the time, but working diligently on a biography [16] of his friend, collapsed when he heard the sad news. Within two months he died.

Ned learned that another friend, the actor Chanfrau, had become a rich man. He was still playing the part of Mose. This Bowery character had been put into three different dramas, and Chanfrau was on the road with all of them. Thus theatergoers across the Union could see him play Mose in *Linda, the Cigar Girl* on one night. Next evening they could watch him as Mose in the old stand-by, *A Glance at New York.* On the third night they could see Chanfrau play *Mose in California.* The actor was putting money in the bank and planning a theater of his own.[17] Ned had done pretty well himself since the old days when Chanfrau had played in *Mysteries and Miseries,* but he had wasted time on those temperance lectures.

Ned went back up the Hudson with a new wife named Kate (or Catherine) Myers. The couple was married by the chaplain at Sing Sing on November 2, 1860. The bridegroom sent word ahead for Chauncey Hathorn to help take his lady to Eagle's Nest. Hathorn, since his winter on Eagle Lake in 1856, had become addicted to the wilderness. Nothing suited him better than prowling alone through the mountains. He had renounced all the advantages of his classical education, and in a lonely cabin was now known as the Hermit of Tallow Lake. He went willingly to town, however, to help Ned bring in his new wife. She proved to be good-looking and intelligent, but Hathorn soon learned that the city girl was unused to a backwoods life. The trip over rough roads to Raquette Lake in a wagon became almost more than she could stand. At the lake Ned arranged to have her go the last ten miles in a boat with Hathorn while he took the trunks around by the road.

The route up the Marion River, through Utowana Lake, was a long pull with oars, and the girl's heart sank deeper and deeper as the gloomy forest wall drifted past the gunwales. Finally Hathorn pulled ashore at a dim trail, a "carry" to the next navigable water. Two carries, he said, were necessary before they reached Eagle's Nest. Mrs. Judson became indignant. She asked her guide what manner of house to expect at the end of such a path. From her husband's glowing description she had pictured a great mansion, but skepticism now overwhelmed her. Hathorn shouldered the frail boat and started up the trail. He realized that this young woman was due for a great shock when she saw the crude log cabin that served as "shooting box" for her lord and master. At periodic rests he talked about the beauties of the view from the cabin, the flat-topped peak behind, the blue lake in front, the dazzling contrast of somber evergreens against autumnal red and yellow maple leaves. Hathorn knew classical literature and could quote the poets. He praised the purity of mountain water, the fresh air, and cool still nights, so restful for sleeping.

Years later Ned himself liked to tell how he got his bride to Eagle's Nest and then stole her shoes so that she could not run away. Whatever the true situation may have been, Ned settled down comfortably with his bride and before long snow cushioned them snugly from the outside world. At Christmas time newspapers reported that "Professor" Ingraham had died from a bullet wound at Holly Springs, Mississippi. The reformed shilling-shocker writer had been shot accidentally by his own pistol. During his last years he had tried unsuccessfully to buy back the copyrights on his trashy romances.[18]

Ned planned a big output of adventure literature during the long quiet winter. With pen and paper he lay on the floor on a bearskin, oblivious to his surroundings. Kate began to complain. Ned tried to flatter her in his stories by calling her "a little fairy I know," and he tried to shame her by saying that she was "one of those *she lazinesses* that thinks it necessary to swelter in bed till noon."[19] It was no use. The new wife did not like Eagle's Nest or understand the exactions of his work. Nagging and squabbling throughout the long winter irritated the couple. During the chilly spring days in the mountains Ned stayed away from the house more and more. Always capricious in his likes and dislikes, and seeking some wrong to combat, Ned vented his accumulating wrath against a party of wealthy sportsmen who rowed their skiffs to his landing. In the bow of each boat he saw bloody hunks of meat, the hindquarters of deer or "saddles" as they were called. "Where did you get them?" Ned asked, spoiling for an argument.

The hunters, proud of their marksmanship, replied that they had killed the deer swimming the lake. They had also killed a doe and a fawn, they said, but the meat of a suckling female was not good, so they had left it.

"Hold on," shouted Ned, drawing up his stubby form indignantly. "Game butchers cannot stop here." He ordered the guides to reload the duffel, and in his best platform manner Ned

Buntline lectured the hunters on conservation until they were out of hearing from the shore.

The practice of shooting deer in the water always incensed Ned, except when he killed his own meat that way. In summer, guides "jacked" deer at night for tourists. After dark the timid animals waded out in the lakes to nibble aquatic plants. Hunters with a bright light fixed on the prow of a boat could often paddle close to them. The dazzling light hid the boat and fascinated the deer. Long before their dun sides became visible, the light reflected in their wondering eyes and disclosed their location to the hunters. Then the boat glided silently toward them until the jacklamp illuminated the deer's shadowy bodies, and the marksmen fired at close range.

In the daytime, guides entertained their customers in another fashion. They stationed the hunters in boats and turned hounds loose in the hills. A chased deer invariably runs to water and crosses it to escape the dogs. Almost always the hunters had a chance to shoot the dripping animal as it emerged on the far shore. Sometimes the boatmen overtook the deer in deep water, and the guide held the swimming animal's tail while the tourist killed it. This holding the deer was necessary to keep it from sinking, for only when covered with a spongy winter coat of hair would the carcass float. Tourists claimed, with good reason, that to run deer with dogs was poor sportsmanship.

Ned's unhappy married life soon led to a bigger quarrel. Buntline sought relief in a bitter feud with a neighbor, a feud that has become traditional in the Adirondacks. Ned's neighbor, Alvah Dunning, a famous guide, was as odd, opinionated, and self-willed as Ned himself. Alvah made his living hounding deer to water for his guests to kill. Ned determined to stop this.

Alvah was an old-timer, descendant of a Tory scout. His vulturesquely beaked nose overshadowed a small tight-lipped mouth. Little, clear bright eyes sparkled with ratlike cunning. He intensely disliked city visitors and complained against their asininities. One ignoramus, he said, had even tried to tell him that the world was round. Yet, strangely enough, his vinegar disposition did not impair his guiding business. Instead, sportsmen boasted about going out with the sour old fellow. To be able to get along with him was a sign that a man had mastered the last difficulty of woodcraft. Ned was unimpressed. He pronounced Alvah an "amaroogian" [20] – a name of contempt that mystified the guides and dismayed city sportsmen who could not find the word in any dictionary. Without doubt Alvah Dunning and Ned Buntline were due for a fracas.

The trouble came to a head when Alvah heard Ned's dictum against hounding deer to water. He told his neighbor guides tartly that no paper-backed pen-pusher could tell him what he could and could not do. Ned heard the acid ultimatum and sent back an alkaline reply. Shortly thereafter he met Alvah in the woods close to Eagle's Nest, with two hounds at his heels. Ned said not a word, but he raised his rifle and shot one dog dead. "The other barrel's ready for you if you are in sight in five minutes," Ned announced stentorianly.

Alvah believed him and raced away, his white beard flying – a frightened man but by no means broken in spirit. Back at his own cabin Alvah told neighbors that he intended to shoot the novelist on sight. The feud got wide publicity. Hunters, fishermen, summer tourists, readers of sporting periodicals, speculated on the comparative deadliness of the grim, determined mountaineer and the noisy, wild fellow of the adventure magazines. Old John Brown had never turned up in the Adirondacks to give campers a happy scare. Instead, he had been hanged in Virginia. Now the Buntline-Dunning feud excited city sportsmen. Cynical guides said that the two principals put in considerable time seeking to avoid one another.

Mrs. Judson's personal observations have not been recorded. The Civil War came as a fortunate respite to her troubles as well as to Alvah Dunning's.

XX

The Civil War

NED BUNTLINE hesitated to join the army at the opening of the Civil War. He was no longer young, and he had watched with disapproval the growing agitation over slavery instead of other issues like intemperance, Catholicism, and immigration. But wherever Ned went, at Lake Pleasant, Glens Falls, Saratoga, and Troy, men talked war, drilled, and marched away. Lumbermen laid down their axes, farmers left the spring plowing. Horace Greeley and his *Tribune* had convinced them that Know-Nothingism was wrong and a crusade against slavery was right.

In June 1861, Ned left for Washington to offer his services for a commission. His wife, expecting a baby at Eagle's Nest, thought that he had only gone to town for supplies. At the capital he wrote a front-page story for the *Sunday Morning Chronicle* [1] – Lincoln's mouthpiece – in the form of a letter from his sister Irene urging him to do his duty, die if necessary for "our *Glorious Constitution.*"

Ned returned to the Adirondacks without dying for the constitution or even getting a commission. On January 10, 1862, a baby girl was born at Eagle's Nest and named Mary Carrollita. In the spring Kate insisted on leaving the woods for a trip. The family traveled down to her old home in Westchester County, and there – at Mount Pleasant, on September 25, 1862 – Ned enlisted as a private in Company K of the 1st New York Mounted Rifles. He gave his age as thirty-seven, cheating by only two years. The government furnished him a dark blue jacket, grayish-blue trousers, a blue flannel shirt, boots, saber, carbine, and a six-chambered revolver.[2] For inclement weather the Mounted Rifles wore cloaks, much more dashing than the overcoats issued the infantry. Yellow braid chevrons distinguished the various non-commissioned officers. Ned was given a horse, a McClellan saddle, and a canvas nose bag with a leather bottom. He would soon show his comrades a novel use for that piece of equipment.

Men and horses were loaded on a steamboat and shipped to Norfolk, Virginia. It was common talk that Union Army officers did not have adequate maps of Virginia. Reprints had been made from an old chart used by Cornwallis[3] in 1781. Another survey, dated 1818, had been found faulty. Buntline was confident that scouts like himself would have a great opportunity to display their woodcraft for their country's glory. The 1st New York Mounted Rifles felt a proprietary interest in Norfolk. The port city, practically an island between the Atlantic Ocean, Chesapeake Bay, and the great Dismal Swamp, had been entered on May 10, 1862, by the Rifles' commander, Colonel Charles C. Dodge. In the fall, when Buntline arrived, Norfolk appeared to be a substantial and wealthy city. The principal hotel had a grandiose front and poor accommodations – a Southern characteristic, Ned thought. Gaping soldiers tramped through the hotel. They noticed a ladies' parlor, a great hall, and two billiard rooms. Signs asked patrons to refrain from all political discussion lest the house be closed.[4] Southern residents were polite to the men in uniform, but the boys in blue suspected that hatred lurked in their courteous eyes.

Cars stood ready to haul Ned and his troop to Suffolk, west of the Dismal Swamp, an outpost close to the enemy, where action could be expected. The train steamed off with soldiers perched on the roofs of the stock cars. Wooden trestles penetrated the swamp, which was a tangle of cypress, black gum, water ash. The troopers stared at marshy meadows in a jungle similar to the Everglades. Trees, dead and bleached, stood with their roots in roily water. High up the trunks could be seen the mud mark of a past flood. "Looks like they all had on stockings," one soldier remarked. The train rattled across the Jericho Canal – stagnant, brackish, brown as tea. Mud-caked turtles slipped off mud-caked logs as the locomotive rushed along. A few minutes later the train twisted and coiled through complicated rifle pits and redoubts, the fortifications surrounding Suffolk.

From the tops of the rocking cars the troopers looked at the dirt and log huts of the garrison. Loafing soldiers made insulting but jovial gestures at the newcomers. The town of Suffolk seemed to be nothing but an army cantonment – new, temporary, utilitarian as a construction camp. Work gangs of soldiers and of Negro laborers, or "contrabands" as they were called, marched along the wagon ruts among tree stumps. West of camp, the muddy Nansemond, like a moat, protected Suffolk from the enemy. A drawbridge led across to the pine forest between the lines. Company K was assigned a campground one mile out of town, back along the Norfolk railroad track.[5]

Ned knew the rudiments of a soldier's life. Older than his fellow privates, he was tough, talkative, and full of mischief. The soldiers liked him, called him "Uncle Ned," soon learned that he saw a story in the dullest everyday event. They liked to hear him splash color in the description of a monotonous tour of guard duty, or add a humorous climax to a petty incident which they did not remember. He knew so much from long experience that they could never be sure when true history ended and Ned's imagination began. He showed them several new uses for the regulation nose bag: how to hide a bottle in it; how to fix it like a nest to tempt hens from the Negro hovels nearby. Ned warned the boys, too, about the danger of letting a thirsty horse stray from the picket line with a nose bag on his head. At the first stream the horse would plunge his nose, bag and all, into the water. The bag would fill, and the horse, unable to free himself from the water, would drown even as his master ran up to save him. Ned could show his comrades a dozen other little things that he had learned by outdoor experience. In short order he qualified as a sharpshooter and became a sergeant.[6]

Ned shared the men's good-natured ridicule of their officers, but he admired Colonel Charles C. Dodge and Major William H. Shieffelin. The colonel was only twenty-four years old, and the major younger still. Both sat their horses like knights of old and pranced through the cantonment leaping obstructions fearlessly. Soldiers who had been in camp all summer told the Company K boys that the young officers planned to take the offensive now that recruits had come. A quick thrust down here would help the main campaign north of the James where General George B. McClellan was trying to capture Richmond with the Army of the Potomac. The grand strategy of the eastern theater was to hold as many Confederate soldiers as possible down on the Nansemond and thus prevent them from going north to participate in the defense of the rebel capital.

The fall weather at Suffolk was piping hot. Clouds of dust followed the four-horse wagons, covered the men's tents, huts, and blankets. Swarms of flies buzzed around the cook tents. The New York Rifles tried to provoke the enemy with a few demonstrations but no engagement was fought. This was the grand strategy. Then dispatches from the North admitted that McClellan's campaign was failing. His great army had maneuvered within sight of Richmond's steeples and then had withdrawn to the shelter of his gunboats on the James. The men at Suffolk talked solemnly about the retreat and passed a mysterious piece of paper from tent to tent. Soldiers read it and their long faces smiled. The paper contained an amusing poem. With pencil and paper in the shade of huts or by the light of burning pine knots at night, they copied and memorized it and laughed. The ditty made fun of McClellan. Entitled "The Craven," it parodied Edgar Allan Poe's popular poem "The Raven." Soldiers repeated over and over:

On that mighty day of battle, 'mid the booming and the rattle,
Shouts of victory and of anguish, wherewith Malvern's Hill did roar,
Did a General now quite fameless, who in these lines shall be nameless,
Show himself as rather gameless, gameless on the James's shore?
Safely smoking on a gunboat, while the tempest raged on shore—
Only this, and nothing more.

The lyric sounded funny to soldiers who had heard Poe's poem recited at evening "socials" and believed it solemn and gruesome.[7]

In November McClellan was succeeded by a new general named Burnside, a handsome man with side whiskers. Down at Suffolk the grand strategy was repeated. Orders were given for another advance on the enemy. The soldiers grumbled at so many false alarms. The fateful day arrived with the men arguing, and some of them betting, that the order would be countermanded. But at dark the men were formed under arms, and at midnight a brigade marched across the drawbridge, the New York Mounted Rifles in the van riding in a column of fours. Behind them followed the 112th New York Regiment and the 39th Illinois.[8] Ned remembered later that he turned in his saddle and looked back. In the dark sky above Suffolk he saw a rocket rise.[9] Some traitor in town was signaling the enemy.

Dawn came with the column swinging along the Blackwater River road, sabers hooked up to keep them from rattling at the trot. Now and again the army tarried at cypress swamps while men and horses splashed through liver-colored water. In the flat pine forest beyond, officers called sharp orders to keep ranks closed and gain the intervals lost at the fords. Finally the column halted. Only a half mile of woodland separated the soldiers from the Blackwater Bridge, a natural place for the rebels to make a stand. The Mounted Rifles wheeled into a depression and formed company front. The colonel asked for volunteers to scout ahead and unmask the enemy. Ned spurred front and center and saluted. The commander let him go alone.[10]

In a few minutes Ned came to the river, a little over a hundred feet wide at this place. The bridge had been destroyed. On the opposite bank Ned saw thick brush but no sign of man. He may have noticed that no turtles were on the logs floating in the Blackwater. Something had scared them away. Ned looked over the bank. The charred stubs of a sawmill stood by the sluggish water. Buntline slid his horse down the steep slope to the water's edge. The animal stretched his head to drink. Sitting silently in the saddle, Ned watched the bushes across the stream. When his horse finished drinking, Ned rode cautiously along the edge of the stream under the bank toward the abutment of the wrecked bridge.

"Halt, you d——d Yank! Halt and surrender!" A Confederate officer stood among the bushes across the water within long pistol range.

"Not much!" Ned replied. "Not quite ready!"

"Fire!" the Confederate commanded. A cloud of smoke rolled out from the bushes. Balls pecked against the clay above Ned's head. His horse bounded like a cat for the crest of the riverbank and thence out of sight of the Confederates. Ned attributed his escape to the fact that men invariably overshoot when aiming down a steep incline. He galloped away to tell his commander that the enemy was unmasked.

The Union soldiers deployed for action. Artillery rolled forward and unlimbered in the brush on the east bank. Across the Blackwater bullets sleeted in from the invisible enemy. Ned and a few sharpshooters slipped forward behind the gnarled trunks of big sycamores. Behind them Major Shieffelin rode along the line of his men, with his blue cloak thrown back over his shoulders, showing the red lining. Ned watched the major's soft boyish face in this, his first battle. An officer of the 39th Illinois warned the major to be more cautious. Shieffelin paused for a moment, his plumed hat a conspicuous mark above the undergrowth. "This is war, is it?" he replied nonchalantly. "Rather hot, but they don't kill every shot." Then the major rode on, passing the tree where Ned lay hidden.

The artillery ceased firing after ten minutes. Apparently the enemy had retreated. Cavalrymen were ordered to cross and investigate. Ned, back in ranks, knew that swimming horses in formation was ticklish business. Perhaps someone had given a rash order, but nobody murmured. Obediently the riders loosened their saddle girths so the horses could swell with air while swimming. Then all remounted, wondering if the enemy had really evacuated the opposite shore. Ned watched the first rank enter the water. The horses waded to their knees, to their bellies, to the points of their shoulders. They stretched out their heads to drink or sniff the water. The blue-clad riders jerked the reins and spurred them forward. Down they went into the deep water, horses' tails floating out behind like seaweed. The next moment horses and riders were out of sight except for their heads. Recruits noticed the unusual quiet – no rattling arms, no horseshoes striking rocks, only the lisping water and the suppressed voice of a rider encouraging his swimming mount. Now was the time for a sharpshooter to upset the column, but no shot broke the silence.

Ned's turn came. Riding beside his platoon, he watched the ranks of swimming men and horses, wondered if the leaders would reach the far shore before a panic started. Ahead of him he saw Surgeon Boyd's horse disappear, sink like a rock. The surgeon, floundering in the deep water, turned toward Ned, his face distorted with surprise and despair. Ned reached out his hand and towed the frantic man along. Already on the far bank the lead horses were coming up out of the water, dripping wet, shaking themselves, making the saddle leathers flap. Ned and his companion waded ashore in the wake of the horses.

The first platoon galloped through the enemy's works and reported them deserted. An advance detachment set off up the road, dripping water from their accouterments. Others unsaddled, refreshed their mounts with a roll on dry ground, poured water out of cavalry boots, wrung their shirts, then followed. Soon word came that the enemy had fallen back on their reserves and were making a stand at the little town of Ivor. The Union officers talked over the situation, decided that they were outnumbered, and ordered the column back to Suffolk – a grand offensive indeed! The men returned to their tents and cabins, doctored their crippled horses, talked about the expedition, wondered if they would get gold "battle stripes" to wear on their sleeves,[11] played cards, bet on cockfights, and grumbled about the sutlers, who had nothing on their shelves, not even a stick of peppermint candy, for sale at less than a dime: robbers, all of them!

Ned noticed that these soldier boys talked often about dimes and quarters. In his youth people had talked about "shillings" and "bits." The war was doing something to the thinking habits of the new generation. Little books called dime novels (no longer shilling shockers) [12] came to the camp in bales like hay.[13] Soldiers sprawled in the dirt and read them hour after hour. They were published by a firm known as Beadle and Company. The Beadle brothers had achieved success in Buffalo, where they published a dime songbook. This was followed by game and joke books, housewives' manuals, and almanacs. In 1856 the Beadle firm moved to New York, where printing and distributing costs were said to be economical. Here in the heart of the twenty-five-cent nouvellette area, they dared, in 1861, to offer the first "dime novel," entitled *Malaeska, the Indian Wife of the White Hunter*. The author, Ann Sophia Winterbotham Stephens, was an old hand in the cheap literature field. Her story had been published twenty years before and Ned could have told her that an up-to-date nouvellette writer did not require ten pages to get the hero in a position where he could say, "Touch but a hair of her head, and by the Lord that made me, I will bespatter that tree with your brains." The Beadle Company had put this old Stephens production in a new saffron cover ornamented with the picture of a ten-cent piece to prevent sutlers from overcharging soldiers. The experiment worked.

In 1862 the firm reorganized as Beadle and Adams, with a diligent and undistinguished editor, Orville Victor,[14] who perfected a clean and moral formula for a wide variety of new and sensational titles. Then he experimented with advertising on a scale new for cheap literature. The sudden soldier market which sprung up for these little books made a fortune for the publishers almost overnight.

Ned Buntline, free-lance writer of the shilling-shocker school, saw this new firm burgeon at a time when he was "hitched" to the army. Colonel Dodge showed remarkable consideration for the literary genius in his regiment and gave him a studio cabin. Ned tried to outwrite the Beadle bunch, but to no avail. Military routine cramped his mind. Scouting duties and his own uncontrollable perversity kept him from writing as he had previously. His best Civil War book was entitled *Life in the Saddle; or, The Cavalry Scout*, with himself a leading character.[15]

The early winter of 1862 was mild, almost balmy. Sergeant Judson got a furlough and sailed for Manhattan with a light heart. Northbound boats were crowded with soldiers on vacation, sutlers, generals, and camp followers. All seemed gay and confident after a year of almost continual war reverses. The lower decks were filled with coffins in charge of professionals who made a business of haunting battlefields to retrieve and ship the dead bodies of soldiers north to relatives at a handsome profit.[16] Veterans had seen too much of warfare to let the sight distress them. Ned looked forward callously to relaxation in the fleshpots of New York, where a wife awaited him.

Manhattan in the winter of 1862–1863 prided itself on being the Sodom and Gomorrah of the North. In this seething mass of carousing soldiers Ned Buntline disappeared, and a strange account of the termination of his furlough has been preserved by

T. P. McElrath, a young officer who hoped to be a great writer some day.

Lieutenant McElrath commanded the provost guard at Fort Hamilton, a prison for petty offenders. Disorderly characters, drunkards, and men who overstayed their furloughs were lodged there in charge of the Invalid Corps – soldiers incapacitated for active battle duty. McElrath disliked the onerous police-station assignment, but he made the most of it by writing stories about his experiences with the characters in his care. One fine afternoon, he recorded later, a corporal's guard brought in a prisoner grotesquely dressed in a combination of uniform and civilian clothes. The culprit had not only overspent his furlough, but he had irritated his wife and she had reported him to the provost guard. McElrath ordered the ragamuffin locked up in one of the fort's bomb cells – a casemate furnished with iron bedstead, a couple of chairs, and other conveniences. A few minutes later the sentry on duty handed a slip of paper to McElrath. It read:

> If Lieutenant McElrath will have the kindness to loan me a book or two I shall be sincerely obliged.
>
> Respectfully, etc.,
> EDWARD Z. C. JUDSON [17]

McElrath would not have been more impressed had he learned that he held in custody Alexandre Dumas, John Ruskin, or John Greenleaf Whittier. He sent an armful of books to the dungeon and promised a fresh supply whenever the prisoner desired it. The next day a woman introduced herself at the commandant's office as Mrs. Judson. She brought a roll of foolscap for her husband. Ned accepted the writing material cheerily and set to work. Every day Lovanche came with more paper and took away his manuscript to sell to Street and Smith, publishers of the *New York Weekly*, a periodical competing with Beadle and Adams in the ten-cent field.

Lovanche had met Ned by accident on the streets of New York

on January 14, 1863. The two stopped for a few minutes' conversation. Ned appeared pale and haggard in his gay cavalry uniform. He was reduced in weight to only ninety-five pounds. Lovanche wanted to mother him, told him her address. Ned said that his furlough was already over, but Lovanche insisted that he was in no condition to return to army fare. That afternoon he went to her residence and the two were again married, this time by the Reverend Dr. Isaac H. Tuttle, pastor of St. Luke's Episcopal Church on Hudson Street. Moreover, Lovanche kept the certificate.[18] She was not going to be defrauded again by technicalities as she had been when Ned deserted her for Josie Juda during the Know-Nothing campaign. In February, after a month, Ned's health seemed thoroughly restored and he himself showed signs of incorrigibility. In fact, Lovanche learned that he had visited his other wife, Kate, at Chappaqua, New York. No one could goad Lovanche without fear of punishment. Maliciously she reported her husband to the authorities as a deserter, and the provost guard, as has been said, jailed him at Fort Hamilton.[19]

During the summer, after Ned had been returned to his company down South, Lovanche moved out to Chappaqua where she happened to meet Mrs. Kate Judson, who still claimed to be the novelist's wife, and, what was more, expected a baby. The two women lived in the same house for a week, becoming more jealous with the passage of each day. Yet mutual regard for Ned held them together. Lovanche formed an attachment for nineteen-month-old Mary Carrollita, the Eagle's Nest baby. She liked to say later that the tiny tot showed more affection for her than for its own mother.[20] Kate's second baby, another girl, arrived on November 10, 1863, and was named Irene Elizabeth for Ned's sister. Lovanche always maintained that Ned was not the baby's father.

Back in Suffolk, Ned found the New York Rifles in a bad way, under censure for insubordination and needless destruction of noncombatants' property. The charge had been denied by handsome young Colonel Dodge, who reported his men eager "to belie the injustice.[21] Sergeant Judson was promptly tried for desertion, and clapped into prison at Fort Norfolk.[22]

During Ned's absence from duty, exciting events occurred. General Longstreet was coming down the James.[23]

Soldiers at Suffolk knew that Lee, in northern Virginia, was sparring for position with the Union General Hooker. The Confederates were outnumbered two to one and it seemed strange to send Longstreet against Suffolk instead of reinforcing Lee. But whatever the reason, Longstreet's men soon invested the full length of the Blackwater. His engineers began to lay pontoon bridges, and scouts from the New York Rifles spied Confederate vedettes in the pine forest. Perhaps the grand strategy was to lure Burnside from across the James and thus keep him from aiding Hooker in the north. Perhaps the invaders planned only to fortify the James and prevent enemy vessels from approaching Richmond.

Deserter Buntline and his fellow soldiers did not know that Longstreet was staying away from Lee deliberately so as to prevent him from gaining a great victory and a great name. On April 11, Longstreet's van drove in the Suffolk pickets. Hopelessly outnumbered, the Union garrison waited behind their defenses. At night Northern soldiers could hear Confederate work parties shoveling on new fortifications. Soon enemy earthworks appeared around the city. Confederate bugle calls echoed across the Union encampment from dawn to dusk. Boys in blue listened to the rebel bands play and the enemy cheer as reinforcements arrived. Grimly the New York Rifles hoped to survive and at the same time divert Longstreet from aiding Lee in the great battle shaping up into what was to be known as Chancellorsville.

One day Confederate artillery opened on the Suffolk works, geysers of dirt spouting from embankments where shells hit. Several Union sorties attempted to stop the bombardment but Confederate muskets crumpled the thin blue line. Disheartened, the Union men withdrew, leaving broken bodies in the field. From the Suffolk fortifications, they looked back at the sprawled bodies left behind, saw some move and resolved to rescue them after dark.[24]

For almost three weeks the enemy besieged Suffolk and then withdrew.[25] Northern scouts followed the retreating regiments cautiously. Then came work parties with spades, bars, and picks. The railroad that had brought Longstreet's army was torn up, loaded on barges, and shipped across to Fortress Monroe. While the men worked they learned that the great battle between Hooker and Lee had been fought. Indeed, it had started on the day Longstreet withdrew from before Suffolk. The general had been compelled to go at last and reinforce Lee, but he was too late to help. Lee, despite inferior numbers, had outgeneraled and badly beaten Fighting Joe Hooker. Both sides would now lick their wounds, rest and reorganize. Another battle could not be expected for some time.

In prison Ned claimed illness and was hospitalized [26] when news came of the terrible battle of Gettysburg. Many officers Ned had known were listed among the slain. Ned read their names and regaled his wardmates with anecdotes about his intimacy with them. Nurses said that Brigadier General Lewis Addison Armistead had died in Pickett's charge, marching jauntily with his cap on the tip of his sword. Ned had known Armistead's father in the Seminole War — very distantly — but now he remembered him fluently.

Late in August Ned was on his feet again, his lameness much worse than in the days before the war. He transferred to the Veterans Reserve Corps — the Invalids who had arrested him in New York — and was assigned to the 74th Company in Scranton. On October 4, 1863, he wrote to his sister wistfully: [27] "It is about 40 miles from here to the old Beech Woods farm where we spent our happiest days." Ned had not forgotten the boyhood heartbreak at being taken from the woods to Philadelphia.

Unfit for further active service, Ned continued to be insubordinate. He wrote little, drank much, and traveled when and where he willed. In Washington he was photographed in a colonel's uniform, sitting in Lincoln's chair at Brady's studio. In Baltimore the provost guard found him drunk, warned him to be less noisy, and marched away. On their next round of the beat the guard found him in worse condition. Limping along in his uniform, he made the streets ring with wild rebel yells. He danced from saloon to printing office telling about his literary ability. Drunkenly, he tried to make arrangements to publish *Buntline's Own.* A crowd gathered around him, laughing, hooting. The provost halted his guard. Soldiers clipped the insignia from Ned's cap. Thus unidentifiable, he was abandoned. For several days he hobbled through the barrooms, stumbled up and down printers' stairways mumbling about *Buntline's Own.* Finally, with bleary eyes and swollen face, he returned to quarters.

On August 23, 1864, he was honorably discharged with a service record that showed no military engagements. In New York Ned displayed his picture in uniform with eagles on his shoulders. He told people that he had been "Chief of Scouts with the rank of a Colonel." [28] The identical words would be used a generation later by another adventurous storyteller named Tom Horn when he, too, became "chief of scouts" in the army and had leisure to read Buntline nouvellettes. Ned, after his discharge, returned to Kate and the two children, Mary Carrollita and Irene Elizabeth, but he kept in touch with Lovanche. Certainly he sent her a valentine in February, 1865. Both women believed themselves legally married to Ned and trouble loomed for him.

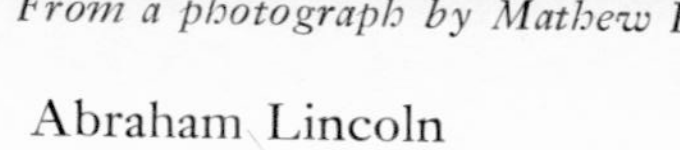

From a photograph by Mathew Brady

Abraham Lincoln

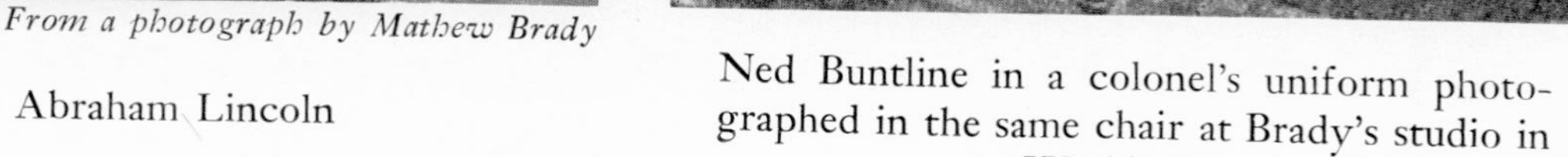

Ned Buntline in a colonel's uniform photographed in the same chair at Brady's studio in Washington

XXI

Ten-Cent Millionaire

MAN OVERBOARD! Man overboard!" A wharfinger waved his lantern above the inky waters and peered below. Men clambered into a dinghy, rowed along the dock, and rescued a dripping form in a soldier's uniform. The excitement attracted a theatrical troupe on the way to their lodgings after their evening performance. One of the actors, Fred Mather, a youthful veteran who hoped to give up trouping for writing stories about angling, recognized the sodden figure as Ned Buntline, nationally known writer and fisherman. Mather's fantastic explanation of the motive behind Ned's ducking in the Hudson at Albany that midnight of May 1, 1865, will be told later. Lovanche's very different interpretation must also be considered. Buntline had reached the pinnacle of his fame and an attempt to commit suicide seems preposterous except for his marital difficulties and certain irregularities in his publishing contracts. He contributed regularly to the *New York Mercury*, and in April 1865 he had revived *Ned Buntline's Own*, adding to the old bannerhead a picture of himself in a Civil War soldier's uniform. A story he wrote on Lincoln's assassination, entitled *The Parricides*, attracted the attention of the editors of Hilton's Ten Cent Books, a new firm competing with Beadle for the dime-novel market. Hilton's offered to absorb the *Own*, relieve Ned of printers' problems, and issue and distribute a *Ned Buntline's Own* series through their organization. The deal sounded good to Ned, and, what was more, he continued to write stories for the *Mercury* under the name of Judson. And this was not all. One "Jack Brace" began writing sea stories that resembled Ned's. Moreover, *Street and Smith's New York Weekly* featured a series by one Edward Minturn, admittedly a pseudonym, whose style also bore a strong resemblance to Ned's works.[1] In all probability Ned was up to an old trick of selling a monopoly on all the writings of "Ned Buntline" and then writing under other names for other publishers. He was said to be making $20,000 yearly, and boasted that he wrote six stories a week,[2] some of them continued. Occasionally he put his characters in the wrong narrative, and more than once failed to sober up in time to meet a publishing deadline. In one instance a ghost writer carried on, and with malice, so tradition says, he killed Ned's hero and gloated over the great novelist's predicament. But Ned read the copy before writing his next installment. Unabashed, he made his hero's ghost take an active part in the story to its end.

Ned prided himself on the devil-may-care speed with which he dashed off his stories, scarcely stopping to eat or sleep. "I once wrote a book of six hundred and ten pages in sixty-two hours," he told an interviewer.

> I never lay out plots in advance. I shouldn't know how to do it, for how can I know what my people may take it into their heads to do? First, I invent a title. When I hit a good one I consider the story about half finished. It is the thing of prime importance. After I begin I push ahead as fast as I can write, never blotting out anything I have once written and never making a correction or modification. . . . If a book does not suit me when I have finished it, I simply throw it in the fire and begin again without any reference to the discarded text.[3]

Ned's work showed his haste, but the money rolled in. He spent it lavishly, making few if any investments, but there is little reason to suspect a genuine suicide attempt unless Lovanche's interpretation is true. She maintained that Ned followed his valentine in person and was received coolly. She asked for an explanation of Mrs. Kate Judson's last child, Irene Elizabeth, and another one she was obviously expecting.

A less resourceful man than Buntline might have been chagrined, but not Ned. He denied fathering any of her children except Carrollita. Lovanche pointed out that Irene was a Judson name. Ned replied that a woman could name her children anything she wished. Then Lovanche sobbed into Ned's arms. She was the sole witness of the meeting, so she may have imagined Ned's denial of parenthood. However that may be, Lovanche determined to stop Ned's double life. At least she wanted support – or was it blackmail? In any event, she explained later that Ned tried to commit suicide because she moved from New York to Albany. Ned followed her, she said, sat for two hours in the dark on the steps before her bolted door, then went down and jumped into the Hudson. That was her story! [4]

At the time of his rescue Ned told the crowd on the dock that he had slipped on an orange peel. He boasted that he was a great swimmer and had no fear of drowning. He showed them the strength of his arms, flexed his biceps and displayed the depth of his chest, said he had fought in the Seminole War, in the war with Mexico, and in the Civil War had been chief of scouts with the rank of colonel. Ned aimed his conversation especially at the actors, enlarged on his exploits and invited the troupe to dine with him in the best hotel in Albany.

Fred Mather remembered later how Ned grew expansive from champagne during the meal. He called on each guest to perform. One of the players, Tom Pendergast, a minstrel tenor, stood up and sang: "Father, Dear Father, Come Home with Me Now." The tipsy men sniffled. A war veteran covered his face with his only hand. Ned jumped to his feet, threw his arms around Pendergast, and kissed him on both cheeks. "That is the best temperance song ever written – or sung," Ned sobbed. Tears streamed down his prematurely seamed cheeks. "Waiter, waiter," he called. "Another quart of Heidsieck for the gentlemen." [5]

Next day Ned and Mather went bass fishing together.[6] They caught some monsters hiding behind submerged logs. Ned showed his young friend how to drop a lure in shallow water where the big bass crept through the reeds, feeding on insects. Mather did not consider Ned's mishap in the Hudson River an attempted suicide, but rather a desire to attract attention, meet people, be the center of a dramatic scene, and glory in the luxury of a great meal after a sordid ducking in the Hudson. Whatever Ned's motive, the years after the war proved exciting and prosperous for him. He seems to have visited his Adirondack camp, but never settled there permanently. Youthful A. Nelson Cheney of Glens Falls, later world-famous as a fish culturist, remembered seeing Ned with two companions, all bearded like mountaineers. The trio clattered in from the woods and stopped at his father's summer hotel to end their holiday with a huge dinner. After partaking of a lavish meal and attracting a gang of small boys, the horsemen raced to the edge of the village. Ned hung a bottle from the limb of a tree, then mounted his pony and galloped toward it, breaking the glass with his bullets. Whooping back to town, the three wild fellows rode their horses in and out of the stores and up and down the stairs of the hotel porch,[7] pretending always to be oblivious of the admiring glee of many children.

Ned usually came out of these sprees penniless and far behind on some writing contract, but publishers forgave him and he would soon be at work again. Early in 1868 he was off on another wild goose chase – one that, strangely enough, led to his greatest renown. On May 1, 1868, the *San Francisco Evening Bulletin* announced with a front-page headline: LOOK OUT FOR A VISITOR OF NOTE. Ned Buntline, the article explained, had engaged passage on the next Aspinwall steamer. (William H. Aspinwall was promoter of the Pacific Mail Steamship Company and the Panama Railroad; a town at the railroad terminus bearing his name has since been changed to Colón.) The *Bulletin* said that Buntline had been "copy" for the press during the past thirty years. Now he had bidden farewell to the Eastern states by delivering a temperance speech at Cooper Institute in New York. With an impassioned voice he had concluded by saying that "he must say farewell to his audience and soon to wife and children. [Kate and her youngsters surely, not Lovanche!] He knew the struggle of the foe. If he fell in the struggle, he could leave this legacy to his children. He fell battling for the good of humanity."[8] Ned knew that the first railroad across the continent was due for completion in the early summer of 1869. What a grand opportunity to come back on the first train across North America and write about the experience! Also Lovanche was causing trouble again. Kate had given her third baby a Judson name, Alexander McClintock, after Ned's brother-in-law. Then in 1867 she bore a baby girl whom she named Edwardina. Lovanche felt highly outraged and Ned had good reason for enjoying a Western trip.

Buntline arrived in California as the official guest of the Grand Division of the Sons and Daughters of Temperance "to labor under their auspices in this state." He found San Francisco a cosmopolitan city with a distinct culture, neither Spanish nor American. The population hailed from all corners of the globe. Fortunes were piling up rapidly. Unnaturalized Irishmen had formed an organization to keep Chinese out of the state—a violent extralegal authority like Buntline's American Party but Ned had outgrown his old idea that violence was patriotic, and took no part in the rioting. After all, Irishmen were not true Americans. Instead, Ned sought conservative company.

A tradition of gracious living had come down to the Californians from Spanish grandees. Much leisure time was spent outdoors. Ned watched fashionably dressed women driving in barouches out Mission Road over the Point Lobos turnpike to Cliff House, where their children bathed at the beach under the bluff and Mamma bought gingerbread and sweets in the bazaar. In the fall of the year sea lions came in herds to the Golden Gate. They climbed over the rocky islands in the blue Pacific and barked hoarsely at spectators on shore. Sometimes the seals lay in great rafts, distended heads floating over the ocean swell. Occasionally a breaker rolled toward them – a long line of white water. Ned, a lover of nature, enjoyed seeing the seals duck below the surface as the churning foam approached and then come up again barking behind it.

Here in San Francisco Ned saw many open-air entertainments similar to those at Niblo's Gardens in New York. People drank in open beer gardens with no thought of temperance. They danced on uncovered floors. Local companies presented classical operas, and the best professionals in the world were imported, even as Ned Buntline. Ned learned that J. Ross Browne, his former contributor of sea stories, had become a great man in California. Having written the state's constitution, he was talked about now as possible minister to China. Another of Ned's contributors to the old *Literary Journal* was here too – the *grande dame* of the West, Julia L. Dumont. Now seventy-five, she held her head high among the women writers of the Pacific Coast.

In San Francisco Ned found a paper, the *Golden Era*, which combined fiction and news – the kind of publication Ned had wanted to make out of *Buntline's Own*. Bret Harte had got his start on the *Era*, and Mark Twain had written for it.[9] The *Era* exalted all notables visiting San Francisco and usually got a contribution from them. Orpheus C. Kerr ("Office Seeker"), Prentice Mulford, C. W. Stoddard, and Artemus Ward had been inveigled into contributing, so Ned, as soon as he landed, began a new serial for the paper. Kerr (Robert Henry Newell) had succumbed in California to the charms of a bareback-riding circus poetess.[10] Ned's hope of escape from entangling alliances seemed to be as slim as the hero's in one of his own stories.

Colonel Judson, so called by the California papers, delivered his opening lecture on temperance at the Methodist Episcopal Church on Powell Street. This talk was followed by another in the hall at Powell and Green streets. Then Ned left for Sacramento and the mines. His entire itinerary cannot be traced, but he certainly went up the Sacramento River to Mount Shasta.[11] He also rode in a stagecoach across "the valley" and up the escarpment to the lookout above Yosemite where the chasm gaped below him, blue and misty. Perhaps, too, he rode one of the Western ponies that were hired by tourists for a gallop through the spruce and across the creek to the foot of Bridal Veil Falls.

After two months Ned was back in San Francisco. His record of conversions to temperance was not impressive. In faraway Sierra County in eastern California he reported founding Table Rock Division No. 37 of the Sons of Temperance at Howland Flat. In nearby Martinez, on the upper bay, he organized Hope Division No. 17, but could show the signatures of only fourteen charter members. Ned's audiences during the summer were small. The temperance line he had been able to sell back East was hard to peddle here. Ned added something new. In the interior, he said, he had noticed many ghost towns. Liquor, he boomed, had been the destruction of most of them. He told his audiences, too, that back in New York he had discovered that many of the churches had invested their money in dives of iniquity. He wondered if that was so in San Francisco.[12]

A few Protestant churches welcomed Ned for his old talk against Catholics, but the news notes show plainly that he was not big enough to impress California. Obviously he was lonely, marking time, waiting for the transcontinental railroad to be finished so he could go back East overland. In January 1869, Ned lectured in Oakland. The *Evening Bulletin* reported a hundred in attendance,[13] and that probably meant twenty-five!

To be frank, California was no place for Ned Buntline and his moral lectures. Perhaps the population felt more sophisticated than people back East. Country men out West had not come from nearby parochial communities, and they were not confused and dismayed by mushrooming industrial cities. California immigrants differed from Easterners who had gone from the farm to nearby mill towns and commercial metropolises. Moreover, the cosmopolitan Californians did not favor abstinence. Then, too, both Mark Twain and Bret Harte had scoffed at the Sunday-school fallacy that hard work and virtue always brought success.[14] But Californians had other eccentricities. Cynical of moral reform, they swallowed spiritualism avidly. Here the cult flourished even more luxuriously than in the Eastern states.[15] Miners, prospectors, and gamblers all worshiped the God of Chance. Spiritualism satisfied an urgent instinct. The fad seemed to be dying back East, but here in California spiritualism was part of the state's radical movement, as it had been part of New York's free-thinking a decade before. Spiritualists who noticed their audiences dwindling nightly in the East had toured California with continuous success. In short, the cards were stacked against Ned on the Pacific Coast.

He boarded the train for the East during the summer of 1869.[16] By some miracle he had missed being on the first train to cross the continent, and does not seem to have been present for the driving of the golden spike on May 10, 1869, at Promontory Point in Utah. But it was during that summer that he experienced the most fabulous incident in his career—the discovery of Buffalo Bill.

The Scout of the Plains engaged a good deal of Ned's energy, from the time of his first story about him in December 1869 until they parted company in the spring of 1873, and even after that the lure of the Wild West Show would not quite die. By this time Ned had married his "precious Hazel Eye," Anna Fuller Judson, and had settled down in his ancestral village of Stamford, New York. It was from here that he launched his unsuccessful venture with Arizona Frank and Texas Charlie during the summer of 1873. But neither of them charmed audiences like Bill Cody had, and Ned turned quickly to new undertakings. Actually, the Buffalo Bill incident never loomed as large in his life as the subsequent fame of Cody made it appear, and Ned appears to have been quite happy to retire quietly to Stamford. Presiding over his estate, Eagle's Nest, gave him great pleasure, and his Fourth of July displays of fireworks became a regular civic institution. The road in front of the mansion was always crowded by young and old on these occasions, and with them always came a reckless blade or two driving a half-broken colt hitched to a buggy. A runaway in the dark became as much an expected part of the performance as the pyrotechnics.[17] Then, too, Cousin Pratt Judson could also be counted on to stand at his division line, malign his wealthy cousin, and warn the onlookers against trespassing.

Ned experimented with the trials and tribulations of a country gentleman in the prosperous summer of 1875 and found them diverting. The Judson Library Foundation held its annual meeting in August. A musical performance, followed by a speech and a poem of Buntline's, preceded a dinner. Fifty cents per plate was charged for single people, couples were served for forty cents apiece, families of five or more for thirty cents per head. The crowd was invited to assemble in Seminary Hall.

Two extracts of Ned's poem are typical of the performance:

> Why am I singled out to bear the weight
> Which failure makes so grave?
> Why must I stand, unpitied, meet the fate
> Which others, cautious, would not brave?
> What shall I say beneath the classic roof
> Where Homer's ancient songs are sung?
> How weave the deft poetic web and woof
> Where Virgil's lofty chimes are rung?

Ned apologized in this manner through a hundred and fifty lines, with suitable digressions to remind his audience that next year would be the hundredth anniversary of national independence when "no brave man sought the sword to sheathe till base Kingcraft bent on tot'ring knees." The poem ended with:

I've done at last! Thrice happy be the thought,
The task for task it was, is ended
The duty came to me and came unsought—
Bad though the work, it can't be mended—
I hope it has not marred your appetites
For ices, cakes and candies—
For tables filled with choice and sweet delights
Are set for all but dandies—
Forgetting then this worse than prosy poem,
Haste with your fair ones to the table,
Look at all the goodies there and stow 'em
Just as fast as you are able.[18]

Ned's experiments with gentleman-farming continued into the fall of 1875. In September he drove up to the newspaper office and displayed a cucumber that measured twenty-three inches in length and weighed two and a quarter pounds.[19] But the show business tugged at him, and Ned saw a new angle to promote. Wild Indians and scouts were being replaced out on the plains by cowboys. Each year thousands of cattle came up the Chisholm and other Texas trails to the Union Pacific and Santa Fe tracks. Dodge City and other railroad trail-ends were notorious for wild Western lawlessness. Gun-packing marshals named Wyatt Earp, Bat Masterson, and Bill Tilghman had become famous. Ned decided to see how well they really could shoot, to write some stories about them, and to start another show—the last word, with marshals and cowboys instead of mountain trappers and scouts.

Ned ordered the Colt factory to make him some guns to be named Buntline Specials, which he proposed to present to these eminent officers. The unique weapons were .45 Colt six-shooters with twelve-inch barrels and an over-all length of eighteen inches. A demountable walnut stock enabled the owner to convert each into a small repeating rifle. A buckskin sling was provided to attach the arm to belt or saddle. The name NED was carved on the walnut butt, and each gun fitted into a handsome hand-tooled holster.[20]

Little is known about Ned's trip to Dodge City. In all probability he enjoyed shooting with the Western gunmen, and no doubt made a creditable showing himself. Wyatt Earp was still wearing his Buntline Special over twenty years later.[21] Bat Masterson and Bill Tilghman preferred a shorter arm, and both cut the barrels of their Specials down to eight inches.

Whether "precious Hazel Eye" accompanied Ned on this trip is a mystery. In October 1875, Ned turned up in Stamford for a few days, said that he was backing the local Democratic candidate for the assembly and would do the same for the Democratic Presidential nominee the following year unless the Republicans repudiated the graft and corruption of Grant's administration. Serious political activity did not interest him this year, however. His mind centered on the real gunmen and cow-town marshals for his next show, but he had been unable to employ them and his plans seemed destined to fail. Finally, in desperate impatience, he resurrected and revived the plot of his old play, employed a few Texans – none famous – and in December started on the road with *Scouts of the Plains or Red Deviltry As It Is.* Ned toured New England [22] and his old haunts in Maine, but he was not successful, and he did not try show business again. By spring of 1876 he was back in Stamford writing for Street and Smith, planning his annual excursion to Beaverkill, and content to be a country gentleman, in earnest. Then Lovanche got off the train from Kingston with a court order for overdue alimony and a determination to march out to Eagle's Nest, confront Anna, and demand her rights.

XXII

Country Gentleman

SCANDAL seemed to be the order of the day in 1876. For over two years the newspapers had been full of accounts of the alleged salacious relations of Henry Ward Beecher with the wife of one of his parishioners. Ned Buntline's friends in Stamford wanted to save him from similar embarrassment. The villagers had heard whispers about the literary gentleman's past, but nothing more. The Reverend Mr. Richards knew of Lovanche's alleged marriage to Ned, and so did Editor Champion of the *Mirror*, but both had discreetly held their tongues. Ned's counsel and fishing companion, F. R. Gilbert, made an agreement with Lovanche to give her $50, and an order for $1900 on Street and Smith, if she would leave town as quickly and quietly as possible. With the money, Lovanche boarded the Kingston train, after making it plain that she would return if another lapse in payment occurred, and that the next time Eagle's Nest and Ned's innocent wife, Anna, would not be spared.

Ned planned his usual spring fishing excursion to the Beaverkill – an event that had become classic. Anna Judson liked fishing also. For the first time in Ned's life he had a wife who could match his driving energy, or perhaps his own vitality was slowing down. Ned became enthusiastic about "female fishermen." He wrote an article for the *American Angler* describing several famous fisherwomen, great fly casters. He recommended that more women enter the sport. Ned said that a neat bathing suit with skirt to the knees was modest and at the same time ideal for the sport.[1]

All summer long, with a camp outfit in a light wagon, Ned and his wife jogged along soft dirt roads, visiting trout streams in the Catskills and also in the Poconos of Pennsylvania. He heard fishermen talk about a new sport, "dry-fly casting." The lures had been introduced abroad in 1859 in a book by W. C. Stewart entitled *The Practical Angler*. To use dry flies it was necessary to cast upstream instead of down the riffles as most Americans did. Ned tried the curiosities and wrote an article condemning them. Newfangled gut leaders, ready tied with loops, Ned liked, and he wrote another article on their admirable misty invisibility. He found them especially useful in early spring when cold water numbed his fingers until he could no longer tie on a fly.

In his traveling rig Ned always packed a large American flag. Whenever he stopped at an inn in the fishing country the banner was hoisted. City sportsmen soon learned to look for this emblem of the great fisherman.

For sports magazines Ned wrote a chatty directory of hunting and fishing resorts. Guides whom he had known in the Adirondacks were cited. Chauncey Hathorn's camp, near the now famous Blue Mountain Lake House, got free advertising, as did many other places. "At the famous Murray hostelry," he wrote, "you will have fine trout and black bass fishing, pointed out close at hand. You will live well and do well. Ask Rockwell. If you wish to fish to music," Ned added, "where rattlers are almost as plenty as pretty girls, stop off at Mast Hope, just below, for a day or two."[2]

A fortnight prior to the Fourth of July, 1876, Ned went back to Stamford and planned his Independence Day performance—the hundredth anniversary. He looked forward to it with relish. But his ballooning enthusiasm was punctured by the exciting news of Custer's "last stand" out on the Little Big Horn. Ned went at once to the Delaware Inn. A dozen barefoot boys congregated in the post road outside, scratching and squinting, waiting for Ned to explain the catastrophe. He was irritable; after all, the biggest show on earth had occurred without him. The unhappy writer limped across to the newspaper office and left a card for publication. The Buntline pyrotechnic display, so the card announced, would be better than usual. Special attractions were planned.[3]

To make the celebration unusually impressive, Ned began it on the afternoon of the third by speaking on the lawn near his birthplace. Pointing dramatically to the flag above his head, he told the assembled townsmen that its fluttering shadow caressed the house where he was born, and that within the sound of his voice lay the bones of his ancestors buried nearly seventy years ago. Then Ned described the changes since that time, the pioneer settlement with Revolutionary traditions that had been raided by Tories and their Indian allies, and the present prosperous farming community with its large income from "city boarders," foreigners from New York, "many of whom had crossed the far rolling waves of the ocean to enjoy freedom in Freedom's chosen land." [4]

Without doubt Ned had become reconciled to foreigners now that they brought money into the country. In his speech the colonel also referred to the time when these peaceful hills were filled with bears and deer. "We have the 'deers' with us still," he was reported as saying, and he thanked heaven they were tame enough to be caught by the "bears" who roamed over the land. Next day the *Stamford Mirror* complimented the community on a celebration that ended without a fight or a runaway. Two weeks later Ned sent the editor a copy of his "Impromptu Lines" of poetry delivered on the memorable occasion.[5]

Buntline soon learned that his old partner, Buffalo Bill, had used the Custer massacre to promote his own fortunes. Cody had not forgotten Ned's lesson about keeping himself remembered as a scout, not an actor. On receipt of the news of Custer's death, Buffalo Bill closed his show to join the soldiers. Soon the papers announced that he had taken "the first scalp for Custer." This fight had occurred at Hat Creek, and the matinee idol, wearing "a handsome Mexican suit of black velvet, slashed with scarlet, and trimmed with silver buttons and lace," was said to have challenged Chief Yellow Hand to single combat and to have killed him, between admiring lines of red men and white. James Gordon Bennett gave his old friend almost a column in the *Herald.* Fifty years later, survivors of the fight declared that Yellow Hand was murdered by a squaw man in the Indian village, a day previous to the arrival of the soldiers.

After the skirmish Cody undoubtedly had a scalp, which he carried in his pocket, but whether it was taken from a live Indian or a dead one is open to question. One of the officers tendered him $50 to throw it away, and a sergeant in the troop remembered begging Cody to ride on the other side of the column where the wind would not blow in his direction.[6] Having obtained this and other trophies, Cody abandoned the campaign and returned to enjoy the most successful theatrical season he had yet known, terminating it the following spring by a quarrel with his wife over "the manner in which he bade good-by to some of the actresses."[7]

Wild Bill Hickok, this same year, was shot in the back in Deadwood, Dakota Territory. He had given up the show business to join the gold rush. People said that Buffalo Bill would avenge his death,[8] but that was newspaper talk. Why should he? Of all the Leatherstocking performers Buffalo Bill alone prospered.

But Ned, in his new surroundings, was doing quite well. The life of a country gentleman gave him leisure – time to write and to play. Tourists occasionally strolled over to Eagle's Nest to watch the great man, climbed Ned's fences, and rambled across the meadows. On days when Ned felt friendly he hobbled out to chat with them. More often he lurched up with a warning to beware, a blunt reminder that he frequently shot a high-powered rifle for practice and would not be responsible if anyone got hurt.[9]

All through the summer of 1876 the colonel wrote steadily for the *New York Weekly*, never overlooking an opportunity to aggrandize himself. Late in July he brought to the editor of the *Stamford Mirror* a letter from a friend abroad who suggested translating his writings into Dutch and Flemish.[10] Ned hoped that Editor Champion would publicize this new honor. Surely it was more important than the latest achievements of Buffalo Bill.

In the fall of 1876 Ned visited the Centennial Exposition in Philadelphia.[11] He wrote a story about the Fair as he rode the cars and sold it to the *New York Weekly* when he reached the city – a common practice of Ned's, this earning of current expenses. Back in Stamford, he offered his services to the Republican Party in the local campaign. The county chairman arranged a rally, where Ned spoke fluently for the Democratic candidate, thus ending his political usefulness. Read out of the party,[12] Ned retired to Eagle's Nest and to his writing.

Exercise kept the old scout fit. Ned limped to town each morning, called for the mail and drank a milk punch at the tavern. Then he stumbled over to the Delaware Inn and sat in the office while he read the paper. By midmorning he was home again writing, listening to the bare branches of silver maple slash and scrape on the big house.

Stamford reveled in a white Thanksgiving, and by Christmas snow made walking difficult. But staying in the house suited Anna, for she knew that a baby was coming with the spring of 1877. In January three-foot drifts covered the roads, and in some fields snow had piled up twenty feet deep. One morning Ned slipped on his own front steps and broke two ribs.[13] Confined to the house with Anna – now busy letting out the seams in her dresses – Ned complained in letters to his friends, "The winter here has been simply terrible, the thermometer below zero all the time." Old wounds, Ned said, especially a bullet embedded in his spine since June 1863, aggravated his sciatica. "God helping me, 'tis my last winter in the North."[14]

If Anna suffered, too, no record of it has survived. On April 4 the doctor was called to deliver her baby – a girl, named Irene by the proud couple. (Ned's second child by Kate had the same name.) Spring came early but Ned, crippled as he was, brooded over the prospect of the Fourth of July – the first since the nation's centennial celebration had been spoiled for Ned by the curtain-dropping climax of Custer's Last Stand. Irritably Ned complained that he could not finance the entire performance himself this year. Stamford villagers offered to make the display a civic one, with Colonel Judson chairman of the Gun and Fireworks Committee. Buntline was also scheduled to deliver an oration,[15] but felt unhappy about the entire holiday. In June, as plans progressed, Anna, with two-month-old Irene, drove to a neighbor's home to call. On her way back the horse ran away, throwing mother and child out of the carriage. Mrs. Judson broke her arm at the elbow, but tiny Irene rolled to the roadside unhurt. Ned wept, thanked God, cursed himself for permitting his wife to drive alone, then forgot it in his preoccupations – his writing, his plans for speeches, games, and luncheons for the Fourth. The accumulating irritations upset his nerves. To work with other obstinate people always irked Ned, and on the third of July he blew up, spoke his mind to the entire committee, and resigned. To his chagrin the performance went on without him.

Ned's failing health began to give him serious trouble. In August he was confined to bed with a foot infection, probably gout, but he reported it the result of an old wound received in the service of his country. The sickness and quarrel with the committee left him a little lonely, and he renewed his efforts to serve the Judson Library Foundation with a lecture program.[16] As the cold weather approached, his sciatica became worse. Ned determined to go South, preferably to Georgia, for the winter.

Guns and fishing tackle were packed in his carriage along with a flag to hoist at headquarters, wherever that might be. Ned made arrangements to write sporting sketches and a log of his journey for the local newspaper.

The family drove first through the Catskills to Kingston, then south toward New Jersey, averaging about thirty miles a day. Ned reported the roads to be bad, but the inns good, and he read familiar names of Stamfordites on the registers for the first two hundred miles. At Rosendale, New York, the carriage ran over a man. Ned was sure that the fellow had been drinking, and moreover the villain swore terribly when hit. These two things, Ned said, convinced him that his victim had a low moral character, so "no bad dreams" [17] disturbed Ned's sleep. The next day the little family spun along for forty-six miles with a flurry of snow in the air. At Chalfont, Pennsylvania, Ned enjoyed learning that this was the purported burial place of Chief Tammany, good Indian of the early days, now prominent in New York politics.

Ned planned to skirt Philadelphia, and he promised the readers of his newsletter that in the next "I will tell you how the great Battlefield of Gettysburg looks at the present time – for thither and beyond am I bound." At Pottstown he marveled at the ironworks, but not at the city: "Plenty of whiskey and no milk. Poor fare for temperance folks." [18] Inns along the way had picturesque names, the Grape Hotel, the White Horse, the Eagle. Ned found Lancaster County the garden spot of Pennsylvania, and he slept sentimentally at a hotel which he heard had sheltered Martha Washington. In the city of Lancaster Ned was interviewed by the press.

The Judsons crossed the Susquehanna on a new bridge a mile and a half long and saw the first remnants of the fearful battle of Gettysburg. The old bridge, Ned learned, had been burned to keep Confederate General Jubal Early from penetrating into eastern Pennsylvania. In the National Cemetery Ned inspected the old earthworks, and a guide "aided me easily in mastering the details of the fight."[19] Trees, walls, and fences had been left torn and splintered as on the day of battle. Houses in the town were chipped and pocked with bullet scars. Ned collected many odd relics for the Stamford museum. He found the inn hospitable and the rates reasonable, only $3.50 for his family's dinner, bed, and breakfast. In the morning, rain pattered down on the brick houses. Ned decided to stay for several days until it cleared. At Gettysburg he smacked his aging lips over Pennsylvania Dutch cooking – scrapple, schmierkäse and panhas – i-yi-yih-yi! In his room he caught up with his writing, promising his readers to expect more later about "a grand old time among the deer, bear, and turkeys."[20]

From Gettysburg Ned drove to Emmitsburg, Maryland, through mud hub-deep, but all the way he gloried in the fact that he was following the road used by Lee in his retreat. From Emmitsburg the road was smooth as marble to Frederick. Here the Judsons learned that the Potomac bridges were out, so they drove down to Washington where they visited some friends, the Englishes from Stamford. Mr. H. J. English was employed in the Patent Office. His daughter, Miss Hattie, accepted an invitation from the Judsons to accompany them as far as Warrenton, Virginia. The road lay across famous Civil War battlefields – Centerville, Bull Run, and Second Bull Run.[21] Ned enjoyed the vista of rolling hills. The Piedmont of Virginia looked to him like good hunting country. At last he came to a hill higher than the others, and drove to the top, where a porticoed courthouse stood against the sky. This was Warrenton. Ned turned the horses down a narrow street between brick houses and stopped in front of the long gallery of the Warren Green Hotel. A Negro boy, dressed in rags but with pearls for teeth and satin highlights in his eyes, scampered to hold the horses. Mine host, James Maddox, stepped out on the piazza to greet his guests and help the ladies down from the carriage. Ned, round as a bear in his fur coat, gave directions for the feeding of his team, then clumped into the hotel.

The holiday season was approaching. Ned noticed at once how Southerners made more of this than people up North. That evening the family dined on two quails apiece, wild turkey, and oysters. Anna put the baby to bed, and Ned, with a stub pencil, scribbled away at his "letter." The thermometer on the portico, he wrote, registered sixty-four degrees. Think of that for December, when icicles hung on all the eaves in upstate New York! Ned told his readers that he had fallen in love with Warrenton and thought he would stay a few days.

Two weeks later Ned wrote again. He had decided now to stay all winter at the Warren Green; he said he had shot a twenty-pound turkey and was enjoying "delightful society." On the long gallery he had met Colonel Mosby, the Confederate guerrilla, and General William E. Payne, commander of the Black Horse Cavalry. Ned found both of them friendly and courteous, with no shade of malice for the Lost Cause. On Christmas Ned gave a little party of his own with iced lemonade for his guests to sip while he recounted stories of great gamebags. For Northern readers he noted that ice did not sell here by the pound but by the bushel, as it seldom froze more than half an inch thick.

A fortnight later Ned wrote another "letter" for his column. This time he described the five churches in Warrenton and complimented all of them for their hospitality and devotion.[22] Ned told his readers up North, too, that he planned driving out toward the Blue Ridge, twenty miles away. Deer and bears could be found there to add to the milder excitement of quail in the lower country.

A week passed and Ned wrote another "letter." He had not gone west as yet to the Blue Ridge. A blizzard had whistled across the Virginia hills, covering the roads with snow, freezing ice four inches thick. A few sleighs appeared on the roads, but the sun soon shone and Ned maintained that the climate was much warmer than "Old Delaware" and he did not suffer. Then, too, General Robert S. Granger, a retired officer from the regular army, came to the inn with his family for the winter. Ned met him with extended hand. "It is a delight," he wrote home, "to talk with the old hero of our early days in Florida and Mexico, for we both saw hard as well as jolly times in those wars." [23]

Ned's next "letter" to the press described Warrenton's schools. He had told his readers about spiritual life in town earlier, now he depicted the schoolgirls who paraded the streets in a column of twos under command of their teachers. "I've met Stuart, Ashley, and Hampton's cavalry many a time in deadly fray," Ned lied in his letter, "but I tell you what, old friend, were I not protected by the golden shield of matrimony, a charge of flashing glances from the dark eyed daughters of the sunny south would conquer one who never surrendered to the heroes named above. But I must stop this, or I'll get my hair pulled." [24]

Spring came early in the Southland. In the middle of March Ned prepared to return home by a new route. He wrote the paper that he did not know when he would arrive, as he intended to stop at good trout streams, so luck would determine his speed. The Hambletonians seemed eager for the road. "When once our gallant bays take the road the dust will fly, you bet, as we head Northward." [25]

Ned followed spring across Maryland and Pennsylvania. Early in April he turned the team into the lane leading to Eagle's Nest. His fur coat felt good up here. With Anna he prowled through the cold, gloomy house noting how things had been neglected in their absence. Little Irene crawled eagerly across the cold floors, and stood swaying, chubby hands clutching Mamma's long dresses. Ned brought in the trunks and soon he hoisted the flag out on the lawn.[26] Let Stamford know that the Master had returned! The next day Ned drove to town, called at his favorite tavern for a milk punch, and quarreled with Editor Champion—

or at least the *Mirror* ceased to carry complimentary notices about the Judsons. In May, Ned's story "Guiletta the Waif; or The Girl Wrecker" was announced for publication by *Street and Smith's New York Weekly*. Champion referred to the story in the *Mirror* as "the best story he [Ned Buntline] has ever written – so he says and what he says must be true." Obviously Ned was not welcome at the newspaper office, and during the summer of 1878 he loafed, when in town, on the long porch of the Delaware Inn. Old-timers remember that he sat there one day when an Italian organ-grinder started to make the mountain air hideous with canned music. Ned tried to read his mail, but the sound distracted him. He offered the musician a quarter to go. This was accepted, and Ned paid the price. The organ-grinder moved to the other end of the porch and began his dolorous harmony again amid gusts of laughter from all the guests.

Ned remained aloof from community life during the summer. Editor Champion allotted him no space in the paper, and the Fourth of July celebration was enacted without him. At Eagle's Nest the great writer scribbled for hours on his copy and came to town only for mailing it. He did not go South during the winter.

The next spring, 1879, he suffered a slight attack of "gold fever." The Black Hills had been opened by soldiers after the Custer massacre. Buffalo Bill, as has been said, reaped a rich harvest of publicity. Dozens of new mining companies were issuing prospectuses of opportunities in the newly opened Indian lands. Ned bought fifty shares of the Cheyenne Gold Mining Company in March 1879. In May, he and other investors sent out a man to investigate the diggings. A report came back that the company was a bonanza.[27]

Waiting for the Final Shock

NED BUNTLINE displayed himself as a nonchalant bonanza king. In fact it may have been all pose, for there is no evidence that real wealth came to him from the mines. He aged rapidly in his late fifties, complained of sciatica and his old wounds, preached patriotism, and promised to work against James G. Blaine in the political campaign in the fall of 1880 if that Plumed Knight received the nomination. During the spring and summer Ned lectured on "Woman in the Parlor and over the Washtub," ostensibly to raise money to purchase an organ for Richmondville school, and he repeated the performance for the benefit of Stamford's Cornet Band.[1] Stage appearances were still easy for Ned, but the rough action of a Wild West Show no longer appealed to him. During the summer he read about the death of Texas Jack in Leadville, Colorado. The silver city was at the height of spectacular exploitation. Buffalo Bill still strode the boards behind footlights – the best of the Leatherstocking troupers, perhaps, but as yet no great thespian. Certainly Ned was a bigger man in Stamford. To his regular publishers he added another, *Brentano's Monthly*, which accepted a story entitled "Maud Granger – How I Saved Her."

The villagers did not include Ned Buntline in their plans for the Fourth of July in 1880. The great man countered the rebuff by sponsoring the activities of the band, purchasing their uniforms and instruments, and proclaiming that he would celebrate

Washington's Birthday in a manner that would make Stamford's Fourth look like Sunday afternoon.

In the fall of 1880, with election day approaching, politicians took to the hustings. Blaine had not been nominated, so Ned agreed to stump for the Republicans, and he divided his time between speeches for Garfield and Arthur and short stories for his publishers. Always he could spare a few minutes to stop with boys burning leaves and tell them about the West. As a great man of the present he liked to talk about his great past, and his Western years had become more romantic in his mind than his earlier days on sailing ships.

In 1881 a new publisher came for Ned's work. Frederick Pond, who wrote under the name of Will Wildwood, had left the West for New York, to edit *Turf, Field and Farm.* He knew Ned by reputation and quickly made the acquaintance personal. Pond, at twenty-five, had written two books for sportsmen and had edited a third – one by Frank Forester – yet he looked on the prolific Buntline with awe. Would the venerable old writer contribute an article to *Turf, Field and Farm?* Pond received the following:

> It has been my habit for years, when no serious hindrance intervened, to spend the last day of the trout season over on the crystal Beaverkill, and the last day of August found me at the famous Tripp cottage, with my cherished Orvis rod,[2] a book of Orvis flies and a big box of genuine grasshoppers, ready to see the season out.
>
> The stream was very low, consequently rather warm and the fishing poor except where cold springs entered the main stream. There it was superb, and knowing the stream as I do from ten years of experience I skipped all places but these very spring-holes, and the consequence was that I came in with a twenty-pound basket full of speckled beauties, mostly of fine size.
>
> Approaching the stream cautiously on the Charley Water's clearing, sheltered from view by a clump of willows, I looked over to the mouth of a cold spring brook running from Robert Seal's farm. In a shallow pool where the ice-cold water from the spring ran in I counted ten trout that would average from ten to twelve inches long

and in weight strike a half pound apiece. There they lay, their dorsal fins quivering with pleasure, in the cool shade, unconscious of danger. I changed a much worn leader for a fresh one, took a single black gnat from my book, shortened my line for a clean lift out, and then, all unseen through the leafy screen, lightly dropped an invitation to the lowest trout in the pool. The fly hardly touched water ere it was sprung for, taken, and *Mr. Salmo Fontinalis* literally *lifted* out by the tough bamboo, without noise or trouble enough to startle the rest of the little "school." Number one deftly secured and basketed, I tried the same game with numbers two, three and four successfully. But the fifth was a little more gamey, or else success had made me careless; and, only half-hooked, he tore away and made the water fly with his wild antics, startling his brethren into other waters and shutting off my rash intention of "cleaning out" the pool.

You cannot, with every six-ounce bamboo rod, *lift* out a half-pound trout; in fact, I never had one before that was pliant enough for a seventy-foot cast, that would bear such a strain; but I believe I have as good a rod as ever fell to an angler's lot. With the tip touching the reel plate, I have proved it, holding a three-pounder in a swift current, away from roots and snags, till I tired and drowned him out.

To me there are two glorious times in the trout season. The *first* is in the early Spring, when the streams are full and rapid, when the trout seem wild and fresh from a long Winter's rest, and like nature herself, full of beauty, strength and *vim!*

The *second* is the last of the season, when the largest trout emerge from their hiding places under dark ledges, mossy banks and deep, well sheltered pools, to seek the sandy spawning beds far up the stream, where they can carry out the procreative laws which prevent our brooks, lakes and rivers from utter depletion, fished as they are, literally "to death." But friend Wildwood, I fear I am spinning too long a yarn for the limited space accorded in your journal to piscatorial lore.

Ere I close let me join the general "boom" in congratulations that you have come *Eastward* for *light*, found it, and are content to give your facile pen play in a field which I trust will add both to your fame and fortune.[3]

In January 1881, Ned planned his Washington's Birthday celebration that was to eclipse the Fourth of July display which had been taken away from him. In the midst of his elaborate arrangements the cup of happiness was snatched from his lips by a sudden misfortune – one of the great sorrows of his life. Wives had come and gone with Ned Buntline always; he took horse-whipping and jailing philosophically; but when little four-year-old Irene died after a two-day illness, Ned collapsed in tears. The tragedy melted the hearts of his neighbors. All came to Eagle's Nest to offer sympathy. Ned and Anna inserted a card of appreciation in the newspaper thanking their friends who had assuaged by words and flowers "the most crushing blow of life." [4]

Little Irene's death, in the big gloomy house on the snow-covered hillside, wrenched Ned out of his dime-novel world and conjured the Victorian Muses of his youth. Street and Smith were forgotten when he tried falteringly to release his own agony in poetry:

> The long days come, the long days go,
> The silent, dreary nights as well –
> They bring no solace for our woe,
> No words of comfort to us tell.
> The light which once upon us shone,
> The music which so sweetly fell,
> Is gone – alas! forever gone –
> We only know her parting knell.
>
> Oh, gloomy day! – Oh, starless night!
> If we could only, only dream!
> In fancy see one ray of light –
> Of faded joys feel but a gleam –
> Could hear the patter of the feet
> That to and fro swift used to go,
> We'd bow our heads, the shadow greet,
> And kiss the Hand that dealt the blow. [5]

The Cornet Band performed loyally at the funeral, and Ned published a letter of appreciation in the *Mirror* stating that he would donate $5.00 each month for the good cause they "are doing to add to the pleasures of those among whom they live. . . . Think," Ned concluded, "that 'The little Angel of the Band' sends it."[6] Ned, penitent and dejected, was elected to the school board.

Washington's Birthday came at last and Ned's spirits revived. He gave, as he had promised, a great dinner at the Hamilton House. The band met him at Eagle's Nest and escorted the celebrity to town. Editor Champion and other townsmen were picked up by the blaring mob. After prolonged toasts and speeches, all sat down at three o'clock in the afternoon to feast. Hours later, when darkness crept up the valley and enveloped Eagle's Nest, the villagers looked at and listened to a fireworks display as good as or better than the performance Ned had formerly given on the Fourth of July.[7]

In March, spring began to stir on the meadow below Eagle's Nest. Another baby stirred under Anna's heart. A glint of fatherhood shone in Ned Buntline's ancient eye. He worked seriously with school board duties, and at the closing exercises presented five-dollar gold pieces with suitable remarks to two students whose records showed meritorious deportment. He announced that he planned six other prizes for constant attendance, faithful study, and good conduct. He urged all pupils to be vaccinated against smallpox, employed a new teacher, and promised that school would be conducted "on principles of kindness and encouragement"[8]—two things which Ned believed had been denied him as a boy.

Ned's civic responsibilities were seriously disturbed in April. Lovanche alighted from the Kingston train with blood in her eye. This time she evaded Ned's attorney and the minister. Registering at the Hamilton House, she announced boldly that she was the lawfully wedded wife of Colonel Judson. Great excitement bubbled through Stamford. At last, after a decade, the scandal was out. To a score of people in the lobby of the hotel and on the street Lovanche repeated her story. The strange yarn was picked up by papers out of town. The *New York Times* headlined it as "Colonel Judson's Life Disturbed." At first some Stamfordites doubted the tale, but soon many of them wagged their heads asserting that she and not Anna, now well along with child, was the legitimate "Mrs. Judson." Newspaper reporters came up from Kingston to get more details. One reported:

> Mrs. Judson appears to be about fifty-five years old, and is crippled and an invalid. One who knew her years ago says she was most beautiful then, but she has no traces of beauty now. She seems to have seen much of the world, is quick-witted, and has a most effective tongue. By most persons she would be considered to be more than ordinarily intelligent.[9]

Ned met Lovanche face to face and fled on the next train. Soon word came from Kingston that he had stopped there long enough to leave in the newspaper office the following explanation:

> EDITOR FREEMAN:
>
> The attempt to blackmail me by false statements and forgeries alluded to in your paper of today has been repeatedly tried but has failed in this as in other attempts of the same woman. She is not, never was my wife, nor has any legal claim upon me. I shall hold my slanderers to a strict account in this matter.
>
> Yours, respectfully,
>
> E. Z. C. JUDSON[10]
>
> *Rondout, 14th April, 1881.*

The editor tried to locate Judson but was unable to find him in town. Ned turned up next in New York, where the press received further notes concerning the woman's attempt to extort money from him. Lovanche, in the meantime, spent all her funds and sent for the Overseer of the Poor. She explained that she could not pay her hotel bill and was destitute. The official agreed to settle her week's account at the Hamilton House and give her $5.00 in cash if she would purchase a ticket out of town. Lovanche took the money, and the officer watched her leave for New York City, where Ned was known to be hiding.

From the terminus of the Ulster & Delaware Railroad Lovanche boarded a steamboat bound down the Hudson. Ned, on another boat, came up and crossed to Stamford. Bristling with indignation, he maintained that important business had called him suddenly from town. He had returned, he said, to fulfill his engagements at various neighboring villages that had been promised concerts from his band.[11] Then with his trotters, and the band in a wagon, he set off. In May he hurried back importantly to receive a shipment of 1500 California trout eggs from Seth Green's Rochester hatchery.[12] A fortnight later a great thing happened. Perhaps it was part of the Buntline luck. Early on the morning of May 19, 1881, Ned came out of Eagle's Nest and hoisted the flag against the stars. The next issue of the *Mirror* announced:

> Eagle's Nest, Col. E. Z. [*sic*] Judson's home, were [*sic*] made happy by the appearance of a young eagle, in good trim and as lively as a cricket. The Colonel felt as jolly as a lark. . . . It's a boy.[13]

During the summer Ned hobbled around the house like a goblin, reciting poetry and peeping under the coverlet at his baby son. Dreaming of posterity, he laid out burial plots for the entire family, including himself, and erected a memorial column to Irene with an angel kneeling on the capital.[14]

Early in the winter Buntline announced that he and his family intended to visit New York, Philadelphia, and Washington. President Garfield had died in September, and the trial of his assassin promised to furnish as good copy as the trial of the Lincoln conspirators sixteen years before.

The Judsons did not return to Stamford until March. Ned brought a bas-relief of Irene reclining on a bed of Italian marble roses, carved by Henry Lindes. He also had boxes and baskets full of toys for Eddie – toys much too complicated for the nine-months-old baby. "I mean that his childhood shall be happy as mine was not," [15] Ned told friends proudly. On the lawn he found the flagpole blown down. He announced that he would raise another, fifty-eight feet tall. In May the colonel made a Memorial Day address at Cobbleskill, then drove over to the Beaverkill for the first spring fishing.

The ensuing summer of 1882 – one of the quietest in Ned's new life – passed monotonously, and the following winter seemed unusually long at Eagle's Nest. Ned's ligaments contracted in the cold weather, torturing his nerves. Anna suffered from a serious illness and convalesced slowly. Ned determined to make good his old resolution and never spend another winter in Stamford. After Christmas he watched for signs of spring and cheered himself by announcing that he had been invited to deliver three Washington's Birthday addresses. In April the papers reported the death of Ned's publisher, Francis S. Street. His estate was estimated at half a million dollars, not counting his interest in the Street and Smith firm – all made on the Buntline type of literature.[16]

When the roads dried Ned set off for the Beaverkill in his buckboard as usual, and returned in time to keep an engagement to speak in Philadelphia on Memorial Day. When he returned to Eagle's Nest, he told townsmen that he would talk next at Valley Forge on the Fourth of July. Then something changed his mind. Perhaps the villagers became more cordial, or Ned thought so. In any event, he suddenly promised to show Stamford a record display of pyrotechnics, the first at his own expense since Custer's Last Stand in 1876.

In September 1883, when frost tinted the leaves, Ned prepared for another Southern trip. He was not going to be caught in the snow this winter. Once again he arranged to report the expedition for the press, and long before the leaves began to fall and blow along the roads, Anna and two-year-old Eddie were packed in the "buck board hunting wagon." Ned in his fur coat climbed stiffly to the seat, tightened the reins over his favorite Hambletonians, and away they went. From Warrenton, Virginia, Ned wrote back with pride. He had driven 710 miles from Eagle's Nest in nine and a half days "measured." Ned might have been reporting his own jump from the third floor of the hotel at Nashville. Only now it was his Hambletonians, not himself, that came through without a blemish. Ned felt at home in Warrenton. The Warren Green Hotel proprietor, James Maddox, was an enthusiastic fox hunter as well as a crack shot at birds. Ned liked to stay at his inn. He had become acquainted, too, with the local banker, Charles Payne, a nephew of his old friend Dr. Alban Payne (Nicholas Spicer). Ned intended to renew his acquaintance this winter with his onetime sporting companion in a brawl at Five Points.

Alban Payne lived at Crystal Water Hall, near Markham, in the shadow of the Blue Ridge. The frozen mountain roads were rough, but Ned determined to undertake the fifty-mile drive. When he tied his team at the trip's end, he found that Crystal Water Hall was a frame farm house instead of a mansion, and that his old friend "Nicolas Spicer" appeared gray and trembly like himself – even more frail, since a recent fall from his horse had sprained both of the ancient physician's wrists. Ned heard that one of the conspirators in Lincoln's assassination had been a guerrilla with Mosby. Between raids he had lived peacefully as an itinerant farm hand with Dr. Payne and when arrested and executed he died under the name of his former host and benefactor.[17]

Late in March, Ned decided to return to Stamford. The way was familiar to him now and the carriage wheels spun along the silent dirt roads. Home again in the Catskills, Anna aired the bedding on the green lawn, while the colonel employed painters to refurbish the mansion,[18] and then announced himself as an Independent Republican who would stump for Grover Cleveland.

Of course Ned could not devote all his time to politics – he had heavy writing commitments with both Street and Smith and the Beadle firm, and Frederick Pond was constantly urging him to send sporting copy to *Turf, Field and Farm.* Ned went to New York during the summer of 1884; when he stumbled up the wooden stairs to the *Turf, Field and Farm* office, Editor Pond had difficulty concealing his surprise at Ned's advancing age. He noticed how the old fellow needed the handrail to help him downstairs to the street. Pond surmised that Ned Buntline would never come to his office again – and he was right.

Back in Stamford, Ned seemed less confused. He settled down to writing, with politics as an avocation. He campaigned, as he had promised, against James G. Blaine, rather than for Grover Cleveland. In skits for the press Ned wrote that he had watched the Plumed Knight's career "from poverty to immense and *fraudulent* wealth." The *New York World* printed a long article about Ned, detailing his importance in the now discredited Know-Nothing movement, and then quoting him as saying that Candidate Blaine had been a fellow Know-Nothing[19] – a statement that lost the candidate many Catholic votes and confirmed the unwise announcement of Blaine's colleague, the Reverend Dr. S. D. Burchard, that the Democrats stood for "Rum, Romanism, and Rebellion."

At the height of the excitement Ned's opportunity to serve was cut short. A similar termination had come to his Know-Nothing career three months before the Cincinnati convention, when he was jailed for bigamy. Now, as the Presidential campaign gathered momentum, an ugly scandal story appeared in the press:

COURTED BY MOONLIGHT:

NED BUNTLINE'S DAUGHTER AND HER FAITHLESS SUITOR

Grief and Terror of a Lonely Girl Deserted Just Before Her Wedding

ROMANCE IN THE GROVES OF WESTCHESTER

Below this heading readers learned that Edwardina J. Judson, youngest daughter of Adirondack Kate, born at Chappaqua in 1867, had "too far trusted" an oily tongued young man. The scamp was being held for a grand jury hearing at White Plains.

"The prominence of her father," the paper continued, "makes the case of interest to all." This alone was enough to ruin Ned's influence in the political campaign, but Lovanche was still to be heard from. A later issue carried the following letter:

MRS. JUDSON ASTONISHED.

To the Editor of the Morning Journal.

My attention was called this evening to an article in this morning's issue of your paper under the heading "Courted by Moonlight," that proved an "tonishing" and "unthought-of revelation" to me, as I was not aware that I do or ever did live in "New Castle" Westchester county, or that I have or ever had a daughter named "Edwardina J. Judson" or "any other name."

But I am and have been the wife of E. Z. C. Judson (better known as "Ned Buntline," "the well-known author," with "many-sided attainments"), for over thirty years, having been legally married to him on the 24th of September, '53, at "Palisade House," West Hoboken, N. J., as can readily be proved to the satisfaction of any person who is sufficiently interested to investigate by calling on me at my residence.

Mrs. E. Z. C. Judson[20]

No. 277 East Eighty-first street, New York city
September 3d, 1884.

Lovanche would barter to the end for her pound of flesh. She knew all about the Mrs. Judson at Westchester and her daughter Edwardina but " 'tonished" or not, with her letter she knocked Ned out of the campaign – although Cleveland won the election, and Ned won a new hat.[21]

Complacent and philosophical about life, he signed a contract to write a series of stories for the Sunday section of the *New York World*. Sunday papers were something new, as dime novels had been a quarter of a century earlier. For other papers Ned wrote stories about the Civil and Seminole wars, fishing trips and snakes he had known – one so big it carried off a trout Ned tossed on the bank.[22]

In June 1885, Stamford citizens read in the paper that none

other than Joseph Pulitzer himself was coming to town as the guest of Colonel Judson. The great editor had bought the *New York World* from Jay Gould in 1883. Part of his phenomenal success was due to the Sunday supplements which he furnished readers on the dime-novel level, and Ned Buntline – as has been said – wrote in this capacity for the *World*. Pulitzer increased circulation for his paper by fearlessly denouncing the aristocracy of money and lauding the aristocracy of labor. Critics considered his paper radical because it advocated taxation of luxuries, of large incomes, of inheritances, and of big corporation profits. Pulitzer had fought in the Civil War and considered himself a Republican, but now, like Ned Buntline, he discovered that he was a Democrat. Ned had progressed through the same cycle.

To interview Ned Buntline at Eagle's Nest became one of the things cub reporters were assigned to do. Young Rufus Rockwell Wilson, learning the newspaper business in his teens, went to see the great man and found him egotistical and self-centered, perpetually striking an attitude on the pedestal of conceit. Ned's one interest besides himself seemed to be little Eddie. Ned noticed that the child liked to make a noise, and forthwith he purchased him a trumpet, a tremendous drum, a banjo, a violin, two guitars, a tambourine, an organette, a xylophone, and a piano. "I get for him all the toys any boy needs," Ned liked to say with an adoring look at his baby son. "During my childhood I never had a kite or a ball, a trumpet or a marble. I never knew how to play." [23]

Almost a legendary figure in his last years, Ned was pumped by publisher Fred Pond for every drop of information about his literary past. Ned, as always, apologized with left-handed excuses for his cheap literature. "I might have paved for myself a far different career in letters," Ned told Pond; then with his usual disregard for truth he added, "but my early lot was cast among rough men on the border; they became my comrades, and when I made my name as a teller of stories about Indians, pirates and scouts, it seemed too late to begin over again. And besides, I made more money than any Bohemian in New York or Boston." [24] Another writer, W. H. Venable, preparing a work on *Beginnings of Literary Culture in the Ohio Valley*, wrote Buntline asking for information about himself and his work. Ned replied to him:

> I have little to write about myself. I detest autobiography. If a man has lived to merit it, his life will live after him, and be written by those who appreciated him. The early struggles of a literary man are only interesting to himself, and success only wipes away their bitter memories.
>
> In my own case I found that to *make a living* I must write "trash" for the masses, for he who endeavors to write for the critical few, and do his genius justice, will go hungry if he has no other means of support. Is it not so? [25]

Ned became very sentimental – and forgetful – about the old flag and the army. Every morning, weather permitting, he marched his little son outdoors to help him hoist a big banner up the tall spruce pole on the lawn. Visible for miles along the valley, the flag informed all travelers that Ned Buntline was at home. After the formality of raising Old Glory Ned led his little boy by the hand on an inspection of the barn. He held him up to pat the Hambletonians' velvety noses. Then Ned harnessed the team for a short drive, usually uptown to get the mail. He liked to feel the horses swinging along at their best on the soft dirt road. By midmorning Ned settled down to write. A pressman who visited Eagle's Nest reported:

> I found him pleasantly surrounded, much as I had been told. He is now sixty-three years old, and a young son, four years old, is the light of the house. He is probably destined for the army, for I had not been in the library ten minutes when the Colonel was putting him through the manual of arms, with wooden sword and toy gun. The youngster has more playthings than any other boy in the state, and many of them are suggestive of mimic battle.[26]

This was in 1885. Ned was not well enough to go South that winter. A heart ailment had come to add to his suffering from sciatica. Beadle and Adams had a new *Banner Weekly* and asked Ned for contributions, but writing was harder than it used to be. In November he sent for a doctor. David Kennedy came up from Rondout, New York, but he did Ned little good. Buntline showed him rare parchment books in his library, pointed to the faces of famous friends on the walls, but failed to strike a spark of interest in the physician's solemn face. Ned displayed his six-ounce Orvis fly rod and showed the excellent suppleness of the tip. It was no use. Dr. Kennedy's eyes did not even kindle when Ned worked the mechanism on a double-barreled elephant gun and handed him a Buntline Special. The professional call served only one purpose. Ned enjoyed lampooning in the press a man who had no interest but pills.[27]

The winter of 1885–1886 dragged painfully, slow, cold, and dreary for Ned Buntline. One day boys coasted down the hill from town and dragged their sleds up to Eagle's Nest. They had organized a club and wanted to tell Ned about it. "Let them in," Ned shouted from the library when he heard their heavy boots stamping off snow at the kitchen door. With his cane Ned hobbled along the hall and stood among them quaffing the fresh air that had come into the house on their clothes. Buntline watched the boys tell, with eager eyes, all about the club. Beads of melted snow trickled from their brass-toed, red-topped boots as Ned offered profound advice and a selection of passwords together with rituals for varicolored degrees. Then Ned watched the boys storm out into the brilliant winter world. With shouts they ran with their sleds, jumped – belly-bumper – and glided away toward Stamford. In March, month of his birth "when thunder loudly booming shook the roof above my head," Ned became ill. He had never felt like this before, and he knew death was coming. One sleepless night he penned a poem for the *Mercury:*

Drifting on the ebbing tide,
Slow but sure, I onward glide –
Dim the vista seen before,
Useless now to look behind –
Drifting on before the wind,
Toward the unknown shore.

Counting time by ticking clock,
Waiting for the final shock –
Waiting for the dark forever –
Oh, how slow the moments go,
None but I, me seems, can know
How close the tideless river.[28]

Ned continued to write as diligently as his suffering permitted. *Forest and Stream* appealed to him for copy, and Ned had to reply that his old speed was cut down.[29] For *Turf, Field and Farm* he sent his regular letter – column it would be called later – on April 30, 1886:

Propped up in my invalid chair by the window of my sick-chamber, where I have battled for life for ten long weary weeks, I look out on opening leaves, bright apple blossoms, and the flashing waters of my private trout brook, while for the first time at this date for years I see no sign of snow on hillside or mountain. To-morrow a hundred rods will bend over bright waters within a radius of four or five miles of me, yet I must look sadly on my pet "Orvis" in the corner, and let the split bamboo rest.

It is hard when sympathizing visitors, and they are many, tell me the streams never before gave better promise of sport in this section.

Stocked liberally by John N. Bennett and John Griffin, aided by myself, the west branch of the Delaware and the many brooks near by are literally alive with speckled beauty. The two first-named gentlemen have died within a year, and here am I, on my "beams' ends," looking sadly, yet not hopelessly, on dark waters ahead.

Strange, is it not? We, who have done so much to fill the waters, past the reward of labor and expenditure! *Telle est vie.*

I don't like to tell tales out of school, but some of the boys hunting leeks for use in school have *seen* "millions of trout," as they wandered along the brooksides. And I am afraid – encouraged by my physician – they may have brought in *one* or *two* for me to *look* at. Just to cheer me up, you know!

I can write no more. Hopeless of bending a rod this season, if, indeed, I ever do again, I am faithfully yours,[30]

NED BUNTLINE

Far in the South "Nick Spicer" read Buntline's letter in the May 7 *Turf, Field and Farm.* He misread the last line to say "hoping to bend a rod" and wrote Ned that he was glad to know of his improved health. Ned replied from Eagle's Nest:

DEAR DOCTOR:

You had best read the *Turf, Field and Farm* more carefully. I have little hope of ever using a rod again. I have been eleven weeks in bed or in my invalid chair, with a combination of heart disease, valvular obstruction, etc., etc. . . . I have been sick all winter, not out of my chamber or able to walk even with crutches for eleven weeks. My case is a bad one, and my physician with counsel finds it hard to baffle. I can write but little, but try my best to keep up. God bless you and yours. My dear wife nurses me like an angel and is my best hope.

Ever yours,
JUDSON [31]

In May 1886, the *Mirror* announced that Ned's illness was very serious. Neighbors in Stamford sent delicacies to Eagle's Nest – a pound of butter, a brace of squabs, a bowl of cottage cheese with a geranium blossom in the center. The boys' club met and decided to catch some early trout for Ned. An official delegation called at Eagle's Nest to present the speckled beauties. Ned himself had become so weak he could write but a few lines at a time, yet his brain was clear and could not rest.

Anna, attentive always, sat by his bedside night and day. Occasionally Ned looked up from the writing board on his knees. He thought of his Orvis rod, the trout streams gurgling with freshet water, his trotters stamping in the stable. The *New York Waverly* sent a contract for a serial. Ned replied that he was incapacitated. The publishers recommended a new invalid chair and said they were expressing it. Ned agreed to send them a continued story, "Incognita," and wrote the publishers on June 18, 1886:

> The chair arrived last night, and I write my first letter in it this morning. It is a great relief to me, and I will soon get used to working in it. "Incognita" will grow very fast now. It will be a grand story, full of mystery, and the best I have ever written. It may be my last serial, and I want the *Waverly* to have my last letter, which this may be. . . . Thanking you sincerely in taking so much care in selecting the chair, I will well repay you in good work on "Incognita." [32]

Ned had received large sums for his writing, but money always slipped through his fingers. Now, when he could not write so much, Anna had trouble meeting expenses at Eagle's Nest. On July 12, Ned applied for a pension for his Civil War services, but it was too late. On July 16, at 4:30 in the afternoon, Ned Buntline died.

The *Mirror* announced his passing. Editor Champion, who had consistently railed at Ned, now changed completely and added to the obituary:

> For many years he had resided here, surrounded by all the comforts that man can enjoy, and ready to do anything to advance the interests of society, and to benefit mankind. He was one of nature's true noblemen.[33]

Pulitzer's *World* contained considerable misinformation about the famous writer. In its columns appeared the entire Buntline story about running away to sea, being promoted for heroism in the Fulton Ferry disaster, dueling his way into the midshipmen's mess, writing "The Captain's Pig" for *Knickerbocker* in 1838 – a palpable error. The article continued:

> Ned Buntline probably carried more wounds in his body than any other living American. He had in his right knee a bullet received in Virginia [a new wound!], and had twelve other wounds inflicted by sword, shell and gun, seven of which were got in battle. He was not

educated for the army or navy. The title of colonel came to him as Chief of Scouts in the Rebellion of 1861–5 [Wrong again!].[34]

Ned's comrades in his G.A.R. Commandery in Philadelphia announced:

> His spirit was wafted to the side of the great patriots of our land who have gone before and whose deeds and works while in the flesh will be remembered in the brightest pages of our national history.[35]

In Chicago, Illinois, Camp 5 of the Patriotic Order of Sons of America passed a long series of resolutions. One stated:

> Brethren, let us imitate his example and follow in his footsteps; let us devote our lives to our country and like him be ever faithful through life and unto death.[36]

Ned's funeral was reported to have been one of the largest ever held in Stamford. The boys' club watched with open mouths as a hundred veterans of the Grand Army of the Republic marched over to Eagle's Nest to accompany the hearse. On the lawn the great flag was flown at half-mast and one of Ned's Hambletonians, with empty saddle and boots reversed in the stirrups, followed the casket to the cemetery as Ned would have wished it. At the Methodist church the Reverend L. E. Richards, Presbyterian pastor who had understood Ned from the beginning, conducted the services. Only half of the mourners could crowd into the church, and during the ceremony Ned's horse cried bitterly, the shrill whinny penetrating the organ music. How Ned Buntline would have enjoyed that final melodrama!

In the cemetery the rugged old sportsman was lowered into his grave. Again his saddle mare shrieked piteously, mane disheveled, excited eyes protruding. A few women shuddered, on the verge of hysteria, and more than one man looked apprehensively at the distraught animal.

Telegraph wires carried news of the obsequies to the nation's large cities. Leading sportsmen's magazines published fitting eulogies. Dime-novel writers paused a moment before deadlines to pay a colleague respect with silence. Lovanche read the news in Kingston and offered to sell her collection of Buntline letters to any prospective biographer. At Eagle's Nest, Anna planned to write a life of her remarkable husband. In the livery barn at the east end of Stamford the boys' club met in solemn conclave behind the manure pile. Tousle-headed, barefooted, with tear-smeared freckled faces, each urchin held up a grimy little hand and swore earnestly never to tell anything bad about the dead author " 'cause he really liked us kids – but gee wasn't that grand how the ol' mare kept crying fer her mate back in the barn just as though her heart was breakin' fer Ned Buntline." [37]

Notes

CHAPTER I

1. Richard J. Walsh, *The Making of Buffalo Bill: A Study in Heroics*, p. 156.
2. George Bird Grinnell, *Two Great Scouts and their Pawnee Battalion*, p. 71.
3. George Bird Grinnell, *The Fighting Cheyennes*, p. 306.
4. Walsh, *op. cit.*, p. 155.
5. William F. Cody, *An Autobiography of Buffalo Bill*, p. 194.
6. The *White Cloud* [Kansas] *Chief* on April 2, 1862, refers to Buffalo Bill Taylor on the *Leavenworth Enquirer*. The *National Police Gazette* cites another Buffalo Bill in the issue of April 18, 1846.
7. Walsh, *op. cit.*, p. 81.
8. Transcript of interview with Lovanche Judson in scrapbook at *Stamford Mirror* office.
9. *Stamford Mirror*, July 4, 1871.
10. *Ibid.*, Sept. 24, 1872.
11. *Ibid.*, Jan. 2, 1872.
12. Walsh, *op. cit.*, p. 162.
13. Transcript of interview with Lovanche Judson in scrapbook at *Stamford Mirror* office.
14. *Stamford Mirror*, Sept. 5, 1871.
15. *Ibid.*, July 4, 1871.
16. *Ibid.*, July 25, Dec. 19, 1871.
17. Transcript of interview with Lovanche Judson in scrapbook at *Stamford Mirror* office.
18. *Stamford Mirror*, Oct. 10, 1871.
19. E. Z. C. Judson pension records, National Archives.
20. Jay Monaghan, "Literary Opportunities in Pioneer Times," *Journal of the Illinois State Historical Society*, XXXIII, No. 4 (Dec. 1940), p. 412.
21. James A. Hadley, "A Royal Buffalo Hunt," *Transactions of the Kansas State Historical Society, 1907–1908*, X, p. 571.
22. Chalkley M. Beeson, "A Royal Buffalo Hunt," *Transactions of the Kansas State Historical Society, 1907–1908*, X, p. 578.

23. Walsh, *op. cit.*, p. 169.
24. George C. D. Odell, *Annals of the New York Stage*, IX, p. 168. The original script of this play gives the authors as "Fred G. Meader & Col. E. Z. C. Judson, Ned Buntline Author of the Story." In a different ink the reference to Judson has been crossed out.
25. *Stamford Mirror*, Feb. 20, 1872.
26. *Ibid.*, March 19, Apr. 2, 1872.
27. *New York Herald*, Feb. 16, 1872.
28. *Ibid.*, Feb. 21, 1872.
29. *Stamford Mirror*, Feb. 13, March 19, 1872.
30. William F. Cody, *The Story of the Wild West*, p. 634.
31. *Stamford Mirror*, Apr. 2, 1872.
32. *Ibid.*, March 19, 1872.
33. *Ibid.*, Feb. 27, May 28, 1872.
34. *Ibid.*, June 4, Aug. 20, 1872.
35. *Ibid.*, Oct. 8, 22, 1872.
36. *Chicago Daily Tribune*, Oct. 19, 1872. *Stamford Mirror*, Nov. 5, 1872.
37. Walsh, *op. cit.*, p. 178.

CHAPTER II

1. Ned Buntline says, in Fred E. Pond, *The Life and Adventures of "Ned Buntline,"* p. 87, that he arrived Thursday and Bill came in the afternoon. December 12, 1872, was Thursday so Ned's memory proves correct.
2. *Stamford Mirror*, Dec. 24, 1872.
3. Dabney H. Maury, *Recollections of a Virginian*, pp. 113–115.
4. M. B. Leavitt, *Fifty Years in Theatrical Management*, p. 160.
5. Walsh, *op. cit.*, p. 179.
6. Pond, *op. cit.*, p. 88.
7. Jay Monaghan, "The Stage Career of Buffalo Bill," *Journal of the Illinois State Historical Society*, XXXI, No. 4 (Dec. 1938), p. 416.
8. *Chicago Daily Tribune*, Dec. 17, 1872.
9. *Stamford Mirror*, Dec. 24, 1872.
10. Walsh, *op. cit.*, p. 180.
11. St. Louis *Missouri Democrat*, Dec. 27, 1872. The quotation has been edited.
12. Records of St. Louis Criminal Court, July 18, 1873.

13. *Stamford Mirror*, Jan. 7, 1873.
14. Cincinnati *Prairie Enquirer*, Jan. 1, 1873.
15. *New York Herald*, Jan. 8, 1873.
16. *Stamford Mirror*, March 11, 1873.
17. *Ibid.*, Apr. 1, 1873.
18. *Chicago Daily Tribune*, Dec. 27, 1872.
19. *Cincinnati Daily Times & Chronicle*, Jan. 4, 1873.
20. The performance opened March 31, 1873.
21. *New York Herald*, Apr. 1, 1873.
22. Monaghan, "The Stage Career of Buffalo Bill," pp. 418–419.
23. *Stamford Mirror*, May 6, June 3, 1873.
24. Walsh, *op. cit.*, p. 182.
25. *Stamford Mirror*, Aug. 19, 1873.
26. *Ibid.*, July 8, 1873.
27. Leon Mead, "How 'Ned Buntline' Turned from Runaway Boy to Writing Genius," *Reckless Ralph's Dime Novel Roundup*, IX, No. 101 (Jan. 1941), p. 5.
28. *Stamford Mirror*, Sept. 2, 1873.
29. *Paterson Daily Guardian*, Aug. 26, 1873.
30. *Stamford Mirror*, June 3, 1873.
31. Transcript of interview with Lovanche Judson in scrapbook at *Stamford Mirror* office.
32. Fred Mather, *My Angling Friends*, p. 61.
33. Frank J. Wilstach, *Wild Bill Hickok: The Prince of Pistoleers*, p. 222.
34. Walsh, *op. cit.*, p. 185.
35. Wilstach, *op. cit.*, p. 189.

CHAPTER III

1. Available facts add to the uncertainty. A statement by Ned's father in 1838 indicates that 1821 was Ned's birth year and this may be so. Ned himself believed all his life that he was born later. In *Cruisings Afloat and Ashore* (1848) he gives the date as 1822. In *Ned Buntline's Life Yarn* (1849) he states that he enlisted at the age of fourteen, which would mean that he was born in 1823. In the summer of 1850 Ned said that he was nearly twenty-seven. This makes his birth year 1823. Ned enlisted for the Civil War giving 1825 for his birth year. Obviously he wanted to be young enough to get into service. A reporter who interviewed him in 1885 recorded his age as

sixty-three, which would mean that he was born in 1822. His pension record file, WO 906 598, gives his age at death as sixty-four years and four months, which puts his birth date in 1822. His gravestone is marked 1823.

2. Pond, *op. cit.*, p. 120.
3. Charles F. Orvis and A. Nelson Cheney, *Fishing with the Fly*, p. 8.
4. Levi Carroll Judson, *Sages and Heroes of the American Revolution*, preface.
5. Pond, *op. cit.*, p. 12.
6. *South-Western Literary Journal and Monthly Review*, I, No. 3 (Jan. 1845), p. 145.
7. *Wayne Enquirer* [Bethany, Pa.], Feb. 17, 1830. Alfred Matthews, *History of Wayne, Pike and Monroe Counties*, p. 587.
8. *Wayne County Herald and Bethany Enquirer*, Dec. 25, 1834.
9. Delaware County Record of Deeds, Book A, p. 414.
10. Frank Luther Mott, *A History of American Magazines*, I, pp. 527–780. Van Wyck Brooks, *The World of Washington Irving*, p. 443.
11. Captain [Frederick] Marryat, *A Diary in America with Remarks on its Institutions*, I, p. 285.
12. "Ned Buntline's Life-Yarn," *Knickerbocker*, XXVI, No. 5 (Nov. 1845), p. 432.
13. *Ned Buntline's Life Yarn* (New York, 1849), p. 92.
14. "Ned Buntline's Life-Yarn," *Knickerbocker*, XXVI, No. 5 (Nov. 1845), p. 434.
15. Ned Buntline, "Editors' Table," *South-Western Literary Journal and Monthly Review*, I, No. 4 (Feb. 1845), p. 250.

CHAPTER IV

1. "Ned Buntline's Life-Yarn," *Knickerbocker*, XXVI, No. 5 (Nov. 1845), p. 437. The dialogue of original has been edited.
2. *Ned Buntline's Life Yarn* (New York, 1849), pp. 36, 178.
3. "Ned Buntline's Life-Yarn," *Knickerbocker*, XXVII, No. 1 (Jan. 1846), p. 37. "A Race on the Bahama Banks," *Ibid.*, XXVI, No. 3 (March 1845), p. 203.
4. Ned Buntline, "The Right of Search," *Western Literary Journal*, I, No. 1 (Nov. 1844), p. 47.
5. Oliver Otis Howard, *My Life and Experiences among Our Hostile Indians*, p. 67.

6. Thomas Corwin Donaldson, *The George Catlin Indian Gallery in the U.S. National Museum*, pp. 214, 221.
7. *Ned Buntline's Life Yarn* (New York, 1849), p. 79.
8. Letter from War Records Division, National Archives, to author, Feb. 11, 1948.
9. John T. Sprague, *The Origin, Progress, and Conclusion of the Florida War*, p. 213.

CHAPTER V

1. Herman Melville, *White-Jacket, or The World in a Man-of-War*, p. 353.
2. *Ibid.*, p. 207.
3. John Fowler, *Journal of a Tour in the State of New York, in the Year 1830*, p. 24.
4. *Ned Buntline's Life Yarn* (New York, 1849), pp. 83–87. A search has failed to find any contemporary account of this accident and records indicate that Judson's father got him the commission.
5. Edward W. Callahan, *List of Officers of the Navy of the United States and of the Marine Corps from 1775 to 1900*, p. 728.
6. The complete record of Judson's naval service is as follows: He enlisted at the Philadelphia Navy Yard, August 7, 1837, as Second Class boy and was detached September 27 for duty on the U.S. Receiving Ship *Hudson* at New York. On October 30 he was detached from the *Hudson* and received next day on board the U.S. Frigate *Macedonian*, which was being fitted as flagship for an antarctic exploring expedition. He was discharged from the *Macedonian* at Brooklyn on March 1, 1838, with the notation "expiration of service." Judson was appointed Acting Midshipman in the U.S. Navy from Pennsylvania, February 10, 1838, and was ordered to report on board the U.S. Sloop of War *Levant*. Later he served on the U.S. Frigate *Constellation* (1838), and the U.S. Sloop of War *Boston* (1838–1839), attached to the West Indian Squadron, and the U.S. Schooners *Flirt* and *Otsego* (1839–1841), naval vessels co-operating with the army during the Seminole War. From September 1841 to April 1842 he served on several ships at Boston, then was ordered to the U.S. Sloop of War *Falmouth* at Hampton Roads. On May 12, 1842, he requested leave of

absence due to his wife's illness. His resignation of May 14 was accepted June 8, 1842.

7. Pond, *op. cit.*, p. 15. This story sounds more like a Buntline romance than a fact. Commander Lester A. Beardslee wrote it before Ned's death, claiming that he got his information from an admiral who admitted that one of Judson's balls marked him for life.
8. Ned Buntline, "Running the Blockade," *Knickerbocker*, XXIV, No. 4 (October 1844), pp. 323–324.
9. Sprague, *op. cit.*, pp. 270–271.
10. Howard, *op. cit.*, p. 83.
11. *Journal of U.S. Cavalry Association*, III (March 1890).
12. Pond, *op. cit.*, p. 25. Ned claimed to have been Executive Officer.
13. Ned Buntline, "Sketches of the Florida War," *South-Western Literary Journal and Monthly Review*, I, No. 6 (Apr. 1845), p. 334.

CHAPTER VI

1. Pond, *op. cit.*, p. 27.
2. Sprague, *op. cit.*, p. 243.
3. Sprague, *op. cit.*, p. 244. A variant of this story is told by Harriet P. Huse, "An Untold Story of the Florida War," *Harper's New Monthly Magazine*, LXXXIII, No. CCCCXCVI (Sept. 1891), pp. 591–594.
4. John Lee Williams, *Territory of Florida: or Sketches of the Topography, Civil and Natural History . . .*, p. 36.
5. Sprague, *op. cit.*, pp. 244–246. Ned Buntline, "Sketches of the Florida War," *South-Western Literary Journal and Monthly Review*, I, No. 5 (March 1845), p. 282.
6. William Tecumseh Sherman, *Memoirs*, p. 18.
7. Sprague, *op. cit.*, p. 259.
8. Buntline, "Sketches of the Florida War," *South-Western Literary Journal and Monthly Review*, I, No. 3 (Jan. 1845), p. 168.
9. Sprague, *op. cit.*, pp. 475–477.

CHAPTER VII

1. An anonymous article, "My Log-book," in the May 1838 *Knickerbocker* refers to the captain's pig. Ned may have written this, but it has little resemblance to his style. Even if he did get the name "captain's pig" from the article, he copied nothing else.

2. "Editor's Table," *Knickerbocker*, XXIII, No. 6 (June 1844), p. 599.
3. Callahan, *op. cit.*, p. 305.
4. Letter from Director of War Records Division, National Archives, to author, Jan. 21, 1948.
5. Pension records in Washington cast a dim light on Ned's marriage. One deposition states that Ned once said that the couple lived about a year in Cuba. Another deposition, also hearsay from Ned, says that the couple lived in St. Augustine, Florida. Neither makes clear whether this was before or after Judson resigned from the service. Both state that the wife died in childbirth about a year after marriage – statements not borne out by the text in later chapters of this book. Some six or eight years after Seberina's death an employee of Ned's, one Thomas Paterson, said that she was an American girl and Ned resigned from the navy on account of her illness when he was ordered to foreign service. (See Thomas V. Paterson, *The Extraordinary Public Proceedings of E. Z. C. Judson, Alias Ned Buntline*, pp. 22, 44, 46.) Ned himself said in his *Life Yarn*, p. 170, that he dallied in Florida with a beautiful Cuban enchantress named Caroline whom he buried later on the banks of the Ohio – a fate that overtook Seberina. This evidence all points to Seberina and Caroline as being the same person. Moreover, it appears that Seberina went to Cincinnati. In the November 1844 issue of the *Western Literary Journal* Ned printed a poem, "A Spanish Song," by Mrs. S. M. Judson, undoubtedly Seberina Marin Judson. Further light is cast on the Marin family on p. 215 of the February 1845 issue, where Ned refers to Donna Antonia Marin, a small planter on the banks of the St. John River in Florida. This was written while Seberina and Ned were together. Later, after her death, Ned refers ("A Dream That Was Not All a Dream," *Knickerbocker*, September 1846, p. 244) to a Captain Marin, "a dark skinned Spanish Creole." In the March 1845 *Knickerbocker*, p. 205, he speaks of "my little Diègo wife."
6. Pond, *op. cit.*, p. 28.
7. *Cincinnati Daily Enquirer*, May 3, 1844.
8. *Ned Buntline's Magazine*, I, No. 2 (June 1844), p. 60.
9. *Knickerbocker*, XXIV, No. 1 (July 1844), p. 102.
10. Brooks, *op. cit.*, p. 470.

11. Marryat, *op. cit.*, III, p. 278.
12. *Ibid.*, II, p. 154.
13. Henry Howe, *Historical Collections of Ohio*, II, p. 113.
14. *Cincinnati Daily Enquirer*, March 5, 1845.
15. Brooks, *op. cit.*, p. 424 *n.*

CHAPTER VIII

1. This same expression appears in Nelson Haley, *Whale Hunt*, p. 23.
2. Brooks, *op. cit.*, p. 429 *n.*
3. *Western Literary Journal and Monthly Review*, I, No. 1 (Nov. 1844), p. 53.
4. Warren G. French, "A Sketch of the Life of Joseph Holt Ingraham," *Journal of Mississippi History*, XI, No. 3 (July 1949), p. 158.
5. Thurlow Weed, *Letters from Europe and the West Indies*, p. 78.
6. Ned Buntline, "The Masked Ball," *Knickerbocker*, XXIV, No. 6 (Dec. 1844), p. 562. It is presumed that Ned described his usual dress in this passage.
7. Marryat, *op. cit.*, II, p. 144.
8. *Ibid.*, III, p. 53.
9. Harriet Martineau, *Retrospect of Western Travel*, II, p. 25.
10. James Parton, *Life of Andrew Jackson*, I, p. 391.
11. William Henry Venable, *Beginnings of Literary Culture in the Ohio Valley*, p. 295.
12. Martineau, *op. cit.*, I, p. 214.
13. Thomas D. Clark, *The Rampaging Frontier*, p. 304. Note also Buntline, *The Volunteer: or, The Maid of Monterrey*, p. 8.
14. *South-Western Literary Journal and Monthly Review*, I, No. 3 (Jan. 1845), p. 189.
15. *Knickerbocker*, XXIV, No. 6 (Dec. 1844), p. 563.
16. *Ibid.*, p. 566.
17. *Ibid.*, pp. 582–583.

CHAPTER IX

1. St. Louis *Missouri Democrat*, Dec. 27, 1872.
2. Ned Buntline, "Reviews and Literary Notices," *Western Literary Journal and Monthly Review*, I, No. 2 (Dec. 1844), p. 113.
3. *Knickerbocker*, XXV, No. 2 (Feb. 1845), p. 179.
4. Venable, *op. cit.*, p. 292.

5. Ned Buntline, "Reviews and Literary Notices," *South-Western Literary Journal and Monthly Review,* I, No. 3 (Jan. 1845), p. 183.
6. The proposed law for government handling of mail failed to pass in 1845.
7. Ned Buntline, "Editors' Table," *South-Western Literary Journal and Monthly Review,* I, No. 3 (Jan. 1845), p. 189.
8. Levi Carroll Judson, *The Probe: or One Hundred and Two Essays on the Nature of Men and Things,* preface.
9. Venable, *op. cit.,* p. 294, states that this was published in Paducah. A search has failed to reveal a copy.
10. Ned was negotiating in October 1845. See *Knickerbocker,* p. 382, for that month. The "Yarn" began in the November issue. No installment appeared in December but the serial was continued in January 1846. Ned's compensation is questionable. Clark seems to have paid for some articles and not for others. Henry W. Herbert (Frank Forester) complained that he was not paid at first. Years later Ned made the same complaint, but in the 1840's, when in dire need, he continued sending stories to *Knickerbocker.* Clark was hard pressed for money much of the time. See Samuel Longfellow, *Life of Henry Wadsworth Longfellow,* I, p. 341.
11. *Knickerbocker,* XXVII, No. 3 (March 1846), p. 277.
12. *Tri-Weekly Nashville Union,* Nov. 18 to Dec. 27, 1845.
13. *Knickerbocker,* XXVII, No. 4 (Apr. 1846), p. 376.
14. *Tri-Weekly Nashville Union,* July 18, 1846.
15. *Ibid.,* Aug. 11, 1846.
16. Pond, *op. cit.,* p. 33.
17. *Knickerbocker,* XXVII, No. 5 (May 1846), p. 466.
18. *Ibid.,* pp. 466–467.

CHAPTER X

1. The 1848 directory lists Levi Carroll Judson as a publisher at 142 North 8th Street. In 1853 he was listed as a publisher in West Philadelphia. From 1855 to 1857 he was "gent" and "author." The fire is referred to in the preface of Levi Carroll Judson's *The Probe,* etc. (See Note 8, Chapter IX, for full title.)
2. The book is reviewed in *Knickerbocker,* XXVIII, No. 4 (Oct. 1846), p. 352.

Fracker Library
Buena Vista College

3. *Cincinnati Daily Commercial Journal*, July 21, 1846.
4. Philadelphia *Spirit of the Times*, July 6, 1846.
5. *Tri-Weekly Nashville Union*, Aug. 11, 1846.
6. *Ibid.*, Aug. 8, 1846.
7. Fowler, *op. cit.*, p. 229.
8. Eyre Crowe, *With Thackeray in America*, p. 49.
9. Pond, *op. cit.*, p. 38. Payne describes this meeting in the *Spirit of the Times* office.
10. Jay Monaghan, "Literary Opportunities in Pioneer Times," *Journal of the Illinois State Historical Society*, XXXIII, No. 4 (Dec. 1940), p. 428.
11. Philadelphia *Spirit of the Times*, Aug. 4, 1846.
12. Brooks, *op. cit.*, p. 437.
13. Pond, *op. cit.*, p. 8. The text has been edited.
14. Philadelphia *Spirit of the Times*, Aug. 4, 1846.
15. *Ibid.*
16. Murray was appointed passed midshipman July 1, 1842.
17. *Boston Daily Times and Bay State Democrat*, Oct. 5, 1847.
18. *Knickerbocker*, XXVIII, No. 5 (Nov. 1846), p. 449.

CHAPTER XI

1. Merle Curti (*The Growth of American Thought*, p. 345) states that there was an average of sixty gift editions annually from 1846 to 1852.
2. *Ibid.*, pp. 346–347.
3. Printed Jan. 9, 1847.
4. *Boston Daily Times and Bay State Democrat*, Feb. 8, 1847.
5. *Ibid.*, March 18, 1847.
6. *Boston Daily Times*, Apr. 2, 1847.
7. P. 16.
8. This advertisement appeared from June 30 to October 10, 1847.
9. Note that Gleason published this in New York.
10. Samuel L. Clemens, *The Adventures of Tom Sawyer*, p. 75.
11. Pond, *op. cit.*, p. 42. Dr. Sewell dates this duel September 17, 1845 — obviously an error, for Ned was negotiating with *Knickerbocker* to publish his "Life-Yarn" in October and he and Seberina had recently moved to Clarksville, Kentucky. Surely he would have made some mention of such a gallant trip at that time if he had made it. Dr. Sewell's entire diagnosis is questionable.

12. *Boston Daily Times*, Oct. 12, 1847.
13. Thomas V. Paterson, *The Extraordinary Public Proceedings of E. Z. C. Judson, Alias Ned Buntline*, p. 46.
14. Pond, *op. cit.*, p. 44.
15. Published by Hotchkiss & Company, of Boston, 1847.
16. Note Captain Lauchlan Mackinnon's *Atlantic and Transatlantic: Sketches Afloat and Ashore.*

CHAPTER XII

1. Ned Buntline, *The Mysteries and Miseries of New York*, V, appendix, p. 92.
2. Ned's application for pension shows this date to have been January 23 and also January 25.
3. Venable, *op. cit.*, p. 295.
4. St. Louis *Daily Organ and Reveille*, Feb. 18, 1848.
5. Ned Buntline, *The Mysteries and Miseries of New York*, II, p. [4].
6. *Ibid.*, pp. 50–53.
7. *Ibid.*, p. 89.
8. *New York Herald*, Feb. 15, 1848.
9. *New York Daily Globe*, Apr. 15, 1848. Arthur H. Quinn (*A History of the American Drama from the Beginning to the Civil War*, p. 305) describes Baker as a prompter at the Olympic.
10. *New York Herald*, Feb. 15, 1848. *New York Globe*, Apr. 17. 1848.
11. Ned Buntline, *The Mysteries and Miseries of New York*, V, p. 14.

CHAPTER XIII

1. *Cincinnati Daily Enquirer*, Jan. 7, 1848.
2. Lewis Collins and Richard H. Collins, *Collins' Historical Sketches of Kentucky*, II, pp. 490–491.
3. Quinn, *op. cit.*, p. 305.
4. Paterson, *op. cit.*, p. 42.
5. Robert E. Riegel, *Young America, 1830–1840*, pp. 47–48.
6. Ned Buntline, *The Mysteries and Miseries of New York*, V, p. 14.
7. *New York Daily Globe*, Sept. 2, 1848. Authorship of this play is given in Quinn, *op. cit.*, p. 306.
8. Ned Buntline, *The Mysteries and Miseries of New York*, IV, pp. 3–4.
9. *Ibid.*, V, p. 112.

10. Ned Buntline, *The Mysteries and Miseries of New York*, IV, pp. 102–106.
11. *Ibid.*, V, p. 12.
12. *Ibid.*, V, p. 18.
13. *Ibid.*, V, p. 83.
14. William W. Sanger, *The History of Prostitution*, pp. 576–584, admits that such a figure was popularly believed but judges it excessive.
15. Ned Buntline, *The Mysteries and Miseries of New York*, V, pp. 88–89, 100–101, 105–106.

CHAPTER XIV

1. Paterson, *op. cit.*, p. 25.
2. The city directory of 1849–1850 lists Ned's residence as 16 Abingdon Place and his office as 309½ Broadway. Buntline's editor, Thomas Paterson, confirms this residence (Paterson, *op. cit.*, p. 29).
3. The name is probably fictitious. François Mauriceau wrote similar books in the seventeenth century.
4. Paterson, *op. cit.*, p. 26.
5. *Ibid.*, pp. 17, 23.
6. *Ibid.*, pp. 32, 39.
7. *Ibid.*, p. 18. Buntline also wrote a book with this title. See also Quinn, *op. cit.*, p. 306.
8. *Ibid.*, p. 28.
9. *Ibid.*, p. 22.
10. *Ibid.*, p. 25.
11. *Ibid.*, pp. 32, 45, 53; *Ned Buntline's Own*, I, No. 30 (Feb. 10, 1849).
12. John Allen Krout, *The Origins of Prohibition*, p. 183.
13. Issue of February 10, 1849.
14. Paterson, *op. cit.*, p. 28.
15. *Ibid.*
16. *Ibid.*, p. 19. The quotation has been put in the first person.
17. St. Louis *Daily Organ and Reveille*, Sept. 8, 1848.
18. Ned Buntline, *The Mysteries and Miseries of New York*, V, p. 126.

CHAPTER XV

1. *Ned Buntline's Own*, I, No. 30 (Feb. 10, 1849).
2. Paterson, *op. cit.*, pp. 53, 58.

3. Paterson, *op. cit.*, p. 28.
4. *Ibid.*, p. 46.
5. *Ibid.*, p. 28.
6. *Ibid.*, p. 52.
7. *Ibid.*, pp. 30, 55.
8. Apr. 4, 1849. *Ibid.*, p. 33.
9. *Ibid.*, pp. 34, 36.
10. *Ibid.*, p. 53.
11. Montrose J. Moses, *The Fabulous Forrest*, p. 232.
12. Meade Minnigerode, *The Fabulous Forties, 1840–1850*, p. 191.
13. *New York Evening Express*, May 8, 1849.
14. *Ibid.*, May 10, 1849.
15. *Forrest & Macready Astor Place Riot*, p. 16.
16. Paterson, *op. cit.*, p. 37.
17. Moses, *op. cit.*, p. 252.
18. *New York Evening Express*, May 15, 1849.
19. *Forrest & Macready Astor Place Riot*, pp. 22–23.
20. Minnigerode, *op. cit.*, p. 198. *New York Evening Express*, May 11, 1849.
21. *Judge* Charles Patrick Daly, "People vs. Edward Z. C. Judson," *Reports of Cases . . . in the Court of Common Pleas for the City and County of New York*, XI, p. 7. *National Police Gazette*, Sept. 22, 1849.
22. *New York Evening Express*, May 11, 1849.
23. *New York Evening Express*, May 15, 1849.
24. *Forrest & Macready Astor Place Riot*, p. 23.
25. *New York Evening Express*, May 11, 1849.
26. One volume of Daly's scrapbooks at the New York Public Library is devoted to the Astor Place Riot. Pp. 50–51 contain clippings, apparently from the *Metropolis*, regarding Judson's imprisonment in the theater. The *National Police Gazette* contains many references.
27. *Forrest & Macready Astor Place Riot* and Daly, *op. cit.*, both record twenty-three killed.
28. Minnigerode, *op. cit.*, p. 208.
29. Moses, *op. cit.*, p. 260.
30. *New York Evening Express*, May 12, 1849. The person has been changed in the quotations.

NOTES

CHAPTER XVI

1. Paterson, *op. cit.*, p. 47.
2. *Ibid.*, p. 56.
3. *Ibid.*, p. 51.
4. *Ibid.*, p. 30.
5. *Ned Buntline's Own*, I, No. 30 (Feb. 10, 1849).
6. Paterson, *op. cit.*, pp. 7, 50.
7. *Ned Buntline's Life Yarn* (New York, 1849), p. 53.
8. Paterson, *op. cit.*, p. 49.
9. *Ibid.*, p. 44.
10. Allan Nevins, ed., *The Diary of Philip Hone, 1828–1851*, p. 874 *n.*
11. Paterson, *op. cit.*, p. 53.
12. *Ibid.*, p. 61.
13. *Ibid.*, p. 62.
14. His visit was in 1852. Crowe, *op. cit.*, p. 12.
15. Ned Buntline, *The Mysteries and Miseries of New York*, V, p. 58.

CHAPTER XVII

1. *National Police Gazette*, Oct. 5, 1850.
2. Pond, *op. cit.*, p. 50.
3. *Cincinnati Daily Enquirer*, Apr. 3, 1851.
4. First published Aug. 9, 1851, as an article in *Ned Buntline's Own*, IV, No. 4, and as a separate volume by Okarmar & Ormsby, New York, the same year.
5. Martineau, *op. cit.*, I, pp. 222, 271–272.
6. Arthur C. Cole (*The Whig Party in the South*, p. 315) states that nativism was popular in New Orleans, but neither he nor contemporary issues of the *Picayune* reveal Buntline's activities.
7. *Cincinnati Daily Enquirer*, Sept. 7, 1851.
8. J. D. B. De Bow, ed., *De Bow's Review* (July 1848), pp. 65–66.
9. J. D. B. De Bow, *The Industrial Resources, etc., of the Southern and Western States*, II, pp. 62, 559.
10. Springfield *Illinois State Journal*, Dec. 10, 12, 1851.
11. *Ibid.*, Apr. 10, 1852.
12. *St. Louis Daily Globe*, Dec. 27, 1872.
13. Springfield *Illinois State Journal*, Apr. 10, 1852.
14. *St. Louis Daily Globe*, Dec. 27, 1872.
15. Springfield *Illinois State Register*, Nov. 11, 1852.
16. Springfield *Illinois State Journal*, Apr. 10, 1852.

17. *St. Louis Intelligencer*, Apr. 8, 1852.
18. St. Louis *Morning Signal*, Apr. 12, 1852.

CHAPTER XVIII

1. Charles O. Paullin, "The National Ticket of Broom and Coates, 1852," *American Historical Review*, XXV, No. 4 (July 1920), p. 690.
2. Brink, McDonough & Co., pub., *History of Marion and Clinton Counties, Illinois*, p. 62.
3. Franklin William Scott (*Newspapers and Periodicals of Illinois, 1814–1879*, p. 42) cites this paper as the *Prairie Flower*. A search has failed to reveal a copy.
4. Letter from Lovanche Judson to Fred E. Pond, Apr. 23, 1887, in author's collection.
5. Transcript of interview with Lovanche Judson in scrapbook at *Stamford* [N.Y.] *Mirror* office.
6. *Ibid.*
7. Springfield *Illinois Daily Journal*, Apr. 6, 1852.
8. *Sister* M. Evangeline Thomas, *Nativism in the Old Northwest, 1850–1860*, p. 124.
9. Springfield *Illinois State Register*, Oct. 14, 1852.
10. Springfield *Illinois State Journal*, Nov. 18, 1854.
11. *Cincinnati Daily Enquirer*, Sept. 13, 1854.
12. *Ibid.*, Nov. 16, 1854.
13. Louis Dow Scisco, *Political Nativism in New York State*, p. 88.
14. *Cincinnati Daily Enquirer*, Sept. 24, 1854.
15. Mead, *op. cit.*, p. 4. The paper Gabriel edited in Boston gave his name as A. B. Newcomb. *Cincinnati Daily Enquirer*, Aug. 10, 1854.
16. *Ibid.*, Aug. 23; Sept. 24, 1854.
17. *Ibid.*, Aug. 27, 1854.
18. Transcript of interview with Lovanche Judson in scrapbook at *Stamford Mirror* office.
19. *Cincinnati Daily Enquirer*, Aug. 17 and 29, 1854.
20. *Ibid.*, Aug. 23, 1854.
21. *Ibid.*, Sept. 24, 1854.
22. Pond, *op. cit.*, p. 49.
23. Chicago *Daily Democratic Press*, Nov. 1, 1854.
24. Bath, Maine, *Daily Mirror*, Oct. 27, 1854.
25. *Ibid.*, Oct. 25, 1854.

26. Boston *Pilot*, Nov. 4, 1854.
27. Bath, Maine, *Daily Mirror*, Oct. 25, 1854.
28. *Ibid.*, Oct. 27, 1854.
29. *Lincoln* [Maine] *Democrat*, Nov. 1, 1854.
30. *Stamford Mirror*, Sept. 23, 1884.
31. *Cincinnati Daily Enquirer*, Aug. 27, 1854.
32. Thomas, *op. cit.*, p. 168.
33. Scisco, *op. cit.*, p. 134.
34. *Lincoln* [Maine] *Democrat*, Dec. 13 and 20, 1854; Jan. 17, 1855.
35. M. Marion Marberry, *The Golden Voice: A Biography of Isaac Kalloch*, p. 36.
36. *Lincoln* [Maine] *Democrat*, Dec. 27, 1854.
37. *Ibid.*
38. *Ibid.*, Apr. 4, 1855.
39. Warren G. French, *op. cit.*, p. 165.
40. D. Quinn, *Interior Causes of the War*, pp. 26–29.
41. Thomas Nichols, *Forty Years of American Life*, II, p. 61.
42. Springfield *Illinois State Journal*, Feb. 3, 1857.

CHAPTER XIX

1. This may have been in the fall of 1855 although Ned claimed to have been at the Ash Hollow fight in September 1855. (See Ned's speech to Judge Primm in St. Louis, Chapter II.) A. L. Donaldson, in *History of the Adirondacks*, II, p. 120, states that Ned settled on Eagle Lake in 1857. This date seems a little late.
2. Donaldson, *op. cit.*, II, p. 129.
3. *Ibid.*, p. 289.
4. Pond, *op. cit.*, pp. 65–67.
5. *Ibid.*, p. 57.
6. "The Lakes of the Wilderness," *Great Republic Monthly*, I (Apr. 1859), p. 347.
7. Pond, *op. cit.*, pp. 115, 116.
8. Letter of Lovanche Judson to Fred E. Pond, July 3, 1887, in author's collection.
9. Donaldson, *op. cit.*, II, p. 100. The author credits the elder Durant with giving this name. Hathorn credits it to Ned. See Pond, *op. cit.*, pp. 115, 116.
10. *Ibid.*, p. 60.
11. Mather, *op. cit.*, p. 60. Donaldson, *op. cit.*, II, p. 122.

12. Pond, *op. cit.*, pp. 111–112.
13. An expression not original with Ned. See James Dugan, *History of Hurlbut's Fighting Fourth Division*, p. 159.
14. Ned Buntline, *Thayendanegea, the Scourge; or, The War-Eagle of the Mohawks*, p. 44.
15. Ned Buntline, *Seawaif; or, The Terror of the Coast*, p. 4.
16. Francis Brinley, *Life of William T. Porter*, p. 267. Announcement of the wedding that caused Herbert's suicide appears in the *New York Times*, Feb. 19, 1858.
17. Chicago *Daily Democratic Press*, May 26, 27, 29, 1858.
18. *Cincinnati Gazette*, Dec. 20, 1862. French, *op. cit.*, p. 170, states that J. H. Ingraham's brother resolved to buy the copyrights after his death but the sudden success of his stories under Beadle and Adams's promotion made this impossible.
19. Ned Buntline, *The White Wizard; or, The Great Prophet of the Seminoles*, pp. 102–103.
20. Donaldson, *op. cit.*, II, p. 122. Buntline commenced coining words of this nature in his earliest works.

CHAPTER XX

1. June 30, 1861.
2. François Victor Adolphe de Chanal, *The American Army in the War of Secession*, p. 23.
3. Alexander Webb, *The Peninsula: McClellan's Campaign of 1862*, p. 51.
4. George H. Gordon, *A War Diary of Events in the Great Rebellion, 1863–1865*, p. 37.
5. Ned Buntline, *Life in the Saddle, or, The Cavalry Scout*, p. 23.
6. Oct. 24, 1862, according to his service record.
7. Charles M. Clark, *History of the Thirty-Ninth Regiment Illinois Volunteer Veteran Infantry*, p. 90.
8. Pond (*op. cit.*, pp. 67–73) adds an Ohio regiment but this seems questionable.
9. Ned Buntline, *Life in the Saddle*, p. 29.
10. This sortie seems to have been the one on November 14, 1862, described in *War of the Rebellion . . . Official Records*, Series I, XVIII, p. 31. Buntline says that the reconnaissance occurred the day he reached the regiment. He enlisted September 25, 1862. If this statement is correct, six weeks must

have transpired before he reached Suffolk. C. M. Clark, (*op. cit.*, pp. 96–97) describes this skirmish.

11. Ned Buntline, *Life in the Saddle*, p. 3.
12. Gilbert Patten, "Dime Novel Days," *Saturday Evening Post*, CCV, No. 35 (Feb. 28, 1931), p. 6.
13. Charles M. Harvey, "The Dime Novel in American Life," *Atlantic Monthly* (July 1907), pp. 37–45.
14. Mott, *op. cit.*, II, p. 467.
15. Ned Buntline, *Life in the Saddle*, p. 4.
16. Gordon, *op. cit.*, p. 34.
17. Pond, *op. cit.*, p. 78.
18. Transcript of interview with Lovanche Judson in scrapbook at office of *Stamford Mirror*.
19. Pond, *op. cit.*, p. 78.
20. Letter from Lovanche Judson to Fred E. Pond, Apr. 23, 1887, in author's collection.
21. *War of the Rebellion . . . Official Records*, Series I, XVIII, p. 180.
22. Washington *Daily Chronicle*, June 19, 1863.
23. *War of the Rebellion . . . Official Records*, Series I, XVIII, p. 556.
24. Gordon, *op. cit.*, p. 42.
25. *War of the Rebellion . . . Official Records*, Series I, XVIII, pp. 682, 690, 692.
26. Ned Buntline has been credited with receiving from one to twenty wounds in the Civil War. None are cited on his service record. Pond, *op. cit.*, p. 100. Venable, *op. cit.*, p. 294. Mather, *op. cit.*, p. 57. His hospitalization is a repetition of the ruse he tried when jailed after the Astor Place Riot.
27. At least two letters written by Ned in Scranton have been found. One is in the National Archives Pension File WO 906598 and the other in the John Russell Young Papers in the Library of Congress.
28. Pond, *op. cit.*, p. 67.

CHAPTER XXI

1. Note the title of one, *Ethelbert, the Wanderer*, a name Pond (*op. cit.*, p. 59) claimed that Ned used as a pseudonym.
2. Pond, *op. cit.*, p. 93. Mather, *op. cit.*, p. 57.

3. Patten, "Dime-Novel Days," *Saturday Evening Post,* CCV, No. 36 (March 7, 1931), p. 33.
4. Transcript of interview with Lovanche Judson in scrapbook at *Stamford Mirror* office.
5. Mather, *op. cit.*, p. 55.
6. *Ibid.*, p. 50.
7. Pond, *op. cit.*, p. 117.
8. San Francisco *Daily Evening Bulletin,* May 1, 1868.
9. Franklin Walker, *San Francisco's Literary Frontier,* pp. 128, 153.
10. *Ibid.*, pp. 169–171.
11. *Stamford Mirror,* Jan. 11, 1876.
12. San Francisco *Daily Evening Bulletin,* July 20, 1868.
13. Jan. 6, 1869.
14. Walker, *op. cit.*, p. 182.
15. *Ibid.*, p. 201.
16. *New York Times,* Oct. 17, 1869, notes that Ned was in Iowa.
17. *Stamford Mirror,* July 6, 1875.
18. *Ibid.*, Aug. 24, 1875.
19. *Ibid.*, Sept. 21, 1875.
20. Stuart N. Lake, *Wyatt Earp: Frontier Marshal,* pp. 145–146.
21. *Ibid.*, p. 367.
22. *Stamford Mirror,* Dec. 14, 1875.

CHAPTER XXII

1. Pond, *op. cit.*, p. 109.
2. *Ibid.*, p. 114.
3. *Stamford Mirror,* July 4, 1876.
4. *Ibid.*, July 18, 1876.
5. *Ibid.*
6. Walsh, *op. cit.*, p. 205.
7. *Ibid.*
8. *St. Joseph Gazette,* Sept. 5, 1876.
9. *Stamford Mirror,* July 27, 1875.
10. *Ibid.*, July 25, 1876.
11. *Ibid.*, Dec. 26, 1876.
12. *Ibid.*, Sept. 19, 1876.
13. *Ibid.*, Jan. 16, 1877.
14. Pond, *op. cit.*, p. 100.
15. *Stamford Mirror,* July 3, 1877.
16. *Ibid.*, Aug. 7, 1877.

17. *Stamford Mirror*, Nov. 20, 1877.
18. *Ibid.*, Nov. 27, 1877.
19. *Ibid.*
20. Pond, *op. cit.*, p. 101.
21. *Stamford Mirror*, Dec. 11, 1877.
22. *Ibid.*, Jan. 1, 1878.
23. *Ibid.*, Jan. 15, 1878.
24. *Ibid.*
25. *Ibid.*, March 19, 1878.
26. *Ibid.*, Apr. 9, 1878.
27. *Ibid.*, March 11, May 6, 1879.

CHAPTER XXIII

1. *Stamford Mirror*, Feb. 17, Apr. 20, 1880.
2. The name Orvis for a fly rod is like Winchester for a rifle. Charles F. Orvis was born in Manchester, Vermont, in 1831. His craftsmanship attracted summer visitors and in 1856 the present Orvis company was organized.
3. Pond, *op. cit.*, pp. 94–96.
4. *Stamford Mirror*, Jan. 18, 1881.
5. Pond, *op. cit.*, p. 121.
6. *Stamford Mirror*, Jan. 25, 1881.
7. *Ibid.*, March 1, 1881.
8. *Ibid.*, March 15, 22, 29, Apr. 5, 1881.
9. Scrapbook in *Stamford Mirror* office.
10. *Ibid.*
11. *Stamford Mirror*, May 10, June 28, 1881.
12. *Ibid.*, May 10, 1882.
13. *Ibid.*, May 24, 1881.
14. *Ibid.*, Aug. 2, 1881.
15. Pond, *op. cit.*, p. 126.
16. *Ibid.*, May 1, 1883.
17. Interview in July 1947, with Curtis Chappalear, Delaplane, Va.
18. *Ibid.*, July 29, 1884.
19. *Ibid.*, Sept. 23, 1884.
20. Reprint from *New York Morning Journal* in scrapbook at *Stamford Mirror* office. The newspaper erred in calling her "Edwindina." This has been corrected to "Edwardina" to conform with the name cited in the pension records.
21. *Stamford Mirror*, March 31, 1885.

22. *Stamford Mirror*, June 16, 1885.
23. Pond, *op. cit.*, p. 126.
24. *Ibid.*, pp. 106–107.
25. Venable, *op. cit.*, p. 295.
26. Pond, *op. cit.*, pp. 125–126.
27. *Stamford Mirror*, Nov. 24, 1885.
28. *Ibid.*, May 4, 1886. Also printed in Pond, *op. cit.*, p. 129.
29. *Stamford Mirror*, June 1, 1885.
30. Pond, *op. cit.*, pp. 127–128.
31. *Ibid.*, p. 133.
32. *Ibid.*, p. 127.
33. *Stamford Mirror*, July 20, 1886.
34. Clipping from *New York World*, July 17, 1886, in scrapbook at *Stamford Mirror* office.
35. *Stamford Mirror*, Aug. 10, 1886.
36. *Ibid.*, Sept. 7, 1886.
37. Interview in October, 1945, with Jesse Gilbert, Stamford, who was one of the little boys.

Bibliography

Books and Articles

Annual Report of the Adjutant-General of the State of New York (Albany, 1863).

Barnes, Gilbert Hobbs, *The Antislavery Impulse: 1830–1844* (New York, 1933).

B. B. S., "A Trip to the Adirondacks," *Stamford Mirror*, August 28, 1877.

"Beadle's Dime Books . . . ," *North American Review*, CCIV (July 1864), pp. 303–309.

Beeson, Chalkley M., "A Royal Buffalo Hunt," *Transactions of the Kansas State Historical Society, 1907–1908*, X, pp. 574–580.

Billington, Ray Allen, *The Protestant Crusade: 1800–1860* (New York, 1938).

Boernstein, Henry, *The Mysteries of St. Louis or the Jesuits on the Prairie de Noyers* (St. Louis, 1851).

Bragin, Charles, *Dime Novels Bibliography: 1860–1928* (Brooklyn, 1938).

Brink, McDonough & Co., pub., *History of Marion and Clinton Counties, Illinois* (Philadelphia, 1881).

Brinley, Francis, *Life of William T. Porter* (New York, 1860).

Brooks, Van Wyck, *The World of Washington Irving* (Philadelphia, 1945).

Brown, Thomas Allston, *History of the American Stage. Containing Biographical Sketches of Nearly Every Member of the Profession That Has Appeared on the American Stage from 1733 to 1870* (New York, 1870).

Brown, Thomas Allston, *History of the New York Stage from the First Performance in 1732 to 1901* (New York, 1903).

Callahan, Edward W., *List of Officers of the Navy of the United States and of the Marine Corps from 1775 to 1900* (New York, 1901).

Chanal, François Victor Adolphe de, *The American Army in the War of Secession* (Leavenworth, Kansas, 1894).

Clark, Charles M., *The History of the Thirty-Ninth Regiment Illinois Volunteer Veteran Infantry* (Chicago, 1889).

Clark, Thomas D., *The Rampaging Frontier* (Indianapolis, 1939).

Clark, Willis Gaylord, *The Parlour Scrap Book: Comprising Sixteen Engravings, with Poetical and Other Illustrations* (Philadelphia, 1836).

Cody, William Frederick, *An Autobiography of Buffalo Bill* (New York, 1920).

Cody, William Frederick, *The Story of the Wild West* (Philadelphia, 1888).

Cole, Arthur C., *The Whig Party in the South* (Washington, 1913).

Collins, Lewis and Richard H., *Collins' Historical Sketches of Kentucky* (Covington, 1874).

Connelley, William E., *Wild Bill and His Era* (New York, 1933).

Cowley, Malcolm, "The Alger Story," *New Republic*, CXIII, No. 11 (Sept. 10, 1945), pp. 319–320.

Crowe, Eyre, *With Thackeray in America* (London, 1893).

Curti, Merle, *The Growth of American Thought* (New York, 1943).

Daly, *Judge* Charles Patrick, "People vs. Edward Z. C. Judson," *Reports of Cases Argued and Determined in the Court of Common Pleas for the City and County of New York*, XI (New York, 1885), pp. 1–91.

De Bow, J. D. B., *The Industrial Resources, etc., of the Southern and Western States* (New Orleans, 1853).

De Bow, J. D. B., ed., *De Bow's Review*, 1848.

Donaldson, Alfred L., *A History of the Adirondacks* (New York, 1921).

Donaldson, Thomas Corwin, *The George Catlin Indian Gallery in the U.S. National Museum* (Washington, 1888).

Dorchester, Daniel, *The Liquor Problem in All Ages* (New York, 1884).

Dugan, James, *History of Hurlbut's Fighting Fourth Division* (Cincinnati, 1863).

Eckenrode, H. J., and Bryan Conrad, *James Longstreet: Lee's War Horse* (Chapel Hill, North Carolina, 1936).

Forrest & Macready Astor Place Riot. Account of the Terrific & Fatal Riot at the New York Astor Place Opera House, on the Night of May 10th, 1849. With the Quarrels of Forrest & Macready, Including All the Causes Which Led to That Awful Tragedy! . . . (New York, 1849).

Foster, T. Henry, *Beadles, Bibles & Bibliophiles* (Cedar Rapids, Iowa, 1948).

Foster, T. Henry, "Collecting Iowa Dime Novels," *Palimpsest*, XXX, No. 6 (June 1949), pp. 169–172.

Freedley, George, and John A. Reeves, *A History of the Theatre* (New York, 1941).

French, Warren Graham, "A Sketch of the Life of Joseph Holt Ingraham," *Journal of Mississippi History*, XI, No. 3 (July 1949), pp. 155–171.

Goodrich, Phineas G., *History of Wayne County* (Honesdale, Pennsylvania, 1880).

Grinnell, George Bird, *The Fighting Cheyennes* (New York, 1915).

Grinnell, George Bird, *Two Great Scouts and Their Pawnee Battalion* (Cleveland, 1928).

Hadley, James A., "A Royal Buffalo Hunt," *Transactions of the Kansas State Historical Society, 1907–1908*, X, pp. 564–574.

Haines, Benjamin F., *Illustrated History of Wayne County* (n.p., 1900).

Haley, Nelson Cole, *Whale Hunt: The Narrative of a Voyage* (New York, 1948).

Ham, Thomas J., "The Story of the Old Cannon," a series of articles on the history of Honesdale, Pennsylvania, in the *Wayne Citizen* from August 11, 1904, to August 3, 1905.

Hamersly, Thomas H. S., *General Register of the United States Navy and Marine Corps* (Washington, 1882).

Harvey, Charles M., "The Dime Novel in American Life," *Atlantic Monthly* (July 1907), pp. 37–45.

Holbrook, Stewart H., "Annie Oakley: She Was the World's Best Woman Shot," *Life*, XX, No. 17 (April 28, 1947), p. 67.

Holbrook, Stewart H., "Life and Times of Ned Buntline," *American Mercury*, LXIV, No. 281 (May 1947), pp. 599–605. Reprinted in *Little Annie Oakley & Other Rugged People* (New York, 1948).

Howard, Oliver Otis, *My Life and Experiences among Our Hostile Indians* (Hartford, 1907).

Howe, Henry, *Historical Collections of Ohio*, III (Columbus, 1891).

Hunt, Freeman, *The Merchants' Magazine and Commercial Review* (New York, 1845).

Huse, Harriet Pinckney, "An Untold Story of the Florida War," *Harper's New Monthly Magazine*, LXXXIII, No. CCCCXCVI (September 1891), pp. 591–594.

Hyde, W., and H. L. Conrad, eds., *Encyclopedia of History of St. Louis* (New York, 1899).

Ireland, Joseph Norton, *Records of the New York Stage, from 1750 to 1880* (New York, 1866–1867).

Johannsen, Albert, *The House of Beadle and Adams and Its Dime and Nickel Novels: The Story of a Vanished Literature* (Norman, Oklahoma, 1950).

Journal of U.S. Cavalry Association, III (March 1890).

Judson, Levi Carroll, *A Biography of the Signers of the Declaration of Independence, and of Washington and Patrick Henry with an Appendix Containing the Constitution of the United States and Other Documents* (Philadelphia, 1839).

Judson, Levi Carroll, *The Masonic Advocate: Being a Concise Exposition and Full Defence of Free Masonry with an Appendix, Containing an Abridgment of Mackey's and Oliver's Lexicons of Free Masonry* (Philadelphia, n.d.).

Judson, Levi Carroll, *The Probe, or One Hundred and Two Essays on the Nature of Men and Things with an Appendix . . .* (Philadelphia, 1846).

Judson, Levi Carroll, *The Sages and Heroes of the American Revolution, in Two Parts Including the Signers of the Declaration of Independence. Two Hundred and Forty Three of the Sages and Heroes Are Presented in Due Form and Many Others Are Named Incidentally* (Philadelphia, 1851. Rev. eds., 1852, 1853, 1854. These plates were being used for new printings as late as 1889 by the John Adams Lee Publishing Company in Boston).

Krout, John Allen, *The Origins of Prohibition* (New York, 1925).

Lake, Stuart N., *Wyatt Earp: Frontier Marshal* (Boston, 1931).

"The Lakes of the Wilderness," *The Great Republic Monthly*, I (April 1859), pp. 335–350.

Leavitt, M. B., *Fifty Years in Theatrical Management* (New York, 1912).

Lehman-Haupt, Hellmut, *The Book in America: A History of the Making, the Selling, and the Collecting of Books in the United States* (New York, 1939).

Life and Public Services of Gen. Z. Taylor (New York, 1846).

Longfellow, Samuel, *Life of Henry Wadsworth Longfellow*, II (Boston, 1886).

McIlvaine, Charles P., *The Chief Dangers of the Church in These Times: A Charge Delivered to the Clergy of the Diocese of Ohio at the Twenty Sixth Annual Convention of the Same* (New York, 1843).

MacKinnon, *Captain* Lauchlan B., *Atlantic and Transatlantic Sketches Afloat and Ashore* (New York, 1852).

Marberry, M. Marion, *The Golden Voice: A Biography of Isaac Kalloch* (New York, 1947).

Marryat, *Captain* [Frederick], *A Diary in America with Remarks on Its Institutions* (London, 1839).

Martineau, Harriet, *Retrospect of Western Travel* (London, 1838).

Mather, Fred, *My Angling Friends* (New York, 1901).

Matthews, Alfred, *History of Wayne, Pike and Monroe Counties* (Philadelphia, 1886).

Maury, Dabney H., *Recollections of a Virginian* (New York, 1894).

Mead, Leon, "How 'Ned Buntline' Turned from Runaway Boy to Writing Genius," *Reckless Ralph's Dime Novel Roundup*, IX, No. 101 (January 1941), pp. 1–9.

Melville, Herman, *White-Jacket, or The World in a Man-of-War* (Boston, 1892).

Minnigerode, Meade, *The Fabulous Forties, 1840–1850: A Presentation of Private Life* (New York, 1924).

Monaghan, Jay, "Literary Opportunities in Pioneer Times," *Journal of the Illinois State Historical Society*, XXXIII, No. 4 (December 1940), pp. 412–437.

Monaghan, Jay, "The Stage Career of Buffalo Bill," *Journal of the Illinois State Historical Society*, XXXI, No. 4 (December 1938), pp. [411]–423.

Moses, Montrose J., *The Fabulous Forrest* (Boston, 1929).

Mott, Frank Luther, "The Beadles and Their Novels," *Palimpsest*, XXX, No. 6 (June 1949), pp. 173–186.

Mott, Frank Luther, *Golden Multitudes. The Story of Best Sellers in the United States* (New York, 1947).

Mott, Frank Luther, *A History of American Magazines*, I, and II (Cambridge, 1938).

Munsell, W. W., and Co., pub., *History of Delaware County, New York* (New York, 1880).

National Police Gazette, 1845–1847.

Nevins, Allan, ed., *The Diary of Philip Hone, 1828–1851* (New York, 1927).

Nichols, Thomas, *Forty Years of American Life* (London, 1864).

Odell, George C. D., *Annals of the New York Stage*, IX (New York, 1937).

Orvis, Charles F., and A. Nelson Cheney, *Fishing with the Fly* (Boston, 1889).

Parton, James, *Life of Andrew Jackson*, III (New York, 1861).

Paterson, Thomas V., *The Private Life, Public Career, and Real Character of that Odious Rascal Ned Buntline!!* (New York, 1849). The title of a second edition begins: *The Extraordinary Public Proceedings of E. Z. C. Judson, Alias, Ned Buntline against Thomas V. Paterson, for an Alleged Libel Contained in a Pamphlet Entitled The Private Life*, etc.

[Paterson, Thomas V.], *A Sketch of a Reformed Gambler, with the Origin, Object and Nature of the Anti-Gambling Association* (New York, 1851).

Patten, Gilbert, "Dime-Novel Days," *Saturday Evening Post*, CCV, No. 35 (February 28, 1931), p. 6.

Paullin, Charles O., "The National Ticket of Broom and Coates, 1852," *American Historical Review*, XXV, No. 4 (July 1920), pp. 689–691.

Pearson, Edmund, *Dime Novels; or, Following an Old Trail in Popular Literature* (Boston, 1929).

Pearson, Edmund, *Queer Books* (Garden City, New York, 1928).

Phisterer, Frederick, comp., *New York in the War of the Rebellion, 1861 to 1865* (Albany, 1912).

Pollock, *Sir* Frederick, ed., *Macready's Reminiscences and Selections from his Diaries and Letters* (New York, 1875).

Pond, Fred E., *The Life and Adventures of "Ned Buntline"* (New York, 1919).

Porter, John W. H., *A Record of Events in Norfolk County, Virginia, from April 19th, 1861, to May 10th, 1862 . . .* (Portsmouth, Virginia, 1892).

Quinn, Arthur Hobson, *A History of the American Drama from the Beginning to the Civil War* (New York, 1923).

[Quinn, D.], *Interior Causes of the War* (New York, 1863).

Rice, Wallace, "Dedication of the Memorial to James Butler Hickok, 'Wild Bill'," *Journal of the Illinois State Historical Society*, XXIII, No. 3 (October 1930), pp. 522–536.

Riegel, Robert E., *Young America 1830–1840* (Norman, Oklahoma, 1949).

Rives, John C., *Appendix to the Congressional Globe, for the First*

Session, Thirty-third Congress, New Series, XXXI (Washington, 1854).

Rusk, Ralph Leslie, *The Literature of the Middle Western Frontier* (New York, 1925).

Sanger, William W., *The History of Prostitution* (New York, 1859).

Schlesinger, Arthur M., Jr., *The Age of Jackson* (Boston, 1945).

Scisco, Louis Dow, *Political Nativism in New York State* (New York, 1901). *Columbia University Studies in History, Economics and Public Law*, XIII, No. 2.

Scott, Franklin William, *Newspapers and Periodicals of Illinois 1814–1879* (Springfield, Illinois, 1910).

Sherman, William Tecumseh, *Memoirs* (New York, 1891).

South-Western Literary Journal and Monthly Review, I, Nos. 3–6 (January–April 1845).

Sprague, John T., *The Origin, Progress, and Conclusion of the Florida War* (New York, 1848).

Starrett, Vincent, "Bertha's Christmas Vision," *Chicago Tribune*, August 19, 1945.

Stephens, Ann Sophia (Winterbotham), *Malaeska; The Indian Wife of the White Hunter* (New York, 1860).

Stevens, Walter Barlow, *Missouri the Center State: 1821–1915*, II (Chicago, 1915).

Stevens, Walter Barlow, *St. Louis: The Fourth City* (St. Louis, 1909).

Strait, Newton A., *An Alphabetical List of the Battles of the War of the Rebellion . . . the Florida War*, etc., . . . (Washington, 1881).

Thomas, *Sister* M. Evangeline, *Nativism in the Old Northwest, 1850–1860* (Washington, 1936).

Thorpe, Thomas B., "Lewis Gaylord Clark," *Harper's New Monthly Magazine*, XLVIII, No. 286 (March 1874), pp. 587–592.

Torrey, *Rev.* David, *Memoir of Major Jason Torrey, of Bethany, Wayne County, Pa.* (Scranton, 1885).

Venable, William Henry, *Beginnings of Literary Culture in the Ohio Valley* (Cincinnati, 1891).

Walker, Franklin, *San Francisco's Literary Frontier* (New York, 1939).

Walsh, Richard J., *The Making of Buffalo Bill: A Study in Heroics* (Indianapolis, 1928).

The War of the Rebellion: A Compilation of the Official Records of the Union and Confederate Armies (Washington, 1887).

Webb, Alexander, *The Peninsula – McClellan's Campaign of 1862* (New York, 1881).

Weed, Thurlow, *Letters from Europe and the West Indies* (Albany, 1866).

Western Literary Journal and Monthly Review, I, Nos. 1 and 2 (November–December 1844).

Wilson, Forrest, *Crusader in Crinoline, the Life of Harriet Beecher Stowe* (Philadelphia, 1941).

Wilson, Rufus Rockwell, *New York in Literature* (Elmira, New York, 1947).

Wilstach, Frank J., *Wild Bill Hickok: The Prince of Pistoleers* (Garden City, New York, 1926).

Wood, James Playsted, ed., *One Hundred Years Ago; American Writing of 1848* (New York, 1948).

Wright, Lyle H., *American Fiction, 1774–1850: A Contribution toward a Bibliography* (San Marino, California, 1939).

Newspapers

Albany [New York] *Argus*, 1865.
Bath, Maine, *Daily Mirror*, 1854.
Boston *Angel Gabriel*, 1854.
Boston Daily Times and Bay State Democrat, 1847.
Boston *Pilot*, 1854.
Chicago *Daily Democratic Press*, 1858.
Chicago Daily Tribune, 1872.
Cincinnati *Daily Commercial Journal*, 1846.
Cincinnati Daily Enquirer, 1845, 1848, 1854.
Cincinnati Daily Times & Chronicle, 1873.
Cincinnati Gazette, 1862.
Cincinnati *Prairie Enquirer*, 1873.
Hawley [Pennsylvania] *Times*, 1876.
The Lincoln [Maine] *Democrat*, 1854.
Nashville *Republican Banner*, 1846.
Daily Republican Banner and Nashville Whig, 1845, 1849.
Tri-Weekly Nashville Union, 1845–1846.
New Orleans *Daily Picayune*, 1850–1851.
New York Daily Globe, 1848.
New York Evening Express, 1849.
New York Herald, 1848, 1849, 1886.
New York Times, 1869–1873.

New York World, 1886.
Paterson [New Jersey] *Daily Guardian*, 1873.
Philadelphia *Spirit of the Times*, 1846.
Quincy [Illinois] *Whig*, 1852.
Quincy [Massachusetts] *Patriot*, 1847.
St. Joseph [Missouri] *Gazette*, 1876.
St. Louis Daily Globe, 1872.
St. Louis *Daily Organ and Reveille*, 1848.
St. Louis Herald, 1852.
St. Louis Intelligencer, 1852.
St. Louis *Missouri Democrat*, 1872.
St. Louis *Morning Signal*, 1852.
San Francisco *Daily Evening Bulletin*, 1868.
Springfield *Illinois State Journal* (*Illinois Daily Journal*, *Sangamo Journal*), 1851, 1852, 1854, 1857.
Springfield *Illinois State Register*, 1852.
Stamford [New York] *and Bloomville Mirror*, 1871–1886. On May 19, 1874, this became the *Stamford Mirror*.
Warrenton, Virginia, *True Index*.
Washington *Sunday Morning Chronicle*, 1861.
Wayne [County, Pennsylvania] *Citizen*, 1904–1905.
Wayne County [Pennsylvania] *Herald and Bethany Inquirer*, 1833, 1834.
Wayne Enquirer [Bethany, Pennsylvania], 1830.
White Cloud [Kansas] *Chief*, 1862.

Unpublished Sources

Civil War records of Edward Z. C. Judson, Division of Military and Naval Affairs of the Executive Department, Albany, New York.
Daly, *Judge* Charles Patrick. Scrapbooks of clippings. One section is devoted to the Astor Place Riot.
Davis, Granville D., "Factional Differences in the Democratic Party in Illinois, 1854–1858" (Ph.D. thesis, University of Illinois, Urbana, 1936).
Hasty, Mary Washburn, "E. Z. C. Judson, Adventurer, Journalist, and Writer of Tales" (M.A. thesis, George Peabody College for Teachers, Nashville, Tennessee, 1937).
Letters of E. Z. C. Judson and (Lovanche) Judson in author's collection.

Military records of E. Z. C. Judson in Office of the Adjutant General, Washington, D. C.

Naval records of Edward Z. C. Judson in National Archives.

Pension file, Edward Z. C. Judson, National Archives.

Stamford [New York] *Mirror* scrapbook.

Sutton, Walter E., "Cincinnati as a Publishing and Book Trade Center, 1796–1880" (Ph.D. thesis, Ohio State University, Columbus, 1947).

Explanation of References in the List of Ned Buntline's Works

Bragin. Charles Bragin catalogs, Dime Novel Club, 1525 West 12th Street, Brooklyn, New York.

Caldwell Collection. Owned by Raymond L. Caldwell, Lancaster, Pennsylvania.

DLC. The Library of Congress.

Hochschild Collection. Owned by Harold K. Hochschild, Blue Mountain Lake, New York, whose summer estate includes the site of Buntline's Adirondack hunting lodge.

Johannsen. Albert Johannsen, *House of Beadle and Adams*, a monumental two-volume study and bibliography.

Pond. Fred E. Pond, *The Life and Adventures of "Ned Buntline,"* which contains the earliest bibliography of Buntline's works.

Sabin. Joseph Sabin, *A Dictionary of Books Relating to America.*

Wright. Lyle H. Wright, *American Fiction, 1774–1850: A Contribution toward a Bibliography.*

Works of E. Z. C. Judson (Ned Buntline)

A complete catalogue of Buntline's works is impossible at this time. For years he contributed almost daily to various periodicals. All such essays and stories have been omitted from the bibliography below unless they were published separately. Also excluded from this list are his poems and separate publications which appeared only under pseudonyms. The first editions of all books and pamphlets have been noted when possible. Occasionally a few later printings are also cited. For generous assistance in compiling this check list, I am heavily indebted to Raymond L. Caldwell of Lancaster, Pennsylvania, whose head and whose home rank among the nation's greatest storehouses of information on dime novels.

Afloat and Ashore. See *Cruisings, Afloat and Ashore.*

Agnes; or, The Beautiful Milliner (N.Y.: Hilton & Co., 1866). Ned Buntline's Own Series.

Andros, the Free Rover; or, The Pirate's Daughter (N.Y.: Beadle & Adams, 1883 – Beadle's Dime Library. Also N.Y.: M. J. Ivers & Co., 1903 – New York Dime Library). Same as *Elfrida.*

Barnacle Backstay; or, The Gray Eagle of the Atlantic (N.Y.: Street & Smith, 1899). Log Cabin Library. Hochschild Col. First pub. in *Street and Smith's New York Weekly*, 1870.

Battle of Hate; or, Hearts are Trumps (N.Y.: F. A. Brady, 1867). Referred to in Buntline, *Morgan* (1861), and printed in *New York Mercury*, 1865.

Beautiful Nun (Phila.: T. B. Peterson & Brothers, 1866).

The B'hoys of New York, A Sequel to the Mysteries & Miseries of New York (N.Y.: W. F. Burgess, 1850. Also N.Y.: Dick & Fitzgerald, n.d. Also Halifax, Milner & Sowerby, 1866, n.p.). First pub. in *Ned Buntline's Own*, 1849.

Big Foot Wallace; or, The Giant Hero of the Border (N.Y.: Street & Smith, 1891). Log Cabin Library. First pub. in *Street and Smith's New York Weekly*, 1874.

Bill Tredegar, The Moonshiner of Blue Ridge (N.Y.: Street & Smith, 1889). Log Cabin Library. Hochschild Col. First pub. in *Street and Smith's New York Weekly* as "Bill Tredegar; or, The Outlaw of the Blue Ridge," 1885. Caldwell Col.

The Black Avenger of the Spanish Main; or, The Fiend of Blood: A Thrilling Tale of Buccaneer Times (Boston: F. Gleason, 1847; also Gleason's Publishing Hall, 1847; N.Y.: S. French, 1847; Boston: M. M. Ballou, 1849; Boston: G. W. Studley, 1892 – Owl Library; Chicago: M. A. Donohue, n.d., as *The Avenger of the Spanish Main.*)

The Boot-Maker of Fifth Avenue; or, A Fortune from Petroleum (N.Y.: Hilton & Co., 1866). Ned Buntline's Own Series. Listed by Caldwell.

The Buccaneer's Daughter (N.Y.: Dick & Fitzgerald, n.d.).

Buckskin Sam, The Scalp Taker (N.Y.: Street & Smith, 1891). Log Cabin Library. First pub. as "The Scalp Taker" in *Street and Smith's New York Weekly*, 1875. Caldwell Col.

Buffalo Bill: The King of Border Men (N.Y.: J. S. Ogilvie, 1881). The People's Library. Reprinted as *Buffalo Bill and His Adventures in the West* (N.Y.: J. S. Ogilvie, 1886. Also N.Y.: International Book Co., [1886]). Reprinted also as *Buffalo Bill* (N.Y.: International Book Co., 1886), Aldine ed. First pub. in *Street and Smith's New York Weekly*, 1869.

Buffalo Bill's Best Shot; or, The Heart of Spotted Tail (N.Y.: Street & Smith, 1890). Sea and Shore Series. Another, dated 1891, in Log Cabin Series. First pub. in *Street and Smith's New York Weekly*, 1872.

Buffalo Bill's First Trail; or, Will Cody, The Pony Express Rider (N.Y.: Beadle & Adams, 1888). Beadle's Dime Library. First pub. as "Will Cody, The Pony Express Rider; or, Buffalo Bill's First Trail," in *Beadle's Weekly*, 1885.

Buffalo Bill's Last Victory; or, Dove Eye, the Lodge Queen (N.Y.: Street & Smith, 1890). Sea and Shore Series. First pub. in *Street and Smith's New York Weekly*, 1872.

Captain Jack; or, The Seven Scouts (N.Y.: Street & Smith, 1891). Log Cabin Library. First pub. as "The Terrible Dread; or, The Seven Scouts" in *Street and Smith's New York Weekly*, 1879.

Captain Sea Waif, the Privateer (N.Y.: Beadle & Adams, 1879). Beadle's Dime Library. Same as *Seawaif*.

The Captain's Pig. No copy found. The story appears as "Eating the Captain's Pig; or, The Reefers in a Scrape," in *Cruisings, Afloat and Ashore* (1848), and in Pond, *Life and Adventures of "Ned Buntline."*

Charley Bray (N.Y.: Hilton & Co., 1865). Ned Buntline's Own Series. First pub. as "The Fireman's Mission, a Story of New York Life," in *Ned Buntline's Own*, 1865.

Child of the Sun, A Tale of Mexico (N.Y.: Hilton & Co., 1866). Ned Buntline's Own Series. Caldwell Col.

Clara St. John (N.Y.: Hilton & Co., 1865). Ned Buntline's Own Series. A Sequel to *Mermet Ben*. See also *Rose Seymour*.

Clarence Rhett; or, The Cruise of a Privateer: An American Sea Story (N.Y.: F. A. Brady, 1866. Also an 1878 printing – New York Boys' Library Series).

The Convict; or, The Conspirator's Victim (N.Y.: W. F. Burgess, 1851. Also N.Y.: Dick Fitzgerald, 1853). First pub. in *Ned Buntline's Own*, 1850. Caldwell Col.

Cruisings, Afloat and Ashore, from the Private Log of Ned Buntline: Sketches of Land and Sea, Humorous and Pathetic; Tragical and Comical (N.Y.: Edward Z. C. Judson, R. Craighead printer, 1848. A second ed., N.Y., 1848, was pub. by R. Craighead. Another,

London: H. G. Collins, 1851, was pub. as *Afloat and Ashore*). The book includes "The Masquerade," "The Smuggler: A True Yarn of the Mexican Coast," "Eating the Captain's Pig, or, The Reefers in a Scrape," "The French Captain's Story; or, Britannia Rules Ze Wave," "The March-born" (poem), "A Race on the Bahama Banks," "The Way I Caught a Wife," "Who the De'il is Buntline?" (poem), "Running a French Blockade; or, The Way They Fooled the Prince de Joinville," etc. See *Navigator Ned*.

The Curse! A Tale of Crime and Its Retribution, Founded on Facts of Real Life (Boston: Roberts & Garfield, 1847).

Darrow the Floating Detective; or, The Shadowed Buccaneer (N.Y.: Street & Smith, 1889). Log Cabin Library. First pub. as "The Floating Detective" in *Street and Smith's New York Weekly*, 1880. Caldwell Col.

Dashing Charlie, the Texas Whirlwind (N.Y.: Street & Smith, 1890). Sea and Shore Series. First pub. in *Street and Smith's New York Weekly*, 1872.

The Death-Mystery: A Crimson Tale of Life in New York (N.Y.: F. A. Brady, 1861). First pub. in *New York Mercury*, 1861. A sequel to *Hilliare Henderson*. Note also *The Secret Vow*.

Elfrida, the Red Rover's Daughter, A New Mystery of New York (N.Y.: F. A. Brady, 1860). First pub. in *New York Mercury*, 1860. Note *Andros*.

Ella Adams; or, The Demon of Fire: A Tale of the Charleston Conflagration (N.Y.: F. A. Brady, 1862 and 1863). Mercury Stories. First pub. in *New York Mercury*, 1862.

English Tom; or, The Smuggler's Secret: A Tale of Ship and Shore (N.Y.: Cauldwell, Southworth & Whitney, 1862). First pub. in *New York Mercury*, 1862. Caldwell Col. Same as *The Smuggler*.

Ethelbert, the Shell-Hunter; or, The Ocean Chase (N.Y.: Beadle & Adams, 1884). Beadle's Boys' Library of Sport, Story and Adventure. See *The Shell-Hunter*.

Fanny, the Belle of Central Park (N.Y.: Hilton & Co., 1866). Ned Buntline's Own Series. Caldwell Col.

A Fiery Heart; or, A Woman's Love and a Woman's Hate (N.Y.: Beadle & Adams, 1877). Beadle's Cheap Edition Popular Authors. Same as *Hilliare Henderson*.

Fire Feather, The Buccaneer King (N.Y.: Beadle & Adams, 1890). Pub. as serial in *Beadle's Weekly*, 1885.

The G'hals of New York; A Novel (N.Y.: DeWitt and Davenport,

1850. Also N.Y.: R. M. DeWitt, 187–). First pub. as serial in *Ned Buntline's Own*, 1850. Caldwell Col.

Grossbeak Mansion, A Mystery of New York (N.Y.: F. A. Brady, 1864). First pub. in *New York Mercury*, 1862.

Guiletta the Waif; or, The Girl Wrecker (N.Y.: Street & Smith, 1890). Log Cabin Library. First pub. in *Street and Smith's New York Weekly*, 1878. Caldwell Col.

Hank Cringle, The One Armed Buccaneer (N.Y.: Street & Smith, 1890). Nugget Library. First pub. in *Street and Smith's New York Weekly*, 1871.

Harry Bluff, the Reefer; or, Love and Glory on the Sea (N.Y.: Street & Smith, 1890). Nugget Library. Hochschild Col. First pub. in *Street and Smith's New York Weekly*, 1882. Caldwell Col.

Harry Halyard's Ruin: A True Tale for the Intemperate to Read (Boston: Star Spangled Banner Office, [1850]). Listed by Wright.

"The Haze and Her Ocean Cruise," A Story of a Rebel Privateer (N.Y.: R. M. DeWitt, 187–). First pub. in *New York Mercury*, 1865.

Hazel Eye, The Girl Trapper (N.Y.: Street & Smith, 1890). Log Cabin Library. First pub. in *Street and Smith's New York Weekly*, 1871. Caldwell Col.

Hilliare Henderson; or, The Secret Revealed (N.Y.: F. A. Brady [1861]). First pub. *New York Mercury*, 1861. Antecedent of *The Death-Mystery*. Note also *A Fiery Heart* and *The Planter's Ward*.

The Ice-King; or, The Fate of the Lost Steamer: A Fanciful Tale of the Far North. Bound with *Not in Despair, For I've a Friend: A Lesson of Life* (Boston: G. H. Williams, 1848. Also N.Y.: R. M. DeWitt, 1869—DeWitt's Ten-cent Romances). Note *War-Eagle, or, Ossiniwa*.

The Indian Queen's Revenge (Cleveland: The Arthur Westbrook Co., 1909). Beadle's Frontier Series. Pub. by George Munro, New York, in 1865 under authorship of L. Augustus Jones.

The Jew's Daughter. See *Miriam*.

The King of the Sea: A Tale of the Fearless and Free (Boston: Flag of Our Union Office, 1847. Also N.Y.: S. French, 1848; Boston: F. Gleason, 1849; Glasgow and London: Cameron & Ferguson, n.d.; London: G. Pierce, 1848; Boston: F. Gleason, 1852). Pub. in *Welcome Guest & Ballou's Dollar Monthly*, 1860.

The Lady Thief (N.Y.: Hilton & Co., 1866). Ned Buntline's Own Series. Caldwell Col.

The Last Days of Calleo; or, The Doomed City of Sin! (Boston: Jones Publishing House, 1847. Also N.Y.: E. Z. C. Judson, 1848). Pub. in *Star Spangled Banner Weekly*, 1847.

The Last of the Buccaneers: A Yarn of the Eighteenth Century (N.Y.: Dick & Fitzgerald, n.d. Also N.Y.: Garrett & Co. [1856?]). First pub. in *Western Literary Journal*, 1844.

Lenore; or, The Highwayman's Bride (N.Y.: Hilton & Co., 1866). Ned Buntline's Own Series. A sequel to *Red Ralph; or, The Daughter of the Night.*

Life, Career and Character of Ned Buntline (N.Y.: 1849). Listed in Sabin.

Life in the Saddle; or, The Cavalry Scout (N.Y.: F. A. Brady, 1864). Also pub. in *New York Mercury*, 1864.

Life on the Plains. A play, 1874.

Life's Peril; or, The Drunkard's Wife. A play in collaboration with F. G. Meader from a serial by Buntline in *Street and Smith's New York Weekly*, 1872.

Little Buckshot, The White Whirlwind of the Prairie (N.Y.: Street & Smith, 1891). Log Cabin Library. Pub. in *Street and Smith's New York Weekly*, 1870, reprinted 1887. Caldwell Col.

Long Mike, the Oregon Hustler (N.Y.: Street & Smith, 1891). Log Cabin Library. Caldwell Col.

Long Tom Dart, The Yankee Privateer: A New Naval Story of the War of 1812 (N.Y.: Beadle & Adams, 1891). Beadle's Dime Library. Caldwell Col.

Love's Desperation; or, The President's Only Daughter: A Romance of Reality (Boston: F. Gleason, 1847).

Love's Desperation; or, The President's Only Daughter, and Other Tales (Boston: F. Gleason, 1848). Also contains "The Tempter and the Tempted: A Tale of a Western Boarding School," "Love and Hate; or, The Emblematic Safety-Guard," "Ellen, The Golden-Haired Pet," "A Letter from a Married Man in the Moon," "A Letter from the Married Ladies in the Moon," and "To the Indomitable Ten." Also "The Boarding-School Miss; or, The Young Backwoodsman's Bride," by Charles E. Averill.

Luona Prescott; or, The Curse Fulfilled (N.Y.: F. A. Brady, 1864).

Luona's Oath; or, The Curse Fulfilled (N.Y.: F. Starr & Co., 1870). Starr's 15¢ Illustrated Novels. Same as next above.

Mad Anthony's Captain (N.Y.: George Munro, 1872 – Munro's Ten-cent Novels. Also Cleveland: The Arthur Westbrook Co., 1908).

Madeline Desha (N.Y.: R. M. DeWitt, 187–).

Magdalena, the Outcast; or, The Millionaire's Daughter: A Story of Life in the Empire City (N.Y.: Hilton & Co., 1866). Ned Buntline's Own Series.

Magdelina, the Beautiful Mexican Maid: A Story of Buena Vista (N.Y.: Williams Brothers, 1846 [1847]). Contains Whittier's poem, "The Angels of Buena Vista," which first appeared in *National Era*, May 20, 1847. See Wright.

Magic Figure Head (Boston: Jones Publishing House, n.d.). Listed by Wright.

The Man in the White Coat; or, The Widder Hunt. A play in one act.

The Man-O'Wars Man's Grudge: A Romance of the Revolution (N.Y.: F. A. Brady, 1858). Caldwell Col.

Mark Myrtle (N.Y.: Hilton & Co., 1866). Hilton's Ten-cent Romances.

Matanzas; or, A Brother's Revenge: A Tale of Florida (Boston: G. H. Williams, 1848). Also contains "Selling a Green 'Un; or, A Sight at Louis Phillippe."

Merciless Ben, The Hair Lifter (N.Y.: Street & Smith, 1882). Log Cabin Library. Pub. in *Street and Smith's New York Weekly*, 1882.

Mermet Ben; or, The Astrologer King: A Story of Magic and Wonderful Illusions (N.Y.: Hilton & Co., 1865). Ned Buntline's Own Series. A sequel to *Rose Seymour*. See also *Clara St. John.*

The Midnight Lamp; or, Life in the Empire City (N.Y.: Hilton & Co., 1866). Hilton's Ten-cent Books. On inside of flyleaf the author gives notice that he holds copyright to a play by the same name. Caldwell Col.

The Miner Detective; or, The Ghost of the Gulch (N.Y.: Street & Smith, 1889). Log Cabin Library. First pub. as "Black Alf; or, The Ghost of the Gulch," in *Street and Smith's New York Weekly*, 1874. Caldwell Col.

Miriam; or, The Jew's Daughter (N.Y.: Dick & Fitzgerald, n.d.)

Morgan; or, The Knight of the Black Flag: A Strange Story of Bygone Times (N.Y.: F. A. Brady, 1860. Also R. M. DeWitt, 1861 – Ned Buntline's Romances). First pub. in *New York Mercury*, 1860.

Mountain Tom: A Thrilling Story of the New Diamond Fields (N.Y.: Street & Smith, 1890). First pub. in *Street and Smith's New York Weekly*, 1872. Caldwell Col.

The Mysteries and Miseries of New Orleans (N.Y.: Okarmar &

Ormsby, 1851. Also N.Y.: F. A. Brady & Co., 1853). Also pub. in *Ned Buntline's Own*, 1851.

The Mysteries and Miseries of New York: A Story of Real Life (N.Y.: E. Z. C. Judson, 1848. Also N.Y.: Berford & Co., 1848; N.Y.: W. F. Burgess, 1849; and Dublin: J. M. McGlashan, 1849).

The Naval Detective's Chase; or, Nick, The Steeple-Climber: A Thrilling Tale of Real Life (N.Y.: Street & Smith, 1889). Secret Service Series. First pub. in *Street and Smith's New York Weekly*, 1886.

Navigator Ned; Cruisings Afloat and Ashore from the Log of Ned Buntline. Same as *Cruisings, Afloat and Ashore.*

Navigator Ned; or, He would be Captain (N.Y.: Street & Smith, 1890). Nugget Library. First pub. in *Street and Smith's New York Weekly*, 1876. Caldwell Col.

Ned Buntline's Life Yarn (N.Y.: Dick & Fitzgerald, 1850. Also N.Y.: Garret & Co., 1859). First pub. in *Ned Buntline's Own*, 1848.

Ned Buntline's Magazine (Pittsburgh: E. Z. C. Judson, 1844).

Ned Buntline's Novelist (St. Louis, Carlyle, 1852). No copies known.

Ned Buntline's Own (Paducah, Nashville, 1845–1846). No copies known.

Ned Buntline's Own. The first series began July 22, 1848, at 309½ Broadway, N.Y. Termination date unknown but an issue in Caldwell Col. is dated Sept. 6, 1851. The paper must have been discontinued for one year commencing Sept. 30, 1849, when Judson was in jail. Second series began Aug. 27, 1853, at 82 Nassau St., N.Y., and ended Apr. 15, 1854, when it was sold to *The True-American.* Third series began Apr. 8, 1865, pub. by Hilton & Co. Caldwell Col.

Netta Bride and The Poor of New York (N.Y.: Hilton & Co., 1865). Ned Buntline's Own Series. Two vols. in one. Each has separate title page: *Netta Bride: or, The King of the Vultures*, by Capt. Cleighmore [pseud.], 1864, and *The Poor of New York*, by Henry Edwards [pseud.] from the play by the same name.

Norwood; or, Life on the Prairie (N.Y.: W. F. Burgess, 1849 and 1850. Also N. Y.: Burgess & Garrett [1849]).

Old Nick of the Swamp (N.Y.: George Munro, 1867 – Munro's Ten-cent Novels. Also Cleveland: The Arthur Westbrook Co., 1908 – Beadle's Frontier Series).

Old Sib Cone, The Mountain Trapper (N.Y.: Beadle & Adams, 1876 – Beadle's Dime Novels. Also Beadle's New Dime Novels, 1885). The same as *Sib Cone.*

Orthodox Jeems: A Tale of Wild Adventure in the Black Hills (N.Y.: Street & Smith, 1890). Log Cabin Library. First pub. in *Street and Smith's New York Weekly*, 1884. Caldwell Col.

Our Mess; or, The Pirate Hunters of the Gulf: A Tale of Naval Heroism and Wild Adventure in the Tropics (N.Y.: F. A. Brady, 1865). First pub. in *New York Mercury*, 1859. Hochschild Col.

The Parricides; or, The Doom of the Assassins: The Authors of a Nation's Loss (N.Y.: Hilton & Co., 1865). Ned Buntline's Own Series.

The Planter's Ward; or, A Woman's Love and a Woman's Hate: A Romance of the Shore Plantations (N.Y.: F. Starr & Co., 1871). Starr's 15¢ Illustrated Novels. Caldwell Col. Same as *Hilliare Henderson.*

Quaker Saul, The Idiot Spy; or, Luliona, the Seminole: A Tale of Men and Deeds of '76 (N. Y.: Beadle & Co., 1869). Beadle's American Tales. The same as *Saul Sabberday, The Idiot Spy.*

The Queen of the Sea; or, Our Lady of the Ocean: A Tale of Love, Strife & Chivalry (Boston: F. Gleason, 1848. Also N.Y.: S. French, 1848; anonymously in Glasgow and London, n.d. Cameron & Ferguson's Ocean Series).

The Queen of the Sea; or, The Female Pirate Captain (Boston: G. W. Studley, 1899). Hochschild Col. Same as next above.

The Rattlesnake; or, The Rebel Privateer: A Tale of the Present Time (N.Y.: F. A. Brady, [1862]). Mercury Stories. Also pub. in *New York Mercury*, 1862.

Rattlesnake Ned, The Terror of the Sea (N.Y.: Street & Smith, 1890). Log Cabin Library. First pub. in *Street and Smith's New York Weekly*, 1876.

Red Dick, The Tiger of California (N.Y.: Street & Smith, 1890). Sea and Shore Series. Also pub., 1891, in Log Cabin Library. First pub. in *Street and Smith's New York Weekly*, 1872.

The Red Privateer; or, The Midshipman Rover: A Romance of 1812 (N.Y.: Beadle & Adams, 1890). Beadle's Dime Library. First pub. in *Banner Weekly* as "The Midshipman Rover," 1885.

Red Ralph; or, The Daughter of the Night (N.Y.: Hilton & Co., 1865). Ned Buntline's Own Series. Caldwell Col. Note *Lenore.*

Red Ralph, The Ranger; or, The Brother's Revenge (N.Y.: Beadle & Co., 1870). Beadle's American Tales. Also Starr's American Novels, 1875. Caldwell Col.

Red Ralph, The River Rover; or, The Brother's Revenge (N.Y.:

Beadle & Adams, 1884). Beadle's Half-dime Library. Caldwell Col. (The same as next above.)

The Red Revenger; or, The Pirate King of the Floridas: A Romance of the Gulf and Its Islands (Boston: F. Gleason, 1847. Also N.Y.: S. French, 1847. Also entitled *Red Avenger*, etc. Later eds.: Boston: F. Gleason, 1848; Boston: G. W. Studley, n.d.; Boston: Tomes & Talbot, 1876?; and Chicago: M. A. Donohue).

The Red Right Hand: A Tale of Indian Warfare (N.Y.: Dick & Fitzgerald, 1861?). Referred to in Buntline's *Morgan*, which was pub. 1861.

The Red Warrior; or, Stella Delorme's Comanche Lover (N.Y.: Beadle & Adams, 1869 — Beadle's American Tales. Also Beadle's Dime Library, 1900). See *Stella Delorme*.

The Revenue Officers' Triumph; or, The Sunken Treasure (N.Y.: Street & Smith, 1891). Log Cabin Library. First pub. in *Street and Smith's New York Weekly*, 1884, as "The Smuggler's Daughter; or, The Wreck of the Mohawk." Caldwell Col.

The Romance of Life; or, The Life of Martha E. Miller (Alias Walker) (N.Y.: Edward Z. C. Judson, [1849]). Listed by Wright. First pub. in *Ned Buntline's Own*, 1849. Caldwell Col.

Rosa, The Indian Captive: A Story of the Last War with England (N.Y.: Hilton & Co., 1866). Ned Buntline's Own Series.

Rose Seymour, The Ballet Girl's Revenge: A Tale of the New-York Drama (N.Y.: Hilton & Co., 1865). Ned Buntline's Own Series. Caldwell Col. See *Clara St. John* and *Mermet Ben*.

Rover Wild, The Jolly Reefer (N.Y.: Street & Smith, 1890). Log Cabin Library. First pub. as serial in *Street and Smith's New York Weekly*, 1885.

Sadia: A Heroine of the Rebellion (N.Y.: F. A. Brady, 1864). First pub. in *New York Mercury*, 1864. Caldwell Col. Same as *True as Steel*.

Sam Ricketty; or, A Well Planned Plot (N.Y.: Street & Smith, 1891). Nugget Library. First pub. in *Street and Smith's New York Weekly*, 1883, with title "To a Hero's Throne, by Water and Fire."

Saul Sabberday; or, The Idiot Spy: A Tale of the Men and Deeds of '76 (N.Y.: F. A. Brady [1858]). First pub. in *New York Mercury*, 1858. Caldwell Col. See *Quaker Saul*.

Saul Sabberday, The Idiot Spy; or, Luliona, The Seminole (N.Y.: F. Starr & Co., 1875 — Starr's American Novels. Also N.Y.: Beadle

& Adams, 1881 — Beadle's Dime Library). The latter is in Hochschild Col. See also *Quaker Saul.*

Scouts of the Plains, renamed *Scouts of the Prairie* and later *Scouts of the Plains; or, Red Deviltry As It Is.* A play first presented in Chicago Amphitheatre on Dec. 16, 1872.

The Sea Bandit; or, The Queen of the Isle: A Tale of the Antilles (N.Y.: Beadle & Adams, 1870 — Beadle's American Tales. Also F. Starr & Co., 1876 — Starr's American Novels. Also Beadle's Dime Library, 1879).

The Sea Spy; or, Mortimor Monk, The Hunchback Millionaire: A Tale of Sea and Land Fifty Years Ago (N.Y.: Beadle & Adams, 1890). Beadle's Dime Library. First pub. in *Banner Weekly,* 1886.

Seawaif; or, The Terror of the Coast: A Tale of Privateering in 1776 (N.Y.: F. A. Brady, 1859). First pub. in *New York Mercury,* 1859.

Secret Circular: To the Know Nothings of Philadelphia (1856).

The Secret Vow; or, The Power of Woman's Hate (N.Y.: F. Starr & Co., 1871). Starr's 15¢ Illustrated Novels. Listed by Johannsen. Same as *The Death-Mystery.*

Sensation Sate; or, The Queen of Wild Horse Range (N.Y.: Street & Smith, 1890). Log Cabin Library. First pub. in *Street and Smith's New York Weekly,* 1884. Caldwell Col.

The Shadow Scout! or, Screaming Moses of the Fishkill Mountains (N.Y.: George Munro, 1869 — Munro's Ten-cent Novels. Also Cleveland: The Arthur Westbrook Co., 1908 — Beadle's Frontier Series).

Shadowed and Trapped; or, Harry the Sport (N.Y.: Street & Smith, 1889). Log Cabin Library. First pub. as "Beguiled and Trapped" in *Street and Smith's New York Weekly,* 1877. Caldwell Col.

The Shell-Hunter; or, An Ocean Love-Chase: A Romance of Land and Sea (N.Y.: F. A. Brady, [1858?]. Also N.Y.: Beadle & Co., 1871). Printed also in *New York Mercury,* 1860. Caldwell Col. See *Ethelbert, the Shell-Hunter.*

Sib Cone, The Mountain Trapper (N.Y.: F. Starr & Co., 1870). Starr's American Novels. Same as *Old Sib Cone.*

"Silver Wing!" The Angel of the Tribes (N.Y.: Street & Smith, 1891). Log Cabin Library. Hochschild Col. First pub. in *Street and Smith's New York Weekly,* 1875. Caldwell Col.

The Smuggler; or, The Skipper's Crime: A Tale of Ship and Shore (N.Y.: F. Starr & Co., 1871). Starr's American Novels. Same as *English Tom.*

Stella Delorme; or, The Comanche's Dream: A Wild and Fanciful Story of Savage Chivalry (N.Y.: F. A. Brady, 1860). First pub. in *New York Mercury*, 1859. Caldwell Col. Same as *The Red Warrior.*

Texas Jack, The White King of the Pawnees (N.Y.: Street & Smith, 1891). Sea and Shore Stories. Horschild has a Log Cabin Library ed., same date. First pub. in *Street and Smith's New York Weekly*, 1873.

Thayendanegea, The Scourge; or, The War-Eagle of the Mohawks: A Tale of Mystery, Ruth, and Wrong (N.Y.: F. A. Brady, 1858. Also London: Beadle & Co., [1862] — Beadle's American Library; N.Y.: Beadle & Adams, 1869; and M. J. Ivers & Co., 1900 — New York Dime Library). First pub. in *New York Mercury*, 1858.

Three Years After: A Sequel to the Mysteries and Miseries of New York (N.Y.: W. F. Burgess, 1849. Also N.Y.: Dick & Fitzgerald, 186–). First pub. in *Ned Buntline's Own*, 1848.

Tiger-Eye (N.Y.: George Munro, 1866 — Munro's Ten-cent Novels. Also Cleveland: The Arthur Westbrook Co., 1909 — Beadle's Frontier Series).

Tombstone Dick, The Train Pilot; or, The Traitor's Trail: A Story of the Arizonian Wilds (N.Y.: Beadle & Adams, 1885). Beadle's Dime Library.

True as Steel; or, The Faithful Sister (N.Y.: F. Starr & Co., 1871). Starr's 15¢ Illustrated Novels. Same as *Sadia.*

The Virgin of the Sun: A Historical Romance of the Last Revolution in Peru (Boston: Hotchkiss & Company, 1847).

The Volunteer; or, The Maid of Monterrey: A Tale of the Mexican War (Boston: F. Gleason, at "Flag of Our Union" Office, 1847. Also Boston: Gleason's Publishing Hall, 1852; Boston: M. M. Ballou, 1860; and Boston: Elliot, Thomas & Talbott, 1863).

The War Cloud; or, Life for Life (N.Y.: R. M. DeWitt, 187–). Referred to in Buntline, *Morgan* (1861) and printed as a serial in *New York Mercury*, 1867.

War-Eagle, or, Ossiniwa, the Indian Brave (N.Y.: R. M. DeWitt, 1869). DeWitt's Ten-cent Romances. A sequel to *The Ice-King.*

The Wheel of Misfortune; or, The Victims of Lottery and Policy Dealers: A Yarn from the Web of New York Life (N.Y.: Garrett & Co., 1853).

The White Cruiser; or, The Fate of the Unheard-of: A Tale of Land and Sea; of Crime and Mystery (N.Y.: Garrett & Co., 1853. Also

N.Y.: Dick & Fitzgerald, [186–]). First pub. in *Ned Buntline's Own*, 1850. Caldwell Col.

The White Wizard; or, The Great Prophet of the Seminoles: A Tale of Strange Mystery in the South and North (N.Y.: F. A. Brady, 1858, 1862. Also N.Y.: F. Starr & Co., 1875 – Starr's American Novels; N.Y.: Beadle & Adams, 1877 – Beadle Dime Library; and London: Beadle & Co., [187–] – Beadle's American Library). First pub. in *New York Mercury*, 1858.

Wild Bill's Last Trail (N.Y.: Street & Smith, 1900). Nugget Library. First pub. as "On the Death Trail; or, The Last of Wild Bill," in *Street and Smith's New York Weekly*, 1880.

Wrestling Joe, The Dandy of the Mines (N.Y.: J. S. Ogilvie, 1881). First pub. in *Street and Smith's New York Weekly*, 1871.

The Wronged Daughter; or, A Wife's Intrigue (London: The General Publishing Co., [186–] – Romances for the Million. Also Beadle & Adams, 1870 – Starr's 15¢ Illustrated Novels; and Beadle's Cheap Edition Popular Authors, 1877).

Stories attributed to Judson have appeared under the following pseudonyms:

Charlie Bowline	Clew Garnet
Jack Brace	Edward J. C. Handelboe
Captain Cleighmore	Mad Jack
Frank Clewline	L. Augustus Jones
Henry Edwards	Edward Minturn
Jiles Edwards	Harrison Gray Buchanan

Other articles "By one who knows all about it," "By the Orderly" and "By a Recluse" are probably Buntline stories.

Acknowledgments

This study could not have been completed without the encouragement of Stanley Pargellis and a Newberry Library Fellowship – a grant from the Rockefeller Foundation. The moral encouragement I received from the former and the financial help from the latter have done more than anything else to make this work possible. Dr. Pargellis has read the entire manuscript and offered suggestions which have been gratefully accepted.

Kenneth B. Bartlett and Elizabeth Drewry, in the War Records Division of the National Archives, furnished me with the recorded details of Buntline's naval service. Charles Bragin of Brooklyn, New York, and Ralph Cummings of Fisherville, Massachusetts, both professionals in the dime-novel field, have been generous with their time in helping a novice. Arch B. Canfield traced Judson land titles and genealogy at Stamford, New York, and shared his information with me.

Raymond L. Caldwell, of Lancaster, Pennsylvania, spent many hours copying titles from his extensive collection and gave me the benefit of his lifelong study of dime-novel writers. I wish also to express my thanks to Henry Foster of Ottumwa, Iowa, and Odell Hathaway of Middletown, New Jersey, for lending me rare books from their personal libraries.

To George Harvey Genzmer, first person to study Judson material critically, I am indebted for knowledge of sources. Harold K. Hochschild, owner of an Adirondack estate including the site of Buntline's hunting camp, pointed out the site of Ned's cabin. Mr. Hochschild's hospitality to my wife and me is a happy memory. Curtis Chappalear, in his pillared mansion on a hill beyond Delaplane, Virginia, told me his memories of Dr. Alban Payne. I fished in Blue Mountain Lake with the well-known guide, Chester Stanton, and from him learned the local gossip of Buntline's residence there.

Albert Johannsen, authority on dime novels, has been generous with his Buntline data. His book, *The House of Beadle and Adams*, is a classic in the field. William P. Kilroy, at the Library of Congress, has searched and researched the newspaper files for Buntline material. I am indebted to Anna Lyon, the late Helen Vermilyea, and Mrs. DeWitt Sanford, for many hours of work in the Stamford (New York) Public Library. Mrs. Sanford's father, Jesse Gilbert, remembered Ned Buntline and told many anecdotes about Ned's later life.

J. Franklin Meine, Chicago bookman extraordinary, generously gave me the titles of unknown Buntline articles he discovered in intricate meanderings through old tomes. Allan Nevins has encouraged this study from the beginning. Harold Hammond, administrative assistant to the President of Long Island University, was good enough to let me read a chapter of his unfinished thesis on Judge Charles P. Daly. David C. Mearns, chief of the Manuscripts Division, Library of Congress, has been bountiful with his understanding of people and sources. With great thoughtfulness he has sent me a number of Buntline references.

Myrtle Newton unearthed much Buntline material for me in the Wayne County Historical Society files at Honesdale, Pennsylvania. She called my attention to a little-known autobiographical series in the *Hawley Times*. Paul North Rice, in the New York Public Library, S. K. Stevens, director of the Pennsylvania Historical and Museum Commission in Harrisburg, R. N. Williams, II, director of the Historical Society of Pennsylvania, Franklin F. Holbrook, of the Historical Society of Western Pennsylvania at Pittsburgh, and Mason Tolman in the Reference Section of the New York State Library, all helped me trace Ned Buntline in the records deposited in their institutions.

Walter Sutton, who knows more than anyone else about early nineteenth-century publications in Cincinnati, helped me with Buntline data in his field. William Wessels, gracious host of the Blue Mountain Lake House, supplied me with pictures of early day scenes in the Adirondacks. Dr. Milton Shutes, of Oakland, beckoned me to California sources. Lyle Wright's *American Fiction, 1774–1850*, proved invaluable, and correspondence with its author is always a pleasure. Guy J. Griffin, of the Committee of Masonic History, Grand Lodge of California, helped me trace Ned's itinerary on the Pacific Coast.

Hugh Flick, New York State Archivist, fisherman and rough rider, also Edna L. Jacobsen, charming chief of the Manuscripts and History Section of the New York State Library, helped me get material on the Adirondacks. The late Rufus Rockwell Wilson generously sent me his clipping file on Ned Buntline and described his personal interview with the dime novelist.

For liberal assistance during the long period of research on this book I also want to thank the following: Dorothy C. Barck, librarian, New York Historical Society; Rose Demorest, Carnegie Library of Pittsburgh; Fanny Dunlap, reference librarian, University of Illinois; Leva M. Ferguson, librarian, the Pennsylvania Railroad; Mable R. Gillis, California State Librarian, Sacramento; Alice J. Haines, California Historical Society, San Francisco; Irene Janes, reference librarian, Free Public Library, Paterson, New Jersey; Henrietta Kueper, librarian in the public library, Carlyle, Illinois; Edith G. H. Lenel, Newberry Library, Chicago; Mrs. Lincoln MacVeagh, Brunswick, Maine; William A. Settle, Jr., Tulsa University; Helen A. Stratton, Binghamton Public Library, Binghamton, New York; Father Walter Tunks, St. Paul's Episcopal Church, Akron, Ohio; Charles T. White, Hancock, New York; and Ernest J. Wessen, Mansfield, Ohio. Thomas E. Dabney, editor and co-publisher of the Socorro County Publishing Company at Socorro, New Mexico, and Nat Fleischer, president and editor of *The Ring*, Madison Square Garden, New York, both helped me in my efforts to trace obscure Buntline references.

As in several earlier volumes I am heavily indebted to Margaret Flint, reference librarian at the Illinois State Historical Library in Springfield. Always versatile and imaginative, she has a rare gift for finding source material and a priceless sense of humor for appreciating it. James N. Adams typed the entire manuscript with his well-proved speed and accuracy.

And last but by no means least, I want to acknowledge the help of my wife, Millie "with the nut-brown hair," who has walked with me along the full length of the aisle to help lay this sacrifice on the altar of Clio. She has been a patient partner in tedious hours of study, a sunny companion in travels along Buntline's way across Fauquier County, Virginia, through Mississippi River towns, and from the Platte to the Catskills and Adirondacks. She has read and reread the manuscript and typed the bibliography. The book's merits — if any — I owe to her. Its errors must be blamed on the author and "that odious rascal Ned Buntline."

— J. M.

INDEX

Index

INDEX

INDEX

INDEX

INDEX

Fracker Library
Buena Vista College